WO
COULD HAVE
HAPPENED

WORSE COULD HAVE HAPPENED

Andrew D Forrest

POOLBEG

Published 1999
by Poolbeg Press Ltd
123 Baldoyle Industrial Estate
Dublin 13, Ireland

www.poolbeg.com

A catalogue record for this book is available from the British Library.

ISBN 1 85371 548 4

Cover design by Artmark
Set by Pat Hope
Printed by Guernsey Press,
Vale, Guensey, Channel Isles, UK

Dedication

To my wife, Mai, son, Andrew, daughter in law, Noreen, daughter, Madeleine and son in law, Andrew and all my grandchildren.

“A Forrest Stands in
The Shade of a Tree”

INTRODUCTION

"Perhaps the best way to start is to introduce myself" Andrew Forrest wrote to me in May 1998. "I am eighty years of age and I grew up a few hundred yards from where your grandparents lived in Dysart: (Dromagh-Banteer)."

He had written, he explained, what he thought was "a true history" of the 1920s and 1030s, – "a period about which there is a lot of 'disinformation' and 'demagoguery'". Set in north Cork, "it is the story of a group of schoolboys who suffered their share for the hated CUPLA FOCAIL". He wondered if I would edit the book to make it suitable for publication.

Much though I liked his letter, I was apprehensive about seeing the book. It is one thing to tell a thirty-year-old aspiring author that a typescript shows promise but needs rewriting. But an octogenarian? And what was more, with multifarious deadlines looming, what sort of lunatic would I be to agree to edit someone else's manuscript? But Andrew had blackmailed me skillfully with tales of my Grandfather O'Sullivan (Jim Flur in his book), so what could I do? I spoke to him and he was funny and I told him to send the typescript. Naturally, when it arrived, I had a pile of urgent work to do that day, but curiosity caused me to have a quick look prior to putting it into the "Oh-God-yes-I'll-get-round-to-it-when-I-have-a-minute" tray and after the first page I was lost. Utterly beguiled, I sat down and read the whole gripping and original reminiscence straight through, pausing only to laugh.

There is no sentiment in Andrew Forrest – just truth, wisdom and humour. His was the rural life I knew from my mother, Síle Ní Shuilleabháin, and from my long summers in the Banteer of the 1950s – a world of brutality, snobbery and hypocrisy, but also of merriment, wit and farce. In her efforts to explain rural life to her urban children, my mother introduced us to the short stories of Guy de Maupassant, which dealt so often with the harshness and savagery of peasant life. But what she passed on to us too was an appreciation of the black humour and general "divilment" that made life in the north Cork of her youth bearable and sometimes joyful.

"We tried to make a joke of every misfortune", Andrew had said to me, "and we had many" (His approach resembles that of the grandmother of a friend of mine whose advice was: "Learn to laugh at everything since there's usually nothing to laugh at".) There is no whinging and no trace of self-pity in Andrew. He may rage about the poor wretches who were sacrificed to the Green and Holy Terror of language and church, but he sees irony, paradox and sheer fun everywhere and, almost always, finds within himself compassion for even the most nightmarish adults of his youth.

This is a book to be read for sheer interest and enjoyment, but it is, also, of real historical significance. Not only is this a rare and truthful account of rural life in the first two decades of the Irish Free State, but it is also written from a deeply unfashionable political standpoint. Where else can one find a rousing and hilarious reminiscence by a proud ex-Blueshirt – one of those who challenged the IRA's "no free speech for traitors" campaign, when "to tear the blue shirt off a lone man was considered a great day's work. The shirt would then be torn into shreds and burned and the owner given a few good kicks for the road home". The breaking up of a public meeting "was always celebrated by the writing of yet another pathetic patriotic verse such as the following:

"The King's assets
Mulcahy's men
They marched it to
Kilmallock
But they didn't come again".

Andrew was one of those Blueshirts regularly packed into lorries "travelling long distances to uphold the right of free speech and the defence of democracy" by whatever means seemed necessary. He looks back on himself and his comrades with the same amused detachment that he affords their enemies, at whom he hoped to have a crack in Spain when he set off to fight for Franco in circumstances of – yet again – high farce.

There was no need for me to edit a line of Andrew's. And finding him a publisher took no effort either, for I was rightly confident that Philip MacDermot of Poolbeg would fall in love with the book as quickly as I had done. No one with a sense of humour who cares about our past could do otherwise.

Ruth Dudley Edwards
5 October 1999

Contents

1

Coffins and Graves

It was the first coffin I ever saw and I could barely reach to it. It was my mother's coffin. Ever after and right up to the present day I have a profound hatred for coffins and graves. No matter how many silver handles and coats of varnish and fine carvings put on for display, there never was and never will be a nice coffin or such a thing as a nice grave.

For a little while we fight a losing battle with nature; our puerile efforts to hold at bay nature's robe of green are all in vain.

"They grew in beauty, side by side,
They filled one house with glee!
Their graves are sever'd far and wide
By mount and stream and sea."

Our house was not filled with glee for very long. My mother's untimely death changed our lives; people looked on us with pity. In all human life and existence there is nothing sadder than the death of a young mother. Every parent's wish is to live long enough to see their children grown up. Our mother was denied her dearest wish, but by the grace of God her "little orphans" survived the ups and downs of life. My brother who was a few years older than me and my sister who is a few years younger are now well past "the three score and ten"; life is now a matter of echoes and warning signs.

Recently I attended the funeral of an old friend; people said he was around "the seventy" and, after digesting this information, middle-aged men who should know better said, "it was a good age" and with more head-shaking confirmed, "it was a good age for a man that went through the world".

Near me were two schoolboys and I said to them "I suppose you think you will never die?" One looked at the other and then acted as spokesman for both. "We don't know yet," said he. "We don't know yet," said the schoolboy as we stood beside the closing grave.

The certainty and inevitability of dying and death is discreetly diluted and diffused by this element of boyish doubt. To the small boy doubtful things are certain and certain things are doubtful and, while on the subject of funerals, I recall attending the funeral of an only son aged only twenty-two years away back in the time when graves were made with great care and respect. As the cortege drew near the graveyard one could hear the hoof-beats of two hundred horses bringing trap-loads of mourners, all wearing black hat-bands or arm-bands, and at the graveside were numerous clergy in full regalia reading from books in Latin which very few people understood. However, we took it for granted that the clergy themselves understood what they were on about.

The funeral service in Latin had the mysterious effect of making the whole thing more sorrowful and I could see the father watching every move from the sprinkling of the holy water until the last green sod was back in place and then a big shopkeeper, a very important man in his own mind, went up to the grieving father to offer his condolence. "Now, now," said the old man, "things could be worse, thank God we had a few fine days for the tantalizing game."

I admired his choice of words; what else is a funeral but a tantalizing experience, a time of torment, of dashed hopes and the shedding of tears.

Home from my mother's funeral to an empty house, my brother said "Mammy is gone to heaven"; even at this early age he was not one to exaggerate.

Next day great and unexpected changes took place. Grown-ups have a habit of making decisions without consulting people.

2

TEMPORARY SEPARATION

My father was a good man, wise in most things but child-care was not one of his strong points. He was not the feminine or sissy type who could spend all his time messing with small children. Common sense prevailed.

I was taken to my father's old home in Coolbane where my grandfather resided on the old family farm, together with three sons and a daughter as yet unmarried.

It was a really wonderful place and I received VIP treatment from all the family.

My brother was taken to my mother's old home in Dromdowney where my mother's mother resided, again on the old family farm with her son Michael and daughter Sissy, both as yet unmarried.

My sister was taken to Gortnascregga where an aunt of ours, my father's sister, and her husband were busy farming and at the same time rearing a large family, so large in fact that my aunt said "one more will not make much of a difference."

I settled in nicely in Coolbane where my Grandad was my principal companion and I soon regarded Coolbane as my own place.

Many great men tell us of their unhappy childhoods and mine being the direct opposite is perhaps one of the reasons why I made such little impact on world affairs – other factors are too numerous to mention.

As we all know, all good things come to an end, happy days don't last for ever and as the reader will notice in due course I was to have a taste of both worlds.

Grandfather spent much of his early life in Australia in company with his four brothers. He alone returned to Ireland in response to an urgent call from his mother. The story is told that he returned on one condition, namely, "*That he would not have to work*" and as far as I could see this was one condition that was strictly adhered to.

Members of the Forrest family made it to high places in Australia and *The Forrest Trail* is clearly marked on early maps of that continent. The Forrests in Australia were famous as explorers and politicians. As a family we seem stricken with a strange wanderlust, while one generation familiarised themselves with Australia north, south, east and west, the next generation set out to do the same thing in that other land of opportunity, namely, *The Wild West*. My uncles David, James and Conor with my father all went out to California, a fourteen-day journey by train from New York in those days and on arrival there one could say with some truth that their travels had only begun. From San Diego my father and Uncle James went south to Papa Squario in Mexico. Here my father turned back and made his way north to a place called Moose Jaw in Saskatchewan where he became paymaster in a thriving copper mine where a large number of Indians were employed.

It so happened that one day the Governor General of Canada, the Duke of Connaught, paid a surprise visit to the mine. It was mid-winter and the Duke of Connaught was covered in furs with only a small part of face visible, and yet he felt the intense cold. He was surprised to see the Indians so scantily clad with most of their bodies bare. He called an Indian aside . . . "Tell me, my good man, how it is that you can go about without coat or overcoat, and without shirt or undershirt and you don't seem to feel the cold?"

He was a cocky little Indian and he outlined his face with his finger saying, "You not cold there?"

"No," said the Duke of Connaught, "but that is my face."

"Well," said the Indian, "me all a face."

My father used to tell this story and needless to say he told it much better.

In the meantime my uncle James continued south to Ecuador, Peru, Chile and finally to Argentina. Here he met a man called Fitzpatrick; both of them knew the town of Kanturk, as a matter of fact Fitzpatrick came from there. They became good friends and together they had many adventures. They were the first to climb the almost impossible peak of the mountain known as *Ojos del Salado*.

Fitzpatrick always maintained that they could see the names over the doors in his native town including the name *Fitzpatrick* in big blue letters over his brother's shop. Seemingly the mountain was so high the curvature of the earth had no effect, it was just a matter of having good sight. My uncle refused to confirm that part of the story.

My Uncle Conor travelled extensively all over the United States but much of his time was spent in *The Wild West*. He made some easy money from an invention which used water under pressure to facilitate some mining operations and procedures; unfortunately it took years to produce one vital part of sufficient strength to withstand the required pressure for long periods. My Uncle David never returned.

At home in Coolbane Uncle Joe looked after the farm while Uncle Michael spent much of his spare time in the village having a few drinks before times got busy on the farm.

When World War II started he volunteered to do his bit, he joined the merchant navy and after some serious escapades on the Atlantic he sailed with the ill-fated "Q17" convoy from Belfast to Murmansk in northern Russia. He was never heard of again; he was one of many who were lost in that desperate voyage. The convoy was under constant attack by plane and U-boat.

3

COOLBANE

From a small boy's point of view there could be no better place than Coolbane. The farmhouse was surrounded by orchards and fruit-trees of every description. Red and black-currant and gooseberry bushes could be found everywhere beneath the apple trees and the hedgerows out around the farm were dotted with plum and cherry.

Always at jam-making time strange women would come and pick baskets of fruit and take away full loads balanced perfectly on their heads. Many years would come and go before I would see the like again, but see it I did in a far-away land.

From the public road a well-kept tree-lined lane wound its way uphill to end in two branches, one leading to the front of the farmhouse where it widened out, forming a large gravelled area at the end of which stood the lofted coach-house with its two large black doors.

The other branch took you round an old orchard and into the farmyard; ancient trees stood like guards of honour surrounding the haggard and yard. It was truly a place of peace and quiet and I was happy there in these marvellous and serene surroundings. One end of the farmhouse extended into an old orchard and apple-branches shaded and at times caressed the windowpanes of the room in which Grandfather and I slept. When spring came and the days and nights became warmer he let down the window and an apple-branch held at bay all winter extended itself into the room. The blossom filled the room with fragrance and in due course little apples appeared and again in due course became ripe, and fell away to roll under our beds. It was my job to crawl under the beds, collect the over-ripe apples and fling them out the window. Alas! The fine summers and warm nights of long ago are truly long gone, the environment has changed, damaged perhaps beyond repair.

From a rustic garden-seat set into a fence and shaded by a canopy of greenery, Grandfather and I spent much of our time looking across the valley at farmers at work in the hayfields of summer and cornfields at harvest time. At times we would hear the romantic rhythm of an invisible man improving the edge of a scythe in some small field. Suddenly the barking of dogs would command our attention, the postman was arriving at some farmhouse bringing the "Rate Demand Thing" from the County Council or the "Rent Thing" from the Land Commission. There was always the chance it would be a letter from England or America with a few pounds or a few dollars enclosed, but by and large, farmers would be better off if there were neither post nor postmen. How times have changed! We could hear all the dog-barking but there was no way of knowing who got bills or reminders or who got a few quid. Sometimes we could detect a change in tone, but this of course was only "circumstantial evidence". However, if the dogs were allowed to chase the postman for half a mile up the road we could take it for granted that it was "the thing" from the County Council.

Every morning our peaceful diagnosis of life across the valley was shattered by the continuous noisy rattle of creamery carts with their iron-shod wheels and bone-dry, worn, screeching axles and load of half-empty milk-cans with loose, badly fitting covers all dancing merrily as the carts were driven at top speed over broken stones and pot-holes. Road repair technology consisted mainly of scattering broken stones all over the road surface in such a way that it was easier to drive over the heaps and patches than to avoid them.

The drivers seemed oblivious of any sound whatever as they urged their animals to even greater speed, secure in the knowledge that they had personally tied down every milk can, using up every inch of the twenty yards of rope with which every creamery cart was equipped. Were these creamery carts driven over a land-mine, the milk-cans would remain in place because the first thing every creamery-boy learned was how to make a *curby-whibble*, and between every two cans the *curby-whibble* was applied and every one knew "God, man or the devil" could not escape the *curby-whibble*.

It took science a long time to obliterate the creamery-cart, but we must not become all melancholy over the loss of one sound, there are a million others more worthy of lament such as the nocturnal song of the corncrake, the musical noise of the horse-drawn mower, even the merry little grasshopper, all gone and forever! Science has a lot to answer for.

4

Dromdowney

While I was enjoying life in Coolbane, my brother was doing equally well in Dromdowney where life was a little more complicated. Here, several men were in constant employment and an oldish woman, Mrs Something-Or-Other, acted as head cook and bottle-washer; the attention she paid to the rise and fall in the temperature of the range was truly amazing. During busy periods such as harvest time extra men were employed and many of these were ex-soldiers, some from the British Army, others from the Free State Army, all of whom became redundant when all the wars were over.

By far the most famous of these was Bill "Seck", a man who spent four years fighting in the trenches in France and Belgium and he had a box full of medals to prove it. He was never seen without his walking-cane. However, as time went on the cane was reduced to an ordinary ash-plant cut to measure, and under certain circumstances Bill had no qualms about bringing down, be it on the head of a guard or the head of a priest. He moved about from farm to farm working for short periods, arriving suddenly and departing even more suddenly. He made Dromdowney his head-quarters and no matter how unexpected, he was always welcome back.

He was one of many men who failed to settle in to the hum-drum existence of most people, after having endured years of terrible war.

My Uncle, Michael O'Brien, owned the farm and he had many friends amongst the racing fraternity; show jumping, point to point meetings, fox-hunting and greyhound racing were for ever the topic of conversation, a topic I found infinitely boring. My brother on the other hand took it all in and in later life he became an expert in these matters.

Those early years had a lot to do with the direction each of us took as time went on, he was never far from racehorses and greyhounds, I was never near them. Grown men converse with each other under the impression that children are too young to understand what is being said – nothing could be further from the truth. As I listened to my father and his brothers tell of their adventures I made up my mind that I too would travel and have adventures of my own to talk about. My brother on the other hand had no inclination to travel, he had an interesting and exciting life surrounded by the best race horses and greyhounds available and "*per aspera ad astra*" we both had what we wanted.

Dromdowney was a place for tomatoes and cold meat, fruit cakes, and lots and lots of whiskey. The men here dressed differently. Most of the men wore riding-breeches including my uncle and there was one big boy, taller than some of the men, still wearing the short pants, which ended far above his knees, because he had not yet reached the required age for a long trousers which would "make a man of him".

These were the days when "a good stepper" was a prized possession, the training of which took a lot of time and "know-how." To catch up with and overtake other drivers was a matter of great pride and almost a matter of principle.

It was well known around the town of Mallow and the surrounding area which he served, that Dr Barry (MRCVS) owned the best and fastest horse on the road.

The speed and confidence of that animal was truly amazing because in actual fact the horse was stone blind. Dr Barry was a regular visitor to Dromdowney and one night he stayed late – it was one of those nights when the cork of the bottle was flung in the fire – and as the good doctor drove home in the early hours he forgot the sharp turn at the Railway arch, his trusting horse strode bravely on right up against the cut-stone wall to be killed instantly.

Many years afterwards a crowd of us were gathered together in an upper room in Healy's Hotel. It was another night of bliss. Nevertheless when the story of the collision with the Railway arch was retold I saw the tears cascade but he quickly wiped them away saying "Too late, too late for sentiment."

"How often the evening cup of joy led to sorrow in the morning." In this upper room at Healy's there was many an argument – not about religion or politics, not about famous people or money – the speed of a horse or the genealogy of a greyhound were of far greater concern. Historic matters were never mentioned. Once somebody had temerity to say something about Irish history, but he was quickly shot down by old Mrs Healy who told him in no uncertain terms "Sure there is no Irish history only the history one would be ashamed of."

They spoke mostly about dogs and horses but their conversation was never dull.

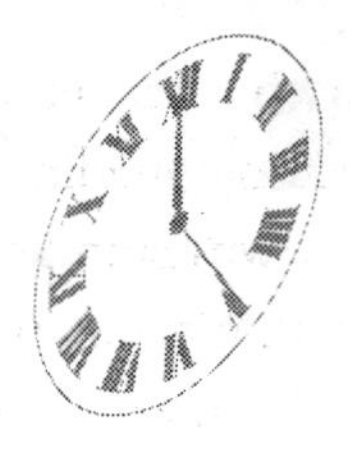

5

The Futility of Brute Force

Unfortunately many story-tellers have given us the impression that farming back in the nineteen-twenties was romantic and easy-going, and that every household had fiddles and bodhráns and more often than not, a gaping hole in the roof – in other words that idleness was the order of the day. This impression was far from correct because once or twice every year every farmyard erupted into a state of pandemonium and the weaker members of the household and staff went about in a state of great confusion and disarray.

As the bacon hanging from the rafters grew less and less the killing of the pig drew closer and closer, and when the local pig-killer finally arrived the whole townland was on red alert. The pig-killer or so-called butcher was always the type of fellow capable of carrying out a massacre without rhyme or reason. The more trouble he created and the more he provoked the women of the household the better for his reputation as a fearless and brutal pig-killer. Never would a friendly word pass his lips and as for a smile! Well, smiling was not the way to maintain the dignity, self-possession and lofty bearing of a pig-killer of any repute.

His method of killing required the assistance of at least half a dozen men with nerves of steel and preferably deaf. The greatest difficulty was in finding a woman with courage and who thought herself capable of holding the bucket to catch the blood, which would be utilised later for filling puddings.

She had to be capable of withstanding all kinds of verbal abuse. The pig-killer had to maintain his domineering and arrogant attitude and so he had to be peevish and surly all the days of his life. For reasons other than economic the pig-sty was always at the far end of the farmyard and from here the pig had to be hauled by two men pulling a long iron gaff inserted with great difficulty inside the pig's jaw-bone; the men pulling on the gaff were assisted by two more men "on the tail" whose job was to lift the pig's hind legs off the ground at regular intervals and so the uneven tug-o-war went on until finally the pig was close enough to the table, which was always right outside the back door of the farmhouse. Suddenly the pig-killer would give the order "*Lift*" and the pig completely surrounded by men, would be lifted on to the table, the men on the gaff maintaining full pressure. As a general rule children fled the scene because it was always a gruesome and repulsive business. When every leg was held firm and the pig was powerless on the table the butcher would go to work. All during this long-drawn-out murder the yelling and screeching of the unfortunate pig could be plainly heard in the local village over a mile away.

I am glad to say I saw the beginning of the end of it. My uncle Conor had seen animals slaughtered in a much more humane manner "out in the wild west" and when the time came to kill a pig in Coolbane the "terrorist" was not invited. Conor set up a contraption which he called a shear-leg and next he rigged out a pair of pulley-blocks and he also provided himself with a short length of chain and a properly sharpened knife. He always said "brute force is no substitute for good edge".

Uncle Joe was not as confident as he should have been and for fear things would go wrong he invited the usual group of unskilled helpers. On arrival they inspected *the gantry* and grave doubts were expressed about its usefulness and one old fellow said "It could be very unlucky to stand under it, worse than I'd say a ladder".

While these sceptical views were being expressed Conor was indoors providing sufficient hot water to "scauld" the pig and so bring about the end of the "hairy bacon" at least in one household.

When Conor emerged he had in his hand a pan containing about half a gallon of fresh milk, he spoke to the men about the weather and other unrelated matters and then one man said, "I suppose I will go on the gaff as usual?"

"No," said Conor, "all I want you to do is stand well back out of my way" and off he went to the pig house. Here he allowed the pig to drink a little of the milk, then he picked up the pan and the pig trotted along beside him right up to *the gantry*. Conor now put down the pan of milk and while the pig was happily engaged drinking the milk he put the little chain around one hind leg and hooked it to the lower pulley-block and in less time than it takes in telling, the pig was hoisted to the proper height and again in less time than it takes in telling, the pig even gave all its blood without a sound and without a struggle. The men collected around the pig, now hanging in mid-air, wondering "what next?" Little did they think they had witnessed the very start of redundancy, but that was not all, they were soon to see a pig properly cleaned and shaved without any of the old-fashioned tugging and lifting. The rope and the pulleys took over, and when the whole operation was over one man observed: "By the Lor, that pig is cleaner an whiter than any Christian I ever saw."

This day tradition was to receive another fatal blow. The blood (which had been collected in a bucket without anybody holding it) together with the head and *crubeens* plus the intestines and other parts of the pig which Conor considered unfit for human consumption, were taken a good distance from the house and buried. From then on the time-honoured practice of filling puddings and distributing parcels of same to all the neighbours went into a steady decline, no more would the receiver be duty bound to give sham thanks to the giver; outside the Church gate one could overhear one woman saying to another: "Oh Mary dear, them were the grandest puddings and Jack said he never ate the like o' them".

Of course he never ate the like of them because the moment the messenger was out of sight the said puddings were immediately thrown to the dogs. This was a foolproof way of letting Jack know that his wife had a poor opinion of the other woman's culinary efforts.

In some bachelor's quarters the gift puddings were well received, there being no woman to undermine the man's appetite. The local blacksmith lived alone and black puddings were the love of his life. When local supplies dried up he had to cycle four miles into town twice a week for the biggest black pudding available and he regretted this greatly because it was a waste of good drinking time. One such evening he was almost home when he noticed the black pudding had fallen from the carrier, "I had no better to do," said he, "than head back into town for another black pudding, at the same time keeping a tight eye on the road for the one I lost. There would be nothing wrong with it unless a lorry drove over it and by the Lor-God just at the mill didn't I spot this little hure of a small dog heading off with my black pudding in his mouth. I put up speed and without getting off the bike I gave him a kick in the behind that rus him ten feet in the air and I was just in time to give him another on the way down. I picked up my black pudding and there was not even a mark on it."

"And do you mean to say you ate it after the dog?"

"You are damm right I ate it."

"Begorra, Dinny, you are a fierce man altogether so you are." From then on Dinny took his rightful place in local folklore.

Those were the times when there was no such thing as cruelty to animals. People remembered the troubled times when farmers and landowners who were in any way unsympathetic to the IRA and the "national cause" had their livestock mutilated during the hours of darkness. Sheep had their tongues cut out, cattle had their legs broken, horses were shot at and left to die. Needless to say, in the aftermath of all this cruelty, there was no sympathy for the poor pig or other farm animals, stray cats had their tails tied together before hanging them over the clothes-line where they spent days fighting and eating each other and I remember a man who got rid of the jackdaws by taking out their eyes. Rural Ireland may have been romantic but it was also very brutal.

In my young days there was no such thing as the de-horning of ordinary cattle. However, as bulls reached four or five years of age they were regarded as dangerous and taking off the horns was a cruel operation. People said "it would quieten them". There was only one man in our area who would undertake the job. He was a wealthy farmer but he probably wanted to be famous for something. Every year he would have a field-day de-horning bulls for farmers from all over the place. His name was Mr Kavanagh and no one dared to address him by his Christian name; as a matter of fact I doubt if he had a Christian name, if he had, I never heard it. He knew how to tie up an animal and render it powerless. Then all the farmers who had brought bulls for de-horning were ordered to sit on the animal being operated on, the heaviest of them sat on the bull's neck and then Mr Kavanagh who had never heard of an anaesthetic would start sawing with an old handsaw and sometimes the base of the horn would be five or six inches across the base. The moment the saw touched the animal the roars of it could be heard in the Down hills. The other bulls awaiting their turn would also start roaring. But the terrifying roars of the animal being de-horned one would not wish to hear ever again. In spite of everything, with blood squirting in all directions, Mr Kavanagh went on sawing with a saw without edge. Five minutes with a good saw would have saved the animal prolonged hours of the greatest torture.

De-horning five or six bulls was a full day's work and the timid people and women living in the surrounding townlands went about all day with the hair standing on their heads.

People who have witnessed this operation are always amazed at the fountain of blood pouring from the wounded animals and unless swift and proper precautions are taken the animal may well bleed to death.

Today, vets come, armed with powders and sprays and with

tweezers to wind up the veins and block off the blood vessels. Mr Kavanagh had none of these, instead he had a bucket of thick yellow mud very much like putty and before the animal was released he made a pancake or doughnut or mud-pie large enough to cover the wound and after making it right sticky he clapped it over the area where the horn had been. Amazingly this completely cut off the flow of blood. It kept the dangerous flies away from the wound and I never heard of it to fail.

It is all too easy to embroider the old days and pretend there was no discomfort, no irritation, no pain. Thanks to men like Conor who always said "Brute force will get you nowhere" things have changed.

However, I must not complain, my young days were happy as I ran about the gardens, the groves and the meadows.

School was still a little way off. I had not yet become a mouse in tar.

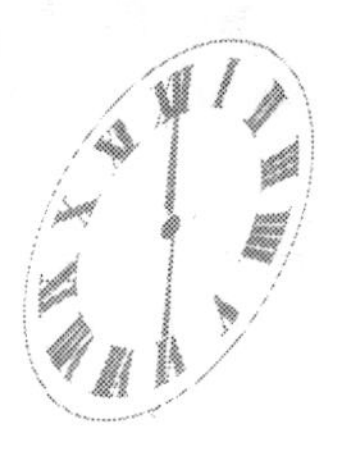

6

LEARNING FROM GRANDAD

It is well known that the very young and the very old get on very well together and my own experience bears this out. During my pre-school days I never heard any fairy stories nor was I ever told about *Little Red Riding Hood* or *Jack and the Beanstalk*. Grandad had a flair for telling true stories and he had hundreds of little anecdotes from ancient history. He would tell of ancient Egyptian kings, and Persian princes, and sometimes he would tell about the ancient Carthagenians and Babylonians and he was never short of a good story about Alexander The Great and his successors.

Like any small boy I enjoyed hearing about blood-thirsty tyrants and their downfall and the stories about great victory celebrations but he never failed to point out how innocent people suffered, be it in victory or defeat. Seemingly, most of the time innocent people suffered under implacable tyranny, but the man I had most sympathy with was poor Socrates and there was the story about a cock but I cannot now recall the details.

Out there in that part of the world where history began, it seems every king was hell-bent on having a monument or sculpture larger and more costly than any of those who reigned before him and it was great hearing about the Pyramids and other magnificent tombs. And then came a king by the name of Demetrius. I will never forget his name because he was in my view a proper spoilsport. He made a law forbidding the building of any more great monuments. However there was no great harm done for when he died the building started all over again. It is ironic that the king who wanted no great monument is better remembered simply because he was the only king without one. Grandad said Demetrius was a clever king who knew what he was doing when he did nothing.

One day I said to Grandad, "Tell me about Belshazzer" and when the story ended he said, "That reminds me, it is time you learned to write your name in preparation for school." Suffice to say, I was able to write my name before I went to school which incidentally was about all I could do the day I finished. Never again during my school days did I hear of Socrates, Cicero, Alexander or Philip and I came to the conclusion Grandad was a great man for the fairy stories.

One day a letter arrived to Coolbane from my father and over the next few days its contents were unfolded. After the summer holidays I was to return home so as to attend school in our own parish. My happy days in Coolbane were numbered. It was farewell *cloud-cuckoo land*.

Under the circumstances, I doubt if I was in any way overjoyed to see my father when he came to take me home because, this was no ordinary visit. I was delighted to see Captain; that was the name of our trap horse, and this was the time when every animal on the farm, nay, every animal in the country had its own name. Every dog and cat, every cow and calf, every goat and donkey were named appropriately. For instance, we had a cat called "Sourey" because it was unfriendly, and a cow called "Narrow-head" because it had a long narrow head.

On arrival, Captain was taken from under the trap and taken to the stables where he was rubbed down and given some oats and bright first-crop hay. Were the Pope of Rome to arrive in Coolbane driving a horse Conor would insist on attending to the horse before giving any attention to the driver. Grandad told a story about a king who when in great difficulty shouted, "A *horse, a horse, my kingdom for a horse*" and Conor chimed in, "One should never underestimate the value of a good horse" and my father, by way of a joke asked Grandad, "I often thought about that king of yours. Were there no tinkers around then to take up the offer?" In due course, we all went indoors and Conor prepared a meal which he called "High Tea". Everything nice that one could think of was on the table.

The conversation was all about foreign countries and *The Wild West*. There was a story about the White Hills which they did not fully explain. My father cut the story short, saying "Never mind, all their clocks are ticking." I was told "take out that bundle of *Wild West* magazines and put them in the box of the trap. When I returned, the story of the White Hills was finished and unfinished.

In all too short a time Captain was back again under the trap and my father and I started out for home. We were not long on the road when it started to rain and my father said, "Cover your knees with the rug" and as an after-thought he added, "This rain is badly wanting." We did not have a long conversation – in fact, we hardly spoke. We each had our own thoughts; mine were mostly conjecture. Saturated and hungry, we reached home. The servant-girl-cum-housekeeper did her best to make us comfortable and as I looked at her I thought one could like her if one went to the trouble of being friendly with her.

I failed to understand the reason why I had to leave my happy *cloud-cuckoo land* to become an exile and a hostage to stupid authority. After my first week – in fact, after my first day in school, I had every reason to believe my misgivings were well-founded. I use the words "stupid authority" deliberately because it seemed to me the sole aim of the educational system at that time was to subjugate and bring under its yoke every boy and girl. And I suppose every boy and girl resented the prospect of attending school as much as I did. I did not realise then that there was such a thing as a necessary evil. Truly the radiance would be taken from the eye of youth, boundless energy sapped and hearts ever-light would in a few short months be dreary, weary, and worn – but more about this later.

I turned my attention to the Herald range with its ornamental oven door and fancy shutters. In Coolbane we had a big open fire, far more friendly-looking than this black monster. However, a range was supposed to make things easier for the housekeeper. That night I went to bed in the same room as my brother and before getting into bed I showed him all my money and treasures. David thought I was rich but gradually my financial position grew worse until finally it disappeared.

David was the possessor of all knowledge. He knew Bill, the workman, and he knew the girl who was here before the present incumbent. He also knew all the boys in school. In fact he knew everything that was worth knowing. There was, however, one thing about which he knew nothing, nor did my father, and Bill like everyone else was equally unaware of what was about to happen.

Mary Sweeney, our cook and housekeeper, had a boyfriend and nobody knew, not even her mother, what these two were planning. People will tell you trouble and sorrow are friends in disguise and if this is true, they were well-disguised the night Mary Sweeney went out the window of her bedroom and into the arms of her boyfriend. Nobody had any idea of where they went until a letter arrived from America after many weeks. Needless to say, when Mary was reported missing her mother arrived by special flight in the donkey and car and she was the first really miserable person I ever saw. Under the circumstances, tears and crying would be understandable but the *olagoning* of Mrs. Sweeney was hard to describe. It was unnatural, abnormal and unprecedented and she went on talking to herself, "Why, why, did I allow my Mary to come to a house where there was no Missus. If there was a Missus in the house she would know what was going on."

The fact that Mary had gone without her wages made matters worse and the mother cried out, "Gone off with some ruffian without a penny in her pocket, what will become of her?" Somehow I knew that for this old woman peace and happiness had vanished. Life previous to this tragedy was normal enough, now it was a lost Eden.

My father had now to find another housekeeper and he consulted a schoolmaster, an old friend of his whom he thought might well be able to recommend a suitable girl who would fill the vacancy as *Cook-General.* The term *Cook-General* was very much in use in those days. She should be trustworthy but above all unromantic.

Straight away the schoolmaster recommended Elly. "Have no fear," said he. "This girl comes from a thrifty hard-working family." Let me introduce our new *Cook-General.* Forget about the "Cook" she was without doubt the greatest "General" slauberauley of all time.

There was little danger of this one going out the window. However, what she lacked in beauty she made up for in health and strength and I may well add, boldness. Unsophisticated, she believed in clothes "tailored to your lifestyle" and by no means flattering.

Clothes at that time were made from long-lasting hard-wearing material and the big danger for young people at that time was that "they would grow out of them." Happily or otherwise, that danger no longer exists. "Butcher Blue" was her favourite material and blue her favourite colour. Her Sunday shoes were light-weight boots suitable for rock-climbing and activities of that nature. Her everyday boots were hobnailed pounders sometimes called beetle-crushers. Kept in repair, this type of footwear lasted for years. The now universal Wellington Boot was still a long way off. She was the first re-cycler I saw in action and one of the first things she did was to make herself what was called a bag-apron from an empty meal-bag. These old jute bags were simply cast away in most farmyards. Worth a few pence if one went to the trouble of collecting them but our new housekeeper seemingly knew the value of what is now known as protective clothing. The bag-apron was also a great labour-saving invention. It was used as a carry-all for firewood, for potatoes and for collecting eggs. In fact, it took the place of a wheel-barrow from time to time.

She had a great dislike for "pets" such as cats and dogs and no way would she allow them inside the house. And to prove her determination on this point she escorted David and myself to the pulper and, pitching in a few turnips, she turned the handle thereby slicing the turnips into little pieces. "Now," she said, "in there goes them cats and dogs if I catch one of them inside the door. The last place I was in I pulped a bloody blasted greyhound, so now I am giving ye timely warning."

"Look out for that one," said David. "She is capable of pulping one of us." And he was not one to exaggerate as we were to find out in due course.

We were not going to like her, and from then on "Savage" was her name as savage was her nature. I doubt if Grandad had discovered her equal in all the pages of ancient history. She was unique and original.

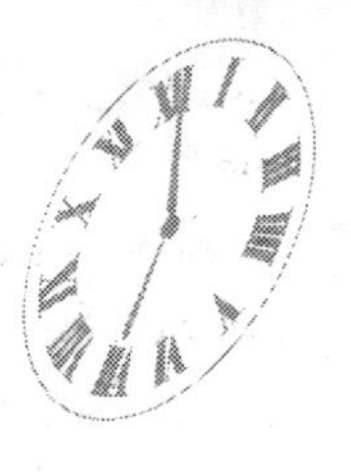

7

SUBMISSION! IMPOSSIBLE

We tried to visualise how Savage would go about pulping a dog or a cat but so far she had failed in nothing she set out to do and we thought it advisable to tie up our dogs for safety sake. Unused to captivity, they spent the night howling.

Next morning we decided to consult Bill, our workman of long standing, whose views were always or mostly always taken into account.

"By the *Croí-an-diabhail*" said Bill, "if she pulps a live dog we will have her put in jail." Any matter that required some thought deserved a complete fill of the pipe and when he had smoke rising steadily he gave us his final decision. "I will have a few words with the boss and who knows, if I can manage it, I will have her packed off home about her business."

Bill's application for her dismissal fell upon deaf ears. My father was of the opinion that in due course she would become a reasonably good housekeeper. Unfortunately she never did; in fact, she grew worse and bolder by the day. There was a sort of hierarchical approach to everything as far as Savage was concerned. She dutifully saw to it that all orders from the boss were carried out, and all others were expected to carry out the very same orders when retransmitted by her. Her orders were never-ending: "Bring in coal, bring in water, go to the shop, sweep the path," etc, etc.

After a dose of these orders I said to her one day, "Why do you have to pick on me all the time?"

"Because," said she and she was full in earnest. "If you don't do as you are told I will give you plenty of the rod across the bare collops."

I thought it best to pull up my stockings and go to work. Her approach to matters under her control was undoubtedly foolproof. Where Savage was in charge, namely around the house and the yard, one obeyed orders.

There were days when she would grab a young cockerel and, holding it between her knees, proceed to saw its head off with a knife repeating over and over, "Ha, me boyo, your dancing days are over! Ha, me boyo, your dancing days are over!" Next day when she had the chicken in the oven she would open the oven door and remind it that its dancing days were over. To make matters worse, my brother tried to intimidate me with stories about school, of how boys and girls were severely punished over trivial matters such as "Not knowing your lessons" or "Being Late for School". Some teachers had long rods, but the Master had an ash-plant the same as those used for cattle on "fair-days." Foolishly I believed he was exaggerating – time alone would tell. "Wait and see," said he.

I had not long to wait. Came the morning when school re-opened, Savage was told to take me to school. This was a kind of "special offer". I would be taken by an adult rather than having to trot along with an older brother like most boys of my age.

My father made it his business to absent himself from the scene and when Savage considered it was time to move she said, "Come on, my boyo, your dancing days are over." I refused to move. "Come on me boyo," said she "your dancing days are over." She grabbed my arm and dragged me all the way to school, giving me no opportunity to dig in my heels. All the sympathy I got during the long haul was, "Come on me boyo, we are nearly there."

The uneven tug-o-war finally ended when she flung me inside the classroom door.

Merciful God, will I ever forget the situation in which I found myself. Infant's class was right inside the door and I found myself surrounded by about twenty closely-cropped, mallet-headed, open-mouthed, wretched and pathetic looking urchins like myself.

In the middle stood Ban Ní Hackendoosh. She formed us into a sort of semi-circle around the blackboard. Then she held up a long rod with the intention of explaining to us, that under certain circumstances the rod would be put to work. One fellow with a rather big head did not seem all that interested in the procedure, turned his back whereupon Ban Ní Hackendoosh gave him a good cut of the rod across the backside after which she was able to cut short her lecture. Fortunately I was aware that people could write and I was not surprised when Ban Ní Hackendoosh wrote something on the blackboard. But! This was different. This was IRISH. Grandad had told me about the great fright Belshazzer got long ago, when the fingers of a hand came forth and wrote upon the wall as if on sand and of how the King's countenance changed and of how his thoughts troubled him as his knees smote one against another. And of how the whole company were filled with terror, fainting and trembling as their hearts panted.

The scene in our school was exactly like the scene in the great hall in Babylon, as Ban Ní Hackendoosh wrote in Irish upon the blackboard. Now we knew how Belshazzer and his friends were afrightened.

But, for us there was no divine illumination. As day followed day things got steadily worse. In 1925 Osborn Bergin complained "*The children on whom the burden of reviving the Irish language was placed, were handed over to a regime of sadists.*" We know he spoke the truth. To us the crack of the stick around our knees and every exposed part of the body was synonymous with the teaching of Irish. One teacher made a practice of bringing the stick down hard on one ear and then on the other and if you moved your head to save your ear you got the stick down on top of your head which was worse; so you stood like a statue and took your beating, be it on the hands, the legs, the ears, the head. We truly suffered on behalf of the Irish language. We suffered even more if that were possible on behalf of the "teachings of the Holy Roman Catholic Church." As far as Ban Ní Hackendoosh was concerned nothing mattered except "your prayers in Irish and the Irish language". In her view, the English had committed so many crimes God would not hear prayers in English; we had fairly good proof that prayers in Irish were also ignored.

Government lackeys called this Compulsory Education. It certainly was *compulsory*. But I have grave reservations about the educational benefit of such tyranny. They failed to make Irish the spoken language of the country and almost succeeded in wiping out the last vestige of true Christianity. Hate and hostility took the place of love and esteem. My uncle Conor could have told them: "Brute force will get you nowhere".

Every child had to attend school every day the school was open until they reached fourteen years of age. And we eagerly looked forward to the day of emancipation. Whenever a child was ill, and perhaps dying, the parents were obliged to send an apologetic note to the Principal outlining the reason for the child's absence. Some of these pathetic little notes were read aloud for the teacher's amusement and the ridicule of parents. Whenever David or myself missed a day from school my father offered the same excuse every time. He simply wrote we were "unavoidably absent" and that was the end of the matter. Every age and generation will produce men capable of circumventing the most rigid rules and regulations, and we were not to be outdone.

Whenever we were kept at home for a genuine reason, we took the opportunity to get two notes instead of one, by demanding a note for the Master before going to bed and demanding another before setting out for school, on the grounds that the original was lost. In this way we mostly always had a note in reserve. With a note in reserve the way was open to take a day off at any time and the temptation was always there especially in summer. To spend a day lying in the sun in some uncut meadow or holed up in some graveyard or better still splashing about in some deep warm pool was something to look forward to. We generally had a tuppenny packet of Woodbines each on the unofficial day off. But we had to be very, very careful. Mitching or "*slinging*" from school was a terrible offence meriting almost the death penalty. Discovery would lead to endless trouble at home and abroad. Nevertheless it was well worth the risk. The happiest days of our lives were spent in old disused lime-kilns, old graveyards and fairyforts but the best days of all were spent around the river. Sooner or later things were bound to go wrong.

It was a lovely warm morning in June and keeping well under cover we made our way to our favourite pool. Needless to say we did not bring our togs but being completely nude made little difference once we were in the water. In a shady place where there were some bushes we undressed, and leaving everything we ran to the pool. We did the breast-stroke and the back-stroke and the crawl and then we turned our attention to floating. Hours must have gone by before we became tired of the water. We ran for our clothes; Merciful God Almighty, our clothes were gone and our schoolbags were gone! In our situation, dear reader, what would you have done? We saw how easy it was for someone to come along and pick up our belongings, not that they were of any great value to anybody except ourselves. We blamed the tinkers. They got blamed for everything anyway.

"The longest day I live," said Jerh D, "I will never ever forgive the b… that took my clothes." And there we sat like three hairless monkeys with our knees drawn up to our chins; but apes and monkeys would not or could not make the mistake we made.

In every parish there is a practical joker, and true to form we had ours. He fancied himself as a funny man. He imagined himself the life and soul of every party. In actual fact he was a proper buffoon.

We saw him coming towards us along the river bank. We decided to hold our seats.

Talk about the innocent story. "I found them clothes, an with the schoolbags and books an all I thought I was doing the right thing – I handed everything in at the school." (Jerh D lived up to his promise.

Twenty years later the "joker" on a return visit from England had good cause to regret his smartness). "Now go back to school," said the joker as he walked off laughing.

We now held what could hardly be described as a council of war but, as the saying goes, we did put our heads together. Of one thing we were certain: we were not marching into school bare-naked thereby giving the teachers a feast and a field-day probably lining us up for all to see before they set to work with rods and canes, and all this before getting our clothes back.

There was only one thing we could do and I was the only one who could do it. Someone of us had to go home and steal some clothes without being caught.

Jerh D lived in the middle of the village and no way could he make it in home and out again unobserved.

Billy's house was a long way away, well over a mile and, taking this into account, he was almost certain to be spotted. I had the feeling I could make it to the house – but what if Savage laid eyes upon me entering the house naked? She would, as a matter of course, side with the enemy. I knew my father would not be in the kitchen. He had a special place where he spent most of his time reading and I knew Bill would be out around the fields with sheep or cattle. I set off.

As I crept nearer the house I saw Savage heading off to the shop. The coast was clear. I rushed upstairs, found a shirt and pants for myself and quickly put them on. Then I collected clothes for Jerh D and Billy. They were more than glad to see me.

In the meantime, the Master had a few swigs from the bottle as he waited to pounce and Ban Ní Hackendoosh was brimming over with excitement. To see us get a right good beating would make her day. The excitement quickly spread to the girls' school and the Principal there was never known by any other name than the "Witch" and seemingly she alone thought it was a matter for the Guards as a first instalment! Her assistant was always called the "Cutler". She never said "hold out your hand for six slaps". She always said "hold out your hand for six good cuts" and giving anything less than six was never considered. She had a head of long red hair and her legs were awful. The fat was bulging out over her shoes and she had no ankles. She is the one who said she "would prefer beating barefoot boys to eating a chicken dinner". All afternoon they waited for us, tension mounting all the time. And, as time went on, the seriousness of the situation began to dawn on them.

The Witch began to ask questions. "What if the boys are still in the river? You should have told that man put the clothes back where he found them. What if they catch a cold or a fever and die as a result? What if they decide on a triple suicide? I told you," said she, "it was a matter for the Guards."

By this time we had worked out a plan and we made our way to the school bridge and here lay in wait for our classmates on their way home.

They told us the Master was as drunk as a kite and this was great news. He never went to the trouble of chastising anyone if he had enough brandy.

The way was clear. We went up to the school to find them all in conference. He stood looking at us in disbelief.

"Sir, we came for our books and clothes." said Jerh D.

"I want a full and proper explanation of this caper", said the Master and he took another sup from the almost empty bottle. Straight away, without pausing for a moment, Jerh D gave the full story.

"Every morning we go for a dip in the river but this morning someone stole our clothes. We tried everywhere but could not find them, and Sir, we nearly died and without our books and without our clothes we – we, were afraid the Priest might come fishing and see us naked and maybe beat us with the fishing-rod an it full of hooks. We nearly died, Sir, without clothes."

"Right," said the Master, "I warn you be more careful in future."

Case dismissed!

8

THE POWER OF THE CÚPLA FOCAL

A number of years ago I attended a poetry reading and many of the poems required a long explanation. The meaning was vague and many were, in my view, meaningless.

One of the "poets" offered to read a poem by any member of the audience if they handed it up before he finished. Straightaway I began to write about *The Old School.*

"It's sixty years ago today
Since we sat down together!
We thought the school a mighty place
But, then we knew no better.
Day after day, day after day,
It was the same old mixture.
The cane was seldom in its place
Behind the holy picture.
Out on the road the tinkerman
Was singing in his caravan.
His children all ran wild and free,
And filled us all with jealousy.
To our old school, it seemed a rule
No scholars came or thinkers.
We often wished to God on high

We'd all been born tinkers."

Perhaps it was the way he read it, but one thing was obvious: the audience appreciated my poem much more than they did other complicated and unnatural verses.

Many of them may have memories of the barbarous tyranny of the teachers and religious brothers during the early days of the Irish Free State.

It is more than likely some readers will misunderstand much of what I have to say in these pages – however, being misunderstood is nothing new. Many better able to explain themselves failed to explain what they were on about. Men like Socrates and Galileo and Newton and other craftsmen in words failed to convince or persuade those who had no wish to learn the truth.

Let there be no doubt about it, our generation suffered their share for the "Faith of our Fathers" and many and many tears were shed because the Irish language was made an essential. Without the *cúpla focal,* all doors were closed firmly against you.

The then Government had visions of an Irish nation speaking the Irish language, but my uncle Conor could have told them: "Brute force will get you nowhere".

Around this time, there was an outbreak of patriotism, the like of which the unfortunate ordinary people found hard to endure. For months before an election of any sort, our principal amusement was listening to political orations after Mass on Sundays. We did not know one party from the other and we were always hopeful the speaker would be heckled and given some verbal abuse from some bold man at the back of the crowd. A rush of angry young men towards the "platform" would be greatly appreciated and to see the "'speaker" getting a few good kicks in the backside was most enjoyable.

As a rule, the man being kicked about was demanding the "Right of Free Speech" and his attackers told him in no uncertain terms "There is no right of free speel or parlance for bloody traitors."

Politicians soon learned that by opening their tirade with some sort of a salutation in Irish which nobody understood was a good way to keep down the temperature of the crowd.

The speaker who opened with "Ladies and Gentlemen" was suspect immediately and he would be told by some infuriated supporters of the other party "This is a free country, the days of the Ladies and Gentlemen are over". A lone voice might be heard: "You can say *that* again."

My father never stood to hear any of their rhetoric; he and a few others of like mind went as always to Nunan's at The Ford where they had a few drinks. Bill, on the other hand even in his old age enjoyed the fighting as much as we did.

One Sunday morning a fight started beside him and he was given a few blows for no reason whatsoever. Next morning my father asked: "Bill, who gave you the black eye?"

"Ah, the *Croí-an-diabhail*, don't have any pity for me. I gave as good as I got. In my young days I would beat the lot of them with my cap."

"Every other Sunday they are speechmaking – come down to The Ford with us. You are too old now and you should have better sense. One speaker who appeared quite often and who later became a minister in de Valera's Government told us one morning "The six counties are not yet free, but if they don't come in shortly, I will personally see to it that they are brought in on a shutter." Great applause followed his announcement. And then someone shouted, "Get off that ditch, you Goddamn bank robber." Quick as lightning, the "bank robber" replied, "Of course we robbed the banks. Who had a better right to the money in the banks than the men who were fighting for, and dying for, our beloved country, our Faith and our Motherland." Prolonged cheers and back-slapping and buck-lepping followed and any schoolboy could see there was little or no sympathy with the banks.

There were plenty of candidates seeking seats in what many of them described as "the corrupt Cork County Council!" Every candidate for Dáil Eireann or the "corrupt Cork County Council" had to learn a few words of Irish or at least the essential "*cúpla focal*".

Without the *cúpla focal,* which very very few understood, there was little hope of being elected.

Many prospective TD's and County Councillors got around the Language Problem by simply learning how to preface all their speeches with a verse or even half a verse of some poem in Irish.

Mise Eire was a great favourite and most impressive when recited by a heavy man with a huge abdomen which came to a point about two feet in front of the rest of his body. Dermot Mick Óg was such a man and to hear him bellowing *Mise Eire* was a never to be forgotten experience. However, Dermot Mick Og was not confined to just one poem. He had another verse and it went something like this:

"*Go d-togfar an baile-si ar ainnsior*
Cill chair brega fis go h-ard
'S go brat no go d-tiocfad an dilionn
Ní faicfear i fis ar lár"

Even when translated this had little meaning but it went down very well with the crowd. No one ventured an interpretation. Nevertheless, men could be heard whispering, "Do you hear that? – the Mick Óg's were always fond of the Irish."

"Yerra me dear boy, that Dermot could talk the Irish to the Pope of Rome."

"And to the Pope of America" butted in another.

"Begorra then he will get my two first preference votes."

"More power to you Ned! More power to you!"

Apart from the *cúpla focal* there were other serious questions which were asked at almost every public meeting. The question most often put to the speechmakers was "Where were you in 1916? Where the hell were you in 1916?"

There were several good answers to this question. One could say, "I was side by side with Paddy Pearse in the GPO". or "I was manning the breach in the wall with Jim Connolly". But by far the best answer was "I was hoping you would ask me that question because there may be a few people unaware of the fact that I was de Valera's right hand man in Boland's Mills during Easter Week and we were the last to lay down our guns and I am glad of the opportunity to dispel any obscurity in relation to that matter."

There were plenty of "begrudgers" who said O'Connell Street would not hold all those claiming to have been in the GPO with Pearse and Connolly. And if all those claiming to have been with de Valera were put together they would completely cover the Dublin mountains. Be that as it may, I remember one old fellow being asked "Where were you in 1916?" The old man looked the heckler straight in the eye and answered "*Do bí me sa bhaile*." The heckler who understood not a single word of Irish was put well and truly in his place. An onlooker shouted "That shook you." The old man was then allowed to finish his speech. Such was the power of the *cúpla focal* all because it was understood by so few. It almost matched Latin, the power of which was known only to the clergy and medical profession.

We were the first tidy towns people. As fast as the various parties put up posters, we tore them down. They responded by nailing their posters higher and higher on the telephone poles. There were no ESB. poles, no electricity, no amplifiers. Our politicians did their own shouting and we saw them in flesh and blood. They were there with us, sometimes bandaged, but they were there. Not like the present shower of silhouettes whom we see on television all dandied up in a kind of suspended animation between cornflakes and washing-up liquid.

Unfortunately, election campaigns don't go on for ever and soon we would be thrown back on our own resources such as hunting, fishing, trespassing, tree-climbing or indeed raiding local orchards. There was one orchard that no one had courage enough to enter day or night because it was haunted by some kind of monk. Many stories were told about a ghost who was to be avoided at all costs. We decided to consult an adult regarding this haunted orchard. As luck would have it, our contact was the greatest liar in the Irish Free State at that time and we were unaware of his great gift.

"Tell us Jerh, did you ever raid Brides' orchard?" A far-away look came in his eyes as he began –

"Will I ever forget the night! Myself and Flur said to ourselves, 'to hell with the ghost! We will raid Brides' orchard.' I warned Flur to bring a good big bag; so we struck off with two bags for Brides' orchard. The longest day – as long as I live I will never forget the day and date! 'Tis stuck in my mind ever since. It was the night of the sixth of May . . ."

Now this date is stuck in my mind too ever since. Could there have been apples in May in Brides' haunted orchard?

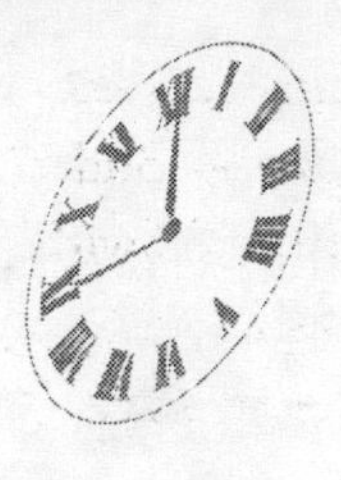

9

Hide Like Elephants

Not all teachers at this time were fluent Irish speakers and some of the older ones hadn't a clue. The Witch was one of these and she justified her ignorance of the language by declaring "There was no Irish in my time."

She supported the idea of an Irish speaking nation and she spared no effort in bringing this about. Her assistant, the Cutler, was able to bluff her way with some few words. In other words, she had the all important *cúpla focal*. The Witch had a poor opinion of her assistant in most subjects but especially so when it came to Irish. To circumvent this drawback, arrangements were made whereby the Witch would march all the "big" girls into our school for a more advanced form of Irish.

We were delighted! This would divert the Master's attention away from us once in a while but the girls were under the false impression that paying attention to his lessons in Irish was a waste of time. One day he lost his temper with them. "Six slaps for each of you." said he and as the first girl held out her hand the Witch spoke, "Sir," said she, "slap them as hard as you can. They have hides like elephants." And this from one who had no word of Irish herself! Is it any wonder then, that a hatred of the Irish Language became buried in our bones. The Witch was a frail old hag; skin where she wasn't bone, with knuckles like burnished steel, and eyes forever riveted on you. The penalty for being late into school was a slap for every minute lost and if you belonged to the Master's classes you had to pass through Ban Ní Hackendoosh's area and she availed of the opportunity to give you a few skelps of the rod around the legs, as you made your way up to the Master for more of the same. Needless to say, most of us were half an hour early rather than half an hour late. There is some truth in the old proverb, "*The devil will find work for idle hands to do*".

One morning as we played about, a few of the bigger boys decided to put some gravel in the locks and so prevent the key turning. The locks were huge affairs and the keys might well be mistaken for the keys of the Tower of London.

We watched him try to turn the key. Time and time again he failed. Kicking and thumping the doors was of no avail. Our spirits rose. We would have at least one day off or perhaps a week while the mighty Board of Works decided what action, if any, they should take in the matter. Remembering what one county councillor said during the recent election when questioned about the failure of the council to act on some serious matter; "Big bodies" said he "move slowly".

We had no reason to believe the Board of Works would suddenly spring to life and provide new doors and locks. Indeed, if things were allowed to run their normal course many of the boys might well have reached school-leaving age before the place was back in business. Alas, those thoughts of joys and longings were soon to end.

When the Master gave up trying the Witch took over. I can still see her mounting the granite steps with her high-buttoned half-empty boots. With her long bony fingers she started to claw out the gravel and in a matter of minutes the doors opened.

The Cutler said, "No girl was involved in this." and Ban Ní Hackendoosh told the Master "My brats are too well-disciplined to try anything like this."

The suspects were thus narrowed down to those under his own personal control.

For us it was a dreadful day; for him it was a day of hard manual labour. He was ruthlessly vindictive and he would turn on a boy in a savage frenzy. Every blow of the ash-plant left a black and blue stripe. All day the brutal treatment went on and on.

Putting gravel in the locks was a dismal failure. We would have to think of something else. We had suffered too much. That very evening it dawned upon us that all that was required to get our own back was one united attack. Forty of us could not fail. There was one who did not approve of the plan. "As regards the stick," said he "my father says we don't get half enough of it."

"You are already beaten into an idiot!" said Jerh D. "Try it," said the Slob "and we will see who is the *eegit*." It is always a set-back when someone gets cold feet. Final preparations for a united attack were put off for the time being.

In the meantime, I decided to talk over the matter with my father, letting him know it was to be a united attack and that there was no ringleader.

"Well," said he "it looks like a good idea. Everyone having a blow at the Master and he crying for mercy, and then pushing him into the backhouse for a few hours."

"We forgot about the backhouse. Would it be a good idea to stick his head down the hole?"

"'Tis a great plan." said he. "The trouble is, it was tried before and it was a failure."

"Why was it a failure?" I asked. "Well," said he "twelve o'clock was zero hour and all eyes were on the clock. When the time came only one boy jumped on the Master and you can guess what happened to him, or can you?"

"I know well what happened to him." said I. "Whatever you do," said he "don't be the first boy to jump on the Master." He went on reading his book to let me know the discussion was over.

I think he knew the Master was quite safe and I must admit good advice costs nothing.

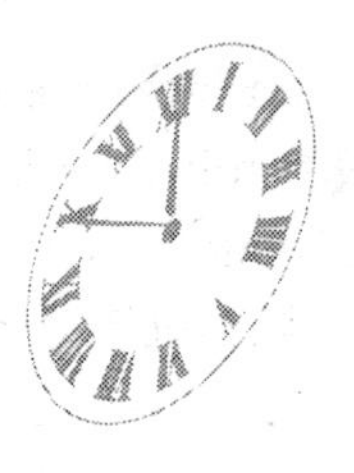

10

THE NEW TAR ROAD

It took "macadamisation" over one hundred years to reach our part of the country and as far as local farmers were concerned it was a very unwelcome development. Jack Pad said it would be no longer safe to take a horse on the road. Jamesy Ben was of the opinion that a donkey without shoes might hold his ground on "them damn slippery tar roads". And Big Mick wanted to know who was paying the rates. "Was it," he asked "the farmers or the county councillors?"

Jack Pad butted in again, "There are only two motor-cars in this parish. One belongs to the parish priest and Captain Leader owns the other. And while Leader owns more land than all of us put together he is not a proper farmer."

"The wrong men were shot!" said Jamesy Ben.

"'Tis not too late to shoot a few more!" said Big Mick. "Imagine going down the Fairfield hill with a load of fat pigs and to have the legs taken from under the horse!"

Every kind of casualty and catastrophe was foreseen and discussed. In spite of much verbal opposition the tarring of the road went ahead. It was a slow process, this being the first operation of its kind in the area.

A local man who had worked all his life for the County Council was put in charge of the tarring machine: a complicated affair drawn by a horse and it containing a huge fire-box for heating the tar and lifting equipment for lifting full barrels of tar onto the machine. There was a hand pump at which one man was employed and most important of all, a long flexible tube with two handles, enabling the man in charge to direct the jet of hot tar to wherever necessary.

Danlie was the name of the man in charge but from then on he would always be known as Danlie Taro. Some people called his machine *d'oul biler*, a derogatory term which Danlie Taro did not like.

Well! It is often said "if you can't beat them, join them". Many people who owned houses along the road would sidle up to Danlie Taro in the local pub, where he spent every night "freeing his thorax from the damn tar".

"And a pint here for Danlie, Bridie, when you have time."

"Thanks you're a decent man . . . God spare you the health!"

"I just thought of it now that I'm talking to you, would you give a "stout or two" of tar into my small gate when ye are passing?"

"I'm not supposed to do it."

"Bridie, a couple a more here . . . I know that Dan, I know that. I wouldn't be asking a stranger now would I?"

To make a long story short, it generally cost about three pints to have a patch of tar outside the small gate. Farmers were not slow to ask Danlie Taro to give the wheels of the cart a good daub of tar as well and this cost about the same. "Macadamisation", as you can see, gave rise to what would nowadays be called "spin off" and the IRA and other political parties were quick to avail of the smooth surface for their different slogans. A bucketful of limewash would paint many various slogans, and crossroads were the main targets.

One night a crossroads near us got a fierce daubing. On one road they printed, or if you like, painted "*Boycott British Goods*". On another they painted "*Up de Valera*" and on the fourth road they painted "*Disband the CID*". A man by the name of John McCabe lived near the crossroads and he was first to see the daubing. John was a proper gentleman and a strong supporter of the Cosgrave Government. Like most farmers, he did not like this daubing. Some horses were very frightened of it and some were known to bolt at the sight of it!

John went home and prepared some whitewash, found himself a wide brush, and returned to the crossroads. His intention was not to blot out the slogans already painted. He wanted to cancel their effect on the public with the minimum of effort. This he did by painting in one word *Bullshit* in large print, in the vacancy between the other slogans.

The tarring of the road had to take place on dry summer days and this coincided with the time when most boys and girls were glad to shed the "ball and chain" of heavy boots. There were a few notable exceptions: the boy with only one leg, who held on to his boot no matter how warm the weather, and one or two who had feet as flat as bread plates – the type of feet which would give any shoemaker a bad name. One day, when I was in the city with my father, I saw some monks wearing sandals and when I told the boys in school about them they came to the conclusion the monks were wearing the sandals as a form of penance – to make up for the sins of the world.

The day came when we could hear the voices of the roadmen outside the school and we could smell the hot tar. A strange smell at that time.

The road was always our playground; boys to the left of the gate, girls to the right and here on the road we all enjoyed our few minutes freedom.

Today all discretion was thrown to the winds. We all collected around Danlie Taro and his tarring machine. For a while, we watched the work in progress. It was not long however until some dare-devil dipped his toe in the pool of tar. Soon boys were stepping in and out of the hot sticky tar. Soon the girls joined in the fun. All except one. She was an only child and everyone said she was a right pet. Now she was standing out with her white legs. A few of the boys got long rods which they dipped in the tar and it was great fun rubbing the tarry sticks across her legs, back and front. She stood still while they did a right job on her!

Things were going great until the Master arrived at the gate and instead of the usual "fag", he put the whistle in his mouth. I never heard a more vicious sounding whistle! There is an old saying "*too much laughing comes to crying*" and this is exactly what happened in this case.

We were ordered into school and the floor was covered with footprints reminding us of Robinson Crusoe and Man Friday.

There we were, male and female, flotsam and jetsam, standing before our four tormentors. Their faces showed we had offended all the gods of ancient Egypt, Greece, Rome and the god of mercy too – especially the latter.

The sour face of the Witch proclaimed the end of the world, for all practical purposes, and no amount of whipping and beating could avert the catastrophe brought about by our paddling in the tar. Ban Ní Hackendoosh had a gleam in her eye in anticipation. The Cutler sat on the table, swinging the big legs as usual. The Master was pale-faced and worried-looking as he replaced the bottle of brandy behind some books. I looked up at the holy-picture and I saw our Saviour looking down on us with great pity, at least that is how it appeared to me.

"Tar," said the Master "can give you skin disease which will turn into cancer. It can also cause eczema and dermatitis."

The Witch gave a loud groan "dermatitis in the school, the school is finished!"

The Master continued "Tar can cause chronic ringworm for which there is no known cure."

The Cutler looked at Ban Ní Hackendoosh while saying in a loud voice "chronic ringworm!" and Ban Ní Hackendoosh answered back "running chronic ringworm."

"O my God!" said the Witch, making the sign of the cross. The Master continued "Apart from these terrible dangers, there is the long term effect of you smearing tar all over yourselves which is the probability that all of you will be completely bald in a matter of weeks. I am now ordering all of you out to the stream and may God help any one of you with a speck of tar on your legs in an hours time!"

Shattered by the gravity of the situation, we were turning to go when the Cutler put up her hand to halt us. "Before you go," said she "I know that the boys are the cause of all this trouble and for this blackguarding any villain who comes back in with tar on his legs will be bastinadoed! I will see to that. Go now and remember what the Master has told you."

No one wanted to be bald for life nor were "running chronic ringworm and dermatitis" pleasant prospects. Needless to say, we went to work with a will using soil for soap. Moss and grass and the bark of trees were all tried out as tar-removers.

All was going well until some lad from the village enquired. "What is that she said she would do to us?"

"I know what it is," said a farmer's son. "I saw it done to ram lambs. We are going to be, you know – splayed."

No one could think of the word she used. Now however, the meaning was clear and things already serious became more so. I could see around me all the boys with solemn frowning faces, working against time trying to remove the deadly dangerous tar, which all of a sudden had become truly fatal, owing to the new definition given to the word which not one of us could remember. There is a proverb which says, "*Men who are unhappy, like men who sleep badly, are always proud of the fact*". Admittedly, we were not yet men and there was little in our present predicament to be proud of. We were devastated. Were all the other diseases rolled into one it would be nothing to compare with this new development in the line of punishment. We returned to the scrubbing with renewed vigour.

The run-away tortured negro slave could follow the north star; and I was just thinking of setting off for the north star myself when we heard another spiteful blast of the whistle.

Awed by authority like sheep, we went inside. The Master and the bottle were both "far gone" and he could no longer focus. The Cutler took over and all the girls were sent off to their own school room. Things did not look good. We were being sorted out. The boy born with only one leg and the couple of lads with the terrible flat feet, who had to wear boots at all times, were also eliminated from the leg inspection. They could now see providence was no longer unfair on them. They would now see the great "runners and jumpers" being humiliated because of our robust activities. Fortunately, they had no idea of the despair prevailing in the ranks of the runners and jumpers. There were times when we wished we were born free like *tinkers*. Now we wished we had been born with only one leg or kind of disabled, with flat feet.

"Delinquency of this nature," said the Cutler "will be stamped out! It is not a mere matter of getting a few cuts of the ash-plant." One by one, we were inspected and after inspection told to stand over at on the right or on the left, as she saw fit. We had no idea which batch would go free . . . talk about the valley of Josephat . . . we got that feeling – a feeling one could never forget.

After the immediate judgement, another kind of general judgement took place during which six of us were moved from one side to the other . . . and we still did not know if this was a good or a fatal move. As it transpired, we were added to that group which would not be wiped off the map.

The group held back for this new punishment looked forlorn; surrounded by the rest of us, now transformed into callous and unemotional brutes, ready to watch them suffer.

My friend Jerh D was one of the unlucky ones and I would have freed him if I could. But also in that unlucky group was the big slob whose father had said that we "did not get half enough of the stick". Even if I had had the power I would not have freed this fellow. That evening he would walk home a tame boy and his father would have no more complaints!

"This lot," said she "face the table, one behind the other, in line." There was some pushing about. No one wanted to be nearest the table. She pretended not to notice this trial of strength. Jerh D was the youngest and weakest. He was forced to stand nearest the table.

The others took their places behind him and the big slob, being the strongest, was last in line. In all, there were six for "capital" punishment.

The Master was admiring the small amount of brandy in the bottle, having completely lost interest in the proceedings.

"Now," said the Cutler "we can learn something new every day and today you will learn what it is like to be bastinadoed. I mean well bastinadoed!"

All eyes were upon her and when she took hold of the ash-plant it was a bit of an anti-climax. After all, we were all well-acquainted with the heavy end of the ash-plant. After this great build-up of fear, one would think there was nothing new under the sun. But once again we were wrong.

"Jermiah," said she "I want you to hold the table and raise one foot so that I can give you two cuts on the sole of your foot." Jerh D did as he was told. She put the stick under his toes to bring the foot to the ideal position. "Now," said she "I will give you two cuts on this foot and then two more on the other. Jimmy, you are next. And there will be two extra cuts for you and so on; two extra for every brat of you until we come to the big *fasthook* at the end. He will receive fourteen cuts!"

"Are you ready Jermiah?"

"Yes, Mam."

He got four slaps of the ash-plant on the bare feet, but true to form he did not shed a tear.

She was working so hard and putting all her strength to work. I was afraid she might run out of energy before she came to the big slob at the end. I need not have worried. Now it was his turn. "Fourteen cuts for you, you big coward, for pushing all the smaller boys to the front. Only a coward would hide behind boys smaller than himself." She took her time delivering the cuts. Soon he was bawling crying and she said, "Stop being a cry-baby or I will give you more!"

Finally, this terrible ordeal was over and things returned to normal.

Worse could have happened.

11

THE KNOCK ON THE DOOR

That evening I was thinking over the events of the day and I decided to have a second opinion about the effect of tar on humans. I told my father about what happened in school. "The Master," said he "need not have been so frightened. In the old days people drank tar-water as a preventative against any diseases. Dean Swift, for instance, was a great drinker of tar-water."

"You know," said I "when the Cutler said we were all to be bastinadoed, we thought something else was going to be done like . . ." and here I hesitated because now it seemed ridiculous.

"Like what?"

"Like Bill does to the lambs."

"What a pack of fools. Take down the dictionary and find the word."

I found the word. *Bastinado – a mild form of corporal punishment; to beat the soles of the feet with a cudgel.* "Ah," said I "the dictionary is wrong. She gave Tim Nolan fourteen hard cuts on the bare feet. Do you think that is '*mild*'?"

"Remember," said he "we are talking about oriental countries where the hand is cut off for stealing and the head for too much talking."

"Well!" said I "if I was as big as Nolan I would attempt to choke her!"

"In that case," said my father "old Nolan might have to thrash the young fellow himself. Perhaps the fourteen cuts were the lesser of two evils."

My father had a good answer to everything. It was implicit in his summing up of things that I should not be too impulsive.

Next morning, we were all sitting down at breakfast, Bill expounding about the weather as usual, when suddenly the old lion-headed iron knocker went *bang, bang, bang*. My father turned to Savage saying "you'd better see who it is." And before Savage reached the door the knocker went mad again. The modernised door bell will never express the urgency or demand admittance on the same scale. The moment the door was opened the "Half Ton", that was the only name we had for her, strode straight into the hall and into the kitchen, carrying in her hand a lively-looking long rod. And believe me, she wasted no time in salutations. Addressing my father directly she began, "Your ruffian of a son was one of the curs who destroyed my little girl, an' she an only child! They daubed tar all over her. Her skin is burnt. Her hair is falling out and now she is in her dying bed. I am not leaving this house until I see skelps taken out of that ruffian." And she pointed the rod at me. "I have been to every house this morning and I have seen some of them curs taken from their beds and reddened from the small of their backs to their heels . . . and you may say Mr. Nolan's son won't grow up a blackguard after what he got this morning! In every house them curs that ruined my little girl were well paid off!"

Now she was waiting for action to be taken.

My father turned to her and said "If things are as serious as you say I have the feeling we will be hearing from you again."

"Are you refusing to chastise that brat or do I have to do it myself?"

"I am asking you to leave."

"I will go when I get satisfaction."

My father turned to Savage. "Elly, will you show this woman out." Savage jumped up, grabbed the "Half Ton" by the hair and with no difficulty dragged her out into the hall, down the steps, down the path to the gate where she had her donkey and cart. Savage waited until the

Half Ton was half-way into the cart and she gave her a powerful kick in the backside, saying "Don't we see you around here again!"

While the rest of the household were getting over the invasion I found myself putting on my stockings and boots. The fun had gone out of going barefoot, for the time being at any rate.

I took the short cut across the fields, creeping like a snail. Truly it can be said that man creates the evil he endures.

I had no notion the Half Ton would make the school her last port of call. From what I had heard, she had had a very successful tour that morning, getting satisfaction everywhere except at our house.

There she was, tying her donkey to the school gate. More than likely she would get the Master to give me the punishment my father thought unnecessary. Alas! I had an exaggerated opinion of my importance. The Half Ton had bigger fish to fry. The moment I stood inside the door it really was as if something had struck the planet. She was already in action. "You drunken bum. You are not fit to teach. You have failed to maintain discipline. You allowed my little girl to be destroyed with tar, by a gang of ruffians under no control while you were filling your belly with brandy."

"That's enough of that from you." shouted Ban Ní Hackendoosh.

"Don't you forget what you are, Hackendoosh — an unqualified JAM also unfit to teach," The Half Ton shouted back and by now the Cutler and the Witch had come in from the girls school to join in the confrontation. The Half Ton was now warning Ban Ní Hackendoosh to keep her big mouth shut.

I never saw any group taken more by surprise and in spite of everything, one could almost feel public opinion veering around in support of our teachers.

"We will have no more of this." said the Cutler. "Get outside the door and stop behaving like a trollop!"

The Half Ton turned on her.

"You ignorant red-handed gipsy. You don't know the meaning of the word *trollop*. You are the one who would not allow my little girl out to the back because she could not remember your *bhfuil cead agam dul amach?*, making her stand all day in wet clothes. Yourselves and your bloody Irish! I have forgotten more Irish than all of you together. By God, I will give you *bhfuil cead agam dul amach?* 'Tis the queer vulgar way you have for teaching Irish. I will have the four of you out of here before long. Remember I spent years up in Dublin in the civil service, working for the Department of Education and 'twas not without Irish I was up there . . . and be bloody sure I still have friends there!"

"You'd better go before I send for the guards." said the Master.

She started again. "May God be with the days when we had proper teachers appointed by the proper people and schools full of well-conducted pupils. I am now going to hand in a written report to the parish priest. Tomorrow morning I will be above in Dublin at the Department of Education. The four of you are for the road."

"The ringleaders have been well-punished." said the Cutler.

"Don't try to cod me." said the Half Ton. "You took care to strike where you would raise no blisters."

The Witch was the first to realise that confrontation was no way to settle the matter.

"Now," said she "we all have a better idea of the problem. Come along with me and perhaps we will think of something else on the way-out."

Slowly the great battleship turned and followed the Witch.

The Master made off for the hall where he always hung his old brown overcoat. Oftentime, the fresh bottle was left in the inside pocket. When he returned, a few minutes later, he looked much better, quite refreshed and cool as could be. "I have an announcement to make." said he. "I will try and change places with Mr Mulcahy. He was very anxious to come here a few years ago."

"Oh my God!" said the Cutler. "Not that awful man! He whips the pupils with the whip he drives to school with – the same whip for boy and beast."

"No way would I stand for that." said Ban Ní Hackendoosh.

"And," said the Witch "I am told, instead of an ordinary stick, he uses a length of whalebone the mark of which never leaves!"

"Well," said the Master "you will have discipline, which many say is lacking here at the moment."

As this discussion went on a great wave of support for the Master could be seen and felt. One of the lads that was bastinadoed the previous day said "I'd prefer the bastinado thing any day to the whalebone. I know a fellow going to Mulcahy in Daraheen school and he said they were often walking over fingertips sheared clear-off by the whalebone."

It took some time for things to settle down again. Seemingly, the parish priest took no action and small blame to him! When the Half Ton saw he had little interest in the matter, she told him that a line or two from herself to his lordship, the bishop, would soon put things right.

We don't know how she was received at the Department of Education. All we know is no action was taken. As a rule, matters of this kind were sorted out at local level.

The Half Ton did remarkably well at local level. Parents believed "her little girl" was very ill-treated and they took a serious view of it. Poor, big, fat, young Nolan came out worst, having suffered in school and at home. Old Nolan told the neighbour "That old schoolmaster is gone soft in the head."

The Half Ton took her little girl to another school. This is usually a case of *out of the frying pan into the fire.*

12

Empty Barrels

The availability of empty tar-barrels marked a turning point in the history of the Irish Free State. For the very first time there was a multi-purpose article on the market and these multi-purpose empty tar-barrels were available from the County Council at affordable prices.

As the new road surface was laid down the empty barrels were snapped up by householders along the way. For the first time many housewives could collect large quantities of rain water. This saved them many a journey to the well.

Among farmers, passive acceptance was the order of the day and the fatalism accorded to the new road gradually died away.

Farmers were the first to spot the great potential of the empty barrels. Tar-barrels were used to hold small amounts of grain, or cut in half were made into two containers. As a matter of fact, the empty tar-barrel had endless possibilities.

The less well-off farmers were able to house their animals for the first time. Whole and complete cattle-sheds were erected almost overnight, without planning permission or, more importantly, without bank loans. When barrels were cut open and flattened out they covered a good area and one farmer was heard to say "The tar-barrel is better than the *galvaneys*."

A quick look around the countryside would lead one to believe Robinson Crusoe was responsible for most of the farm buildings. The same Robinson Crusoe was responsible for our stealing two empty barrels on which to build a raft. We had the ideal place for it. A place where the river made a sharp right-hand turn, locally known as Murphy's Turn Hole. We confused the roadmen by rolling the barrels up and down the road and in the contrived confusion we dumped our two barrels deep in the woods. In due course our raft, now named "*The Ocean Star*", was pushed down the slip-way and many a hilarious hour and evening we spent onboard and overboard, as battles were fought against boarding parties.

All went well until one evening, after a day of very heavy rain, the floodwaters in the river swept "*The Ocean Star*" downstream. All evening the river continued to rise. We had little hope of ever seeing our gallant ship again.

Sic transit gloria mundi.

At this time placing cart wheels in the river was common practice; the idea being that the wood in the wheels would soak the water, causing the whole wheel to expand. This prevented the iron rim from becoming loose and spinning off on its own, leaving the wheel without protection.

People laughed when they heard that Con Doran's pair of cart wheels were swept away by the flood. Some said he was too mean to give Danlie Taro a few pints for tarring the wheels and in so doing, prevent them shrinking in the first place. Late that evening I went to the bridge and Con Doran was there gazing downstream and looking downcast.

"My wheels are gone and God only knows where they are now." He was in the happy position that he, at least, could speak openly of his loss. I, on the other hand, could say nothing about our loss of "*The Ocean Star*".

"Tomorrow morning," said Con "I will have all the lads out here and we will have no trouble finding them wheels, that is if we find them before they reach the bloody Blackwater. If they were carried to the big river they could be in the Pacific Ocean by now. Bad luck to them anyway."

As luck would have it, I met Con again next evening. He was in great humour and glad to have someone willing to listen to his story.

"We found the first wheel no trouble at all, But the other one almost made it to the whooring Blackwater. But the best of it all was that we found two bloody fine barrels tied together, things I badly wanted. One can never have too many tar-barrels."

"What do you want them for?" I asked.

"I will make them into half-barrels for hatching ducks and geese. I was damn lucky to find them. The rats ate every goose-egg I had last spring but next spring the rats will have hungry bellies!"

I then had to listen to a detailed account of how to hatch geese and ducks in half-barrels and what a pity it was that he didn't find three instead of two. Alas! Our fine ship was for the breaker's yard.

No one now thinks of the great debt owed by the people of this country to the empty tar-barrel. It raised the standard of living for man and beast.

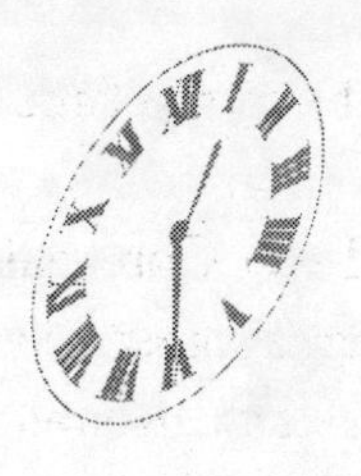

13

The Lost Art

After the confrontation with the Half Ton and the humiliation of our teachers everyone was a little subdued, but for different reasons.

We dreaded the possibility that some morning we would be confronted by the tyrant Mr Mulcahy and his stick of whalebone. We did not like the idea of walking over the severed tops of our fingers and added to this the loss of "*The Ocean Star*". The Master had the privilege of being able to drown his sorrows and this was appreciated by all concerned because he was never known to strike a pupil while under the influence.

In many ways he was a remarkable man, but the rules and regulations prevented him from teaching in the manner in which he would like to teach. When he was very drunk there would be no changing from one subject or another until all understood the lesson. There were other matters not found in school books on which he gave interesting lectures.

"Today," said he "I will tell you about the lost art of doing nothing." We were all attention. The idea of doing nothing appeals to most people but more so to schoolboys.

"Suppose for a moment that I said to fourth class sit down and for the next half hour do absolutely nothing – no reading, no writing, no Irish, no arithmetic, no spelling, no anything, no thinking, no argument, no supervision. What do you think would happen?"

I will tell you what would happen. Before five minutes were up you would be swopping pen-knives, kicking each other under the seats, sticking pins in the boy in front and throwing ink on the boy behind. Before half an hour was up, long before the half hour was up, pandemonium would take over."

He continued, "The loss of the art of doing nothing is so great I doubt if the world will ever recover. Nature has a horror of vacuum. When all is done and the work finished, evil takes over – the hand strays to the pocket . . . for what Jerh D?"

"For cigarettes, Sir."

"Correct. And Billy, the mind strays to the public house for what?"

"Drink, Sir."

"Correct again. And these are just two examples of the misfortune we had when we lost the art of doing nothing. Now will some boy tell us the meaning of the word 'pandemonium'?"

What a pity he was not drunk every day.

14

OUR GREAT HUNTING DOGS

On Friday evenings, on our way from school, the activities for Sunday were usually decided on. Hunting rabbits was a very popular sport and all the lads from the village and neighbouring farms would assemble at our place as soon as possible after Mass. Every boy brought along his dog and sometimes two dogs. Sheep dogs were the most numerous. Next in popularity came the well-known Kerry-blues and the boy who could claim that his dog was a *half-hound* was very proud indeed.

My brother was often home on weekends and he said our two sheep dogs were the only pure bred dogs in the whole "swaree" and, as I said before, he was never one to exaggerate.

A right band of hunters would set off to scour every briary ditch and fursey glen in the surrounding farms. Occasionally we would catch and kill a rabbit – perhaps it was dying anyway – but any kind of kill was good for the morale.

Rarely would we venture into the Leader Estate – not that we were afraid of meeting Captain Leader. He was rarely out around on Sundays. Unfortunately, we always seemed to run into one of the farm workers who would take it upon himself to order us "off home about our business" or if we didn't immediately, he would guarantee we would go with "sore behinds". This was a queer way to address anybody but it was more humiliating to us, who regarded ourselves as successors to Finn of the mighty Fianna, who were "taller than Roman spears". And then to add to the discomfort someone's small brother would start to cry.

Reluctantly we would turn for home with our antagonist shouting "Not one of you was man enough to wait for the boot."

This did not happen very often. But occasionally we would meet a farmer who would rage and fume about broken fences saying "If I catch you around here again it's not home ye will be going!"

"And where will we be going?"

"Ye will be going into hospital. Have I explained things?"

This kind of activity helped us forget school and homework. We went to bed tired, to dream of hares and rabbits and foxes. Needless to say we did no harm to wild life except perhaps make it wilder.

One of our dogs was called Black Shep – probably the best hunting dog in the parish and Murphy's dog Flora was almost as good. Together they enlarged many rabbit burrows, levelling many boundary fences in the process. They deserve to be remembered:

The River and the Wild Wood

The days are gone, and gone for good.
The days are gone for ever.

When we as boys ran through the wood
And played down by the river.

Our swimming pool was deep and cool
And o'er it drooped an elm.

The birds, the bees, the flowers, the trees
Were all within our realms.

We seldom captured any trout
But boy! We did annoy them!

'Twas easy count our biggest catch
And build a fire to fry them.

And when the hunting season came
Mid storms, floods and frogs

The hare and fox left us behind
With our two old hairy dogs.

Black Shep died first; then Flora died
No more we roamed the wildwood.

When we buried those old faithful friends
We buried too our childhood.

All flesh is but dust and men will follow their dogs and horses when the excitement of this life is over. As we grow older we are faced with gloomy alternatives because we know the childhood days of timeless play are gone and for ever. We had many delightful ways of wasting time and all this was before the birth of today's yahoo psychology. It is hard to remember and not feel sad. And what about all the other hunting dogs?

Jerh D he had a lovely dog.
He claimed it was a setter
Fly Head had a half-a-hound
And claimed it was far better
Good dogs we had, there is no doubt.
There was the waiting and the watching
And then the shout.

Most schoolboys suffer from what might be described as compulsion neurosis. In simple terms this means that no matter how enjoyable one sport is, instinctively, they turn to something different. Liming the river was another of our natural outlets. The fact that this was against the law did not matter and in one sense it added to the excitement. For a successful day in the river we had to procure a bucketful of lime; the fresher the better. As no boy wished to steal from his own home, we generally got it from some house where there were no children. People who had no children never developed the habit of putting things safely away.

It required little detective work to locate a supply of lime. People who had lime in stock advertised it by whitewashing the house inside and outside, thus avoiding any clash of colours. Needless to say, the roadside piers were not neglected and this drew our attention to the place. While the people of the house were having their Sunday dinner was our best opportunity to get an ample supply of our raw material for a good day's fishing. Having done this, we made off without delay to one of the good pools.

At the river bank shoes and stockings were removed – and not alone that, the short pants had to be rolled up as far as possible.

Always when out hunting we felt we were keeping up a great Irish tradition. Every effort was made to emulate *Finn McCool and the Fianna* and *The Red Branch Knights*. In other words, we were being patriotic. When liming the river we could make no such claims. However, Jerh D settled the matter by pointing out that liming the river was another way of fishing and in fact, we were now following the example of the twelve apostles.

When all was ready, half the half-naked "apostles" would enter the water upstream and the others, leaving two big boys on the bank, would enter the river downstream. Armed with long poles they worked towards the big pool, prodding and poking the banks and the black roots of the alder and elm. Not even the cleverest trout could remain hidden.

In the meantime, the two big boys on the bank would have prepared the bucket of limewash, and this was allowed to trickle into the upper end of the pool until the water was grey-white in colour. Almost immediately, fish could be seen floating on top of the water and these were raked in with little wire nets.

The cause of their death was always a matter of dispute. Some said they were "blinded-ed"; others maintained they were "poisoned-ed" and there were those who believed they were "stifled-ed".

Apparently the cause of death did not destroy the taste because later that evening there would be some great frying in every house in the village of "illegally-taken" fish.

I didn't dare take home my share of the catch because Savage made it quite clear that the sight of fish gave her "a bad turn". I always gave my share of the fish to Jerh D because I did not want to be responsible for the premature death of Savage. I had often heard it said when some old lady died "Oh, she was grand up to the time she got 'the bad turn'". I could not take such a risk.

Before we leave the river I must tell of my first encounter with Batt McSweeney. Batt owned a farm a long way upstream where the stream was very narrow. Many times I had seen him fishing with a long rod and took little notice of him, but this day he was fishing the pool we had cleaned out the day before. I thought I would tell him to try further down. I was bold enough because it was our field. "You will catch no fish there." I said.

He looked at me and smiled. "I'm not really fishing young man. Sit down here and I will tell you what I am doing."

We sat on the bank, our legs dangling over the water.

"Do you hear it?" said he.

"I hear nothing." said I and that was the truth.

"This time listen very carefully and you will hear the ripple of the stream."

I did listen. And for the very first time I heard the ripple of the stream. "I hear it. I hear it." said I.

"Ah, what a wonderful sound. I come here to listen to the ripple of the stream."

"Why?"

"For four years I heard nothing but the thunder of the big guns, the deadly rattle of machine guns and the *ping* of the sniper's bullet."

"You were in the war?"

"Some day I will tell you all about the Retreat from Mons, the Battle of the Somme and the Hindenberg Line, Festubert and Guinchy brickstacks. Today we will listen to the ripple of the stream."

Did we ever thank Batt or any of his comrades half enough, considering the misery they endured that we might live in a free world?

I listen to the ripple of the stream and think of them.

15

THE COST OF FALSE TEETH

It is true to say that after the two so-called wars the newly established Irish Free State enjoyed by far the lowest standard of living in Europe. With widespread unemployment and other social problems, plus a population well versed in lawlessness, things were absolutely "cat".

In those days, if a poor person wanted to see a doctor they first had to go to somebody who held a book of tickets, usually a big farmer or shopkeeper, and explain all about their problem to them before being handed a ticket. To make matters worse, there were two kinds of tickets. On being handed a red ticket the doctor was obliged to call to the home of the person who was ill; the man responsible for issuing such a ticket had to make sure that someone was on their way either into or out of this world.

Most diseases were taken for granted. Bronchitis – "sure everyone has a touch of bronchitis" and almost everyone had high or low blood pressure, depending on their frame of mind. Rupture was something people brought on themselves and boils, piles and carabuncles were all a matter of time. People had varicose veins or not in much the same way as they either had black or grey hair. Dislocated bones, ringworm, rashes, arthritis and gastritis were attended to by local quacks, more or less free of charge, in local pubs.

There never was any sympathy for those suffering from toothache. "No one," they said "ever died of a toothache." When the pain was at its worst the sufferer, as a last resort, went to the dentist, only to be told "Come back when the swelling is gone." It is partly true that few died as a direct result of sore teeth. No one can deny that hundreds, nay, thousands of people who could no longer endure the excruciating pain, were driven to suicide. In some areas the blacksmith and the publican did trojan work as teeth extractors. However, they never developed the art of capping or filling. They went straight to the root of the trouble.

People appreciated having the work done for free. However, between the work of the dentist and the work of the local operators there was what is called "a grey area" and very few were aware of its existence or ramifications.

Suddenly, out of the blue, Savage got a toothache and she was quiet for the first time in her life. We were wondering what action she would take, now that she had joined the rest of suffering humanity.

Her mind was soon made up. Once and once only would she be thrown out of gear by a so-and-so toothache. After discussing the matter with old Elly Sheehan, who lived near us, fully and frankly they concluded that in view of the fact that all Savage's teeth were very uneven — some in, some out, some up, others down – she would remove the lot and replace them with proper false teeth.

Together they yoked the donkey to the cart and they both set off for town with the intention of interviewing Mr Kelly, the dentist.

"Here, smoke that." said old Elly handing Savage a Woodbine. "'Twill kill the pain." Savage never bought a cigarette in her life and old Elly's packet of Woodbines suffered greatly on the road to town.

After what could be described as far reaching discussions with Mr Kelly, it was agreed that he would extract all her teeth without charge on condition that she would order a complete set of false teeth, which he would provide for her in due course.

After a number of trips to town, availing of old Elly's free transport and free Woodbines, all Savage's teeth were out and Mr Kelly took her measure for a full set – top and bottom. Savage gave him the go-ahead warning him to make the top set first. "He need be in no great hurry with the lower set."

"Tell the postman when you have the top ones ready for fitting." said Savage as she left what she called "the electric chair".

A week later the postman told Savage "Your top set are ready." Again old Elly had to take charge of the transport and that afternoon Savage called to the dentist and the top set were placed in position, never again to move. Well! Not until they were well out of town!

To celebrate the event, Savage bought a packet of Woodbines and clouds of smoke could be seen rising as the two women drove home.

Weeks and months went by and one day old Elly said to Savage "You never told me how much the false teeth cost."

"Well," said Savage. "'Tis like this. You know the pulling was free, and I left him the bottom set in place of the top set, so I think he didn't come out too badly."

Old Elly agreed saying 'twas a great pity more did not know about him.

Soon after Savage got her false teeth I asked Bill "How do you like Savage's false teeth?"

"*Croí-an-diabhail* that they may choke her! She didn't get them for nothing. There is something up with that one."

With her new false teeth in place, Savage decided to go home for a weekend. I was invited along, as she wanted someone to talk to and drive the donkey. Getting a horse or a pony was out of the question even though it was a twelve mile journey.

In a way I was looking forward to the journey and in the meantime I gave plenty of oats to the donkey. The wheels and axle were well-greased least they overheat and the ridgeband well-oiled, and comfortable seats were made from hay for this trip which was into the unknown, as far as I was concerned. Bill said "There was not half the preparation for the *Flight into Egypt*." Behind the scenes, Savage was making her own preparations. The most important consideration was that the trip would cost her or the Savage family – nothing. More than sufficient food along with some tea and sugar would travel with us. Nothing was left to chance. But, of all the people in the world, Savage never learned how to bake nice bread. Sometimes it was only half-baked; more often it was as hard and stiff as concrete.

"The bloody range," she said "is not able to bake bread."

The inflexibility of her judgement was known to all.

Friday came and it was a day off from school for me. No matter how we fared I could forget the hated *cúpla focal* for one day.

I was out early that morning. By now it was easy to locate the donkey. He never went far from the house, expecting to be called in at any time for more oats.

At nine o'clock, fully loaded, we struck out for the hills.

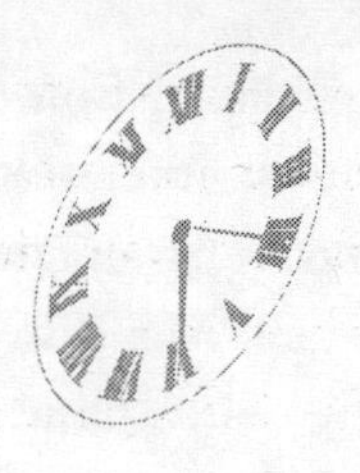

16

AWAY WE WENT AND AWAY WE WENT

There was this old shepherd on the Leader Estate and he regarded himself as a good story-teller. He had only one story, but every time he told it there were many changes. It was all about *the Terrier of the Greenwoods*. The story always and ever had the same introduction – "*Away he went and away he went and away he went*", giving one the impression that this terrier of the greenwoods was half way round the world before its adventures really began.

Much the same could be said about Savage and myself after we set out on our twelve-mile journey to her home in the mountain. We travelled about four miles in an easterly direction. The donkey hopping off the road and sticks hopping off the donkey as we gave it every second belt. Suddenly Savage shouted "Right turn here!" and from there on it was all uphill and we had to reduce speed.

Inevitably, when we had what Savage called *the tispock* knocked out of the donkey we were reduced to walking pace and unlike the terrier of the greenwoods, we had not yet reached the borders of civilisation. This was confirmed when we came across some children on their way from school.

As we drew level with the school I saw a man, whom I took to be a teacher, in the act of closing the gate. Interrupting my profound thoughts, Savage leaped from the cart and in her usual half-trot went straight up to the teacher.

"How the devil are you, Mr Hogan?" said Savage.

"And how the devil are you Miss Elly?" said the teacher as they shook hands like long-lost friends. Now I finally knew the teacher who had found her the job at our place.

"How are you getting along on the job Miss Elly?"

"Grand to the world, Mr Hogan, all my own way. What more could one expect?"

"I'm so glad." said Mr Hogan.

"Sit in here to the cart, Mr Hogan, an' take your legs off the road."

"No thank you, I'm sitting all day. I like the walk."

Giving me a quick glance, Savage said "Drive on after us. I will walk with Mr Hogan as far as the house."

In my wildest dreams I could never have imagined an ex-pupil from our school walking side by side with any of our teachers, or shaking hands with them, in later life. And to make matters worse Savage returned to the cart and opening one of her bags took from it one of her badly baked cakes. Making two parts of it across her knee she returned one half to the bag. In the same manner she made two parts of the remainder and handing one wedge to Mr Hogan said "Be ateing that. You must be starved after the day!"

I never thought I would see the day when a principal schoolteacher would be reduced to munching a lump of dry, badly-made bread on his way from school.

I am sure that Mr Hogan discovered, as many good men before him discovered, there were times when it is really hard to be a gentleman. Rather than hurt her feelings, by flinging the so-called bread as far as he could over the fence, he did his best to nibble at it. No doubt he was a humble man but there is a limit. What he was doing now was enough to humiliate the whole teaching fraternity. At the entrance to his nice house he thanked Savage for the pleasure of her company and especially for the bread. "It was such a nice change and I will have the rest of it for my tea."

Savage made a little hop and once again she was back in the donkey-car.

"A grand man, Mr Hogan." said she. "And never a word of that damn Irish out of him. He found jobs for all his pupils in England and America an' all over. And he always said 'forget about Holy Orders and other sitting jobs.' He always said 'go to work and be beholden to no one.' A grand man, Mr Hogan, everyone knows that."

She surprised me because Savage seldom went to the trouble of explaining anything.

"Turn in here." she ordered. And we entered a kind of sunken lane from which the top-soil had been removed perhaps hundreds of years ago revealing a smooth rock surface, which never needed repairs. Its sides were draped with massive bunches of red, blue, pink, purple and white fuchsia; all the work of nature.

Entering the little farmyard, one could see it was more the work of an excavator rather than a builder. And the dwelling house, were it offered for sale today, would be described as "the original split-level bungalow".

The kitchen was on one level with the farmyard. The fireplace was cut from solid rock. The bedroom was on a higher level and access to it was by means of a ladder which had seen better days. Over the years, whenever a rung or step gave way it was replaced by an old worn-out neck-tie and by now there were four or five colourful neck-ties serving as steps. Looking up along the ladder one would not be surprised to find an arabian prince standing at the bedroom door.

After tea I went on a voyage of discovery. Needless to say, I went to the higher ground and something tempted me to look in the bedroom window. It was obvious the room contained only one bed and as there was no bed in the kitchen, putting two and two together I could see I was not going to have a bedroom to myself – nor did it seem likely I was going to have even a bed to myself.

As the evening wore on, I was getting a little concerned as to where I would lay my head when bedtime came, as come it would. Can anyone tell me the name of the poet who wrote:

"Wearied from doubt to doubt we flee
We welcome fond credulity"?

I felt I had a lot in common with him.

Some might think I was confronted with "a moral peccadillo" at the age of nine; an age at which most of us are sentimental and squeamish. Somehow I foresaw trouble. Yet, something told me I would survive the night.

There were times when my faith weakened during the long hours. Bedtime came early. The older girls were first to mount the ladder, after discarding all footwear. Savage herself was next and last of all the old lady. With one hand on the ladder she said to me, "You stay here with the boys for a few minutes. I will call you when we are ready."

The boys were of course fully-grown men who did all kinds of work on contract. When the old lady had disappeared into the upper chamber one brother said to the other, "You'd better get out eight or ten pounds. We might want it tomorrow." The other brother pulled open a drawer. And it was no small drawer. Never in all my life had I seen so much paper money. I was admiring the money and trying to estimate the amount in the drawer when the old lady shouted "You can come up now."

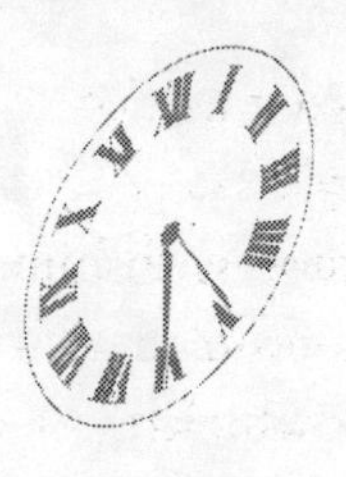

17

A Deadly Night

Slowly I removed my boots and socks as the others had done before mounting the ladder of neckties. The room was dimly-lit as the remains of a candle flared up one minute and died down the next.

There were two rows of heads in the bed; three across the lower end with Savage and her mother occupying the other end. "Jesus" said I to myself. But my blasphemous thoughts were cut short as the old lady moved a slight bit to one side, leaving a small vacancy between herself and Savage. "This is your place." she announced.

Well! As every boy knows when you have nothing on save your shirt you have very little privacy. All I could think of was my complete loss of dignity with five women watching every move I made.

I made a quick dash for the space allotted to me at the head of the bed. I slipped into place like a greased shell into the breech.

Once in place there was no room for movement of any kind. The old lady reached out and choked out the light with her finger and thumb. Then she shouted to the *boys* in the kitchen. "Are ye going to stay up all night burning fire and light?" Now the place was in complete darkness. No one asked me if I was comfortable or otherwise. The bedclothes were drawn tightly across my throat. Savage having a firm hold of them on the inside and her mother more than holding her own on the outside.

I felt as if I were in a coffin many sizes too small and buried alive beneath the Great Pyramid of Egypt with the Sphinx sitting on top smiling that everlasting, inscrutable smile, at my misfortune.

Every inch of space was occupied. Our legs automatically fell into place; each leg between two other legs.

People very ill find the night very long. People with lung trouble such as bronchitis and broncho-pneumonia gasping for air also feel the night almost endless. In other words it is only those who have been at death's door sometime or other who can fully understand all I suffered that night.

My thoughts turned to prayer and to *The Agony in the Garden* and I said to myself "with all his trouble, Jesus was at least able to walk about and speak with the apostles. I had no such comfort. I was going nowhere. I was firmly cased in like a fly in amber.

I thought of the donkey in the field; free to roll over, free to walk about, free to do all the things a donkey might care to do. 'Tis hard lines when one would gladly change places with the donkey in the field.

Sleep was out of the question while the five women with whom I shared the bed was snoring to their hearts content, oblivious to God and the world.

Occasionally, the leg that was between my legs gave a sudden involuntary twitch as if its owner had just expired or was about to do so. In school we were told about heaven and what a Christian might look forward to – mixing with angels and singing hymns all day and all night. No big deal you might say until you consider the alternative. Outside of school we were told that an Arabs' idea of heaven was quite different. In the Arab heaven every Arab would have four or five wives. Well, if that is their idea of heaven one can hardly begin to visualise what the Arab hell is like!

At long last dawn came and rather than have five women see me getting dressed, I shot out of the bed and down the ladder, taking my clothes with me. As I was pulling on my pants one of the men awoke "Ah" said he "I see you are an early-riser." What looked like an old sea-chest last night was now a bed. It was in fact a *settle-bed.* These were quite common in the old days. The other brother also jumped out and they were both dressed in minutes.

I could see that comfortable beds are a great deterrent to early rising. The women now came down the neck-tie ladder with the old lady leading. When all were clear of the ladder she made the sign of the cross and all the family did the same. Then she said "Never forget your prayer for the day." Perhaps this prayer for the day was the secret of their success. After some deliberation, Savage decided we would start out for home fairly early in the day. I was delighted. Years were to come and go before I had the courage to admit I had spent a night in bed with five women.

Listening to teenagers speculating about sharing a bed with a girl and the poor prospects of this ever taking place, I thought the time had come. "I spent a whole night in bed with five women."

"Oh you lucky devil!" they chorused.

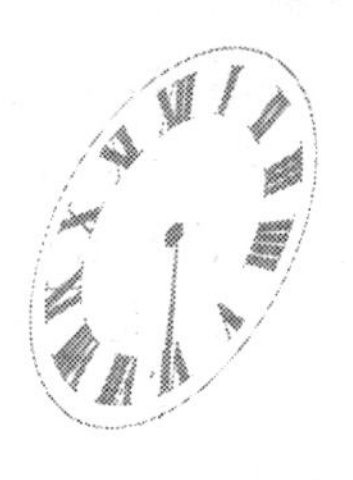

18

The Day of the Inspector

The build-up of tension in the weeks before a visit from the Inspector was unbelievable. Teachers must have suffered great nervous strain as they waited for this man, who had the power of life and death over them and the school and over everyone and everything in any way connected with education.

That is what we were led to believe. And on top of the agenda for survival was our knowledge of the Irish language.

Seemingly, a new breed of inspector was on the loose whose job was "to make the Irish people speak the Irish language".

The teachers were united in thinking that plenty of the stick would work wonders in the weeks previous to the arrival of this powerful autocrat.

During these long weeks the Master would be completely off drink of any kind and if *he* suffered, from lack of alcohol, so did *we* by God. So did *we*.

One mistake in the *cúpla focal* and you were grabbed by the collar of your coat or pullover and bent across the chair and the ash-plant was put hopping off your backside. No one counted the strokes. Sometimes Ban Ní Hackendoosh came up from her end to supervise and encourage. Then she would say "I have a boy who would benefit greatly from a few minutes across the chair."

"Bring the brat up here. I will wake him up."

She would go to her end of the room and pick out a boy and bring him along, with her hand around his shoulders in a protective manner, and put him standing beside the chair.

Sometimes there was a softening-up process which consisted of a good beating on the bare legs after which, for some unknown reason, boys were more easily put across the chair for the principal operation. The cruel punishment would end only when he could no longer stand the wild screaming of the victim. Again Ban Ní Hackendoosh would put her arm around the boy and take him away saying "Now Tommy that little beating will do you the world of good. And you know well, you badly wanted it."

Human nature is hard to understand at times. We had little sympathy for any lad from the junior classes who was brought along for a session across the chair. In our view it was better that he understood and knew what to expect on behalf of the Irish language and other things of national importance, such as the teaching of the Roman Catholic Church. And in due course he might reach what was called "*Pons Assinorum*" or in other words – the bridge of asses.

One evening all four teachers had menacing looks as the Master announced "We are expecting the inspector tomorrow morning. May God help anyone late for school. May God help anyone giving a wrong or stupid answer and I want books in order and everything neat."

We could take it for granted that if all did not go well an outbreak of brutality was inevitable. Calamity was in the air. Ah well! –

"*Time shall unfold what plaited cunning hides*". There was little sleep for any of us that night and to make matters worse Savage had extra work for me next morning.

There was a newly-born white-head calf which refused to drink direct from the bucket. On most farms this matter was easily overcome by giving the calf "the finger". Savage believed in force-feeding and this entailed holding the calf back into a corner while

Savage, using all her strength, held the calf's head well down into the milk. It was a case of drink or drown.

"The inspector is coming to the school today and I will be late." I pleaded.

"Fie blast and blow it. The calf must be fed. And if there is any noise out of that bloody fool of an inspector, give him a good thump in the puss and tell 'em I told you to do it."

Savage had no idea of how much she was out of date. Her militant attitude may have worked in the old days when the people were under foreign rule. Now we had our own Government, our own teachers, our own religion, our own language. Only a traitor could find fault with the system. And woe betide the pupil who would raise his hand against it.

When the calf was fed to her satisfaction I grabbed my bag and made off across the river, using every short cut. Knowing that I was already late, I was delighted to meet Jerh D at the crossroads. There was some consolation in not having to face the firing-squad alone.

"Would you be able to give me a few middle-pages from your jotter?" said Jerh D. Just then I remembered my own jotter was not too healthy. On examination I found that I had exactly one page left. Jerh D had none at all.

Why did this have to happen today of all days? Today would surely see the end of us both. The old Ban Ní Hackendoosh would pretend to be very upset and scandalised; while inwardly she would be delighted to see us being beaten every day for several days as a result of the disgrace we brought upon the school and the "unfortunate teachers".

They say God never closes a door without opening a window. And like Abraham in the old days when he was about to sacrifice his only son, he looked up and saw this ram tied to a bush. Similarly Jerh D looked up and saw two huge posters proclaiming the fact that Duffy's Circus would be in town tonight. Necessity being the mother of invention, we carefully removed the posters and folded them into jotter size, being careful to keep the lions and tigers and clowns hidden away inside the folds. In spite of our best efforts shades of red and blue were visible in places.

With melancholy steps we turned towards the school. The Inspector's car was positioned outside the gate. Things were looking bad.

The moment we entered the school the Master called, "You two up here to the table." We made our way to the table. "Why are you two late this morning?"

I was speechless but my friend Jerh D took up our defence.

"We were in such a hurry Sir we fell crossing the river and we had to go home again for dry clothes and we would still be in lots of time but we had to help Fr. O'Reardon to change a wheel down below the cross."

The Inspector, an oldish man, looked up from his examination of the roll-book and said "So you have done your good deed for today."

"Yes, Sir." said Jerh D without hesitation. As they say in diplomatic circles "the situation was defused". We were allowed back to our usual places. However, we were soon back in more trouble.

The Inspector finished looking over the roll-book and this was the signal for the Master to call out. "Fourth class. Up here around the table for arithmetic." The first question had to do with changing statute or English acres into Irish acres and while we were engaged in patriotic work the Inspector went on walkabout.

He came to a halt in front of Jerh D "I haven't seen this type of jotter before." said he and taking the folded poster from Jerh D he opened it out to its full extent. The Master was so pale one could be forgiven for thinking rigor mortis had already set in.

The Inspector studied the poster for a while. Then turning it towards the class and pointing to a tiger he asked. "Were I to go out to look for this fellow where would I find him?"

"In Duffy's Circus, Sir." said Jerh D.

Everyone laughed, including the Inspector. And the Master managed a very sickly smile. But Ban Ní Hackendoosh was definitely not amused. Continuing with the circus poster the Inspector turned what should have been a dreary half hour of arithmetic into a question and answer session on wildlife. But to make amends for this Indian and African safari he promised the boy who would answer his next question enough money to take him to Duffy's Circus. Believe me the question had nothing to do with wildlife.

"A brick weighs," said he, "a pound and a half and half a brick what is the weight of a brick and a half?"

The moment he finished speaking Jerh D's hand shot up. "What is your answer?" said the Inspector.

Jerh D gave the correct answer.

"Good lad." said the Inspector. "I have asked that question in twenty schools and this is the first time I have got the correct answer."

Amazement spread from face to face and I doubt if the Master had worked out the answer. One thing was certain Ban Ní Hackendoosh, who still had a long way to go before she reached the "bridge of asses", did not know the correct answer. Nevertheless, she took it for granted any answer coming from Jerh D was bound to be wrong.

The Inspector took some change from his pocket and picking out a half-crown handed it to Jerh D saying, "Congratulations. Enjoy the circus." And turning to the Master said "No homework for this good boy tonight." Soon after that he left.

The Master went to the old overcoat in the hall. Things were back to normal, more or less. The Ban came up to our class to oversee the interrogation of Jerh D.

"Where in the Lord did you get the correct answer to that question?"

"It was a good guess, Sir."

"I am warning you. Never again bring a circus poster into school. If we had a young inspector . . ." Ban Ní Hackendoosh cut him short, "If he was still in my class I would whip the life out of him! I tell you he would remember Duffy's Circus . . . Duffy's Circus! What are things coming to! Are you putting him across the chair?"

"No." said the Master. I have a mind to put him at the top of the class." And he went off again to the old overcoat, where refreshment of the right kind was in waiting. Of course, things could have gone *wrong*. Thanks be to God, they didn't.

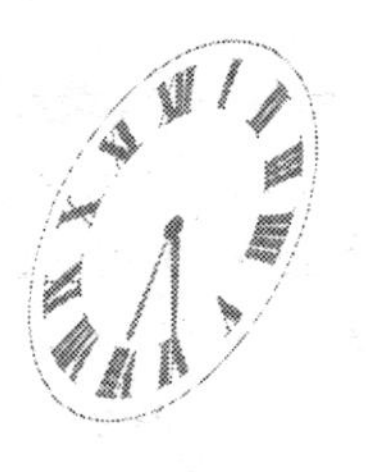

19

THE TICKET FOR CONFIRMATION

The terror instilled into us before the coming of the Inspector was a bizarre deception; a subterfuge, which allowed the teachers to flog, beat, torture and torment. The Irish language had to be imposed; the writings of Douglas Hyde and Patrick Pearse became a new gospel. We were given to understand that in the great days of old everybody spoke Irish and that the people conversed freely with the *Dardheel*, the *Prumpollaun* and the *Kerrogue*, whenever these gentry poked their heads out of the ground. One said "*Vo, Vo.*" Another said "*Ine, Ine*" and the *Keerogue* said "*Ger, Ger.*" Hence the great love for the *cúpla focal*. The true story of the unbelievable tyranny, from which the school children of those days had no escape, will probably never be told.

Perhaps some justification may be found for the beating of Irish into children, by which I mean all kinds of political pressure may well have driven teachers to act as they did.

When it came to religious instruction the combined weight of church and state was upon us.

The ticket for Confirmation was of the utmost importance. Confirmation would make us strong and perfect christians. The clergy seemed to have no doubt about the end-result and they were responsible for the victimisation of so many young people, boys and girls. Preparation for Confirmation was regarded as the "horror of horrors". These are not my words but the words of another much better known writer when describing the run up to Confirmation.

"That you love one another as I love you" was never heard in our school and even the natural love with which every boy and girl is gifted soon died. By Confirmation time it was as dead as a doornail.

In any case, sooner or later everyone had to be confirmed and in order to be confirmed one had to obtain a ticket. The parish priest and the Principal decided who would and who would not get tickets. Everything depended on your knowledge of Christian doctrine and this covered such a wide area that if you got a ticket for Confirmation no great harm would be done if you went straight into Holy Orders.

You had to be on first name terms with so many angels including your *guardian angel*, who somehow kept well away when most wanted.

We had to know how to gain all sorts of indulgences. Some remitted as little as one hundred days in the next nearest place to hell; while others remitted five years or ten years. But best of all was a plenary indulgence which remitted all temporal punishment due to sin. We had to prove the infallibility of the Pope, explain the Principal Mysteries, the Penitential Psalms, the gifts of the Holy Ghost, the Theological Virtues, the Spiritual and Corporal Works of Mercy, the Acts of the Apostles, the Stations of the Cross, the Eight Beatitudes. I could go on and on. Now, if you are familiar with all the above you might be on your way to receiving a ticket.

However, your troubles are far from over. On the *day of the Bishop*, which was a very, very important day in every parish, you and all your comrades, boys and girls, would undergo another examination in the church, carried out by strange priests in full view of all the congregation.

The strange priest would work his way along the seats and every now and then he would withdraw a candidate's ticket. Then the unfortunate boy or girl would have to leave their place and walk down the middle of the church in front of their parents and hundreds of people "a disgrace to their parents, a disgrace to their teachers and a disgrace to their school" and wait another three years for his lordship's return visit. A more traumatic punishment could scarcely be devised. As this strange priest drew near, I could see he had already collected a number of tickets. Everything depended on me being asked a fair question. But very few would be prepared for this one. By the sound of it, I knew he wanted my ticket. "Name," said he. "The nine ways of being an accessory to another's sin." I had a fair idea of what he was on about. I began "by counsel, by command." "Yes." "By consent." "Go on." "By provocation." "And ..." I knew his patience was running out so I let him have the remaining five all in one go. "By praise, by concealment, by partaking, by silence and by defence of the ill done." He moved on.

It was important to have a number of failures and these unfortunates were deliberately humiliated so that fear of failure was uppermost in every child's mind. Those who failed to get tickets and those whose tickets were confiscated were branded as stupid and the failures from the previous *day of the Bishop* were called *catechumens* and other more fancy names. Three years had gone by and many of these youngsters had spent the three years working for local farmers; their knowledge of Christian doctrine had remained static. Yet this time they were all made strong and perfect christians, as good as the best of them.

In our part of the country there was very little class distinction as regards going forward for Confirmation. A likely candidate for the priesthood would not be "put back for another three years." And perhaps a little bribery took place. But by and large it was an ordeal one would not wish to repeat.

In other parts of the country they had different ways of humiliating candidates for Confirmation and seemingly class distinction was not entirely unknown.

In one part of the country that I know about they divided the children into three different classes. Cards of different colours were hung around their necks. There was a colour for the best pupils another colour for the second class. But the third class pupils had to wear *yellow cards*. All the children had to parade up the middle aisle of the church to where the Bishop was. In this way everyone in the church had a good view of the children wearing *yellow cards*. And this was something that would be spoken of for many a long day.

In spite of everything, Christianity survived. I have seen many ordinary men and women "*cross the Jerrico road*" to help people. This is how things were in the 1920's and indeed well into the 1930's.

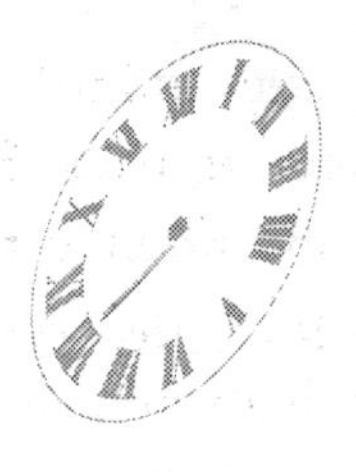

20

Our Visitors

Some visitors were very welcome. Others were not. Among those who were not welcome was the "guard", otherwise known as the attendance officer. His job was to investigate poor attendance. The Inspector was unwelcome because his visit served as an excuse for more and more punishment.

The parish priest and the curate received a half-hearted welcome. The good thing about the priest arriving was the fact that the moment he appeared all those pupils who were sitting jumped to their feet as a mark of respect. And those who were standing also downed tools. Needless to say, the "jump to attention" when the priest arrived might well interrupt a chastisement or save some unfortunate from six cuts.

From time to time a farmer would arrive and request the Master to find out from the pupils if any of them had seen a stray animal on the road.

The Master would hit the table a few belts of the ash-plant to command attention.

"Did anyone see a stray animal on the road this morning?"

Several boys would put up their hands, all claiming to have seen the wayward animal. By the time all the information was sorted out half an hour would be wiped off the curriculum and the farmer would be surprised that of all the stray animals his was none of them. We got good mileage out of stray animals. Beggars and travelling-men were more than welcome and whenever one of them came to the door the beating of some pupil would come to a halt and this in itself should prove to the beggar that when all is said and done they could be very much worse off than they were!

Whenever a tinker or traveller arrived at the door it was always the signal for the Master to hand two pennies to the nearest boy, saying "Give that to the nuisance at the door." A clever boy would always pocket one penny and hand over the other. Times were hard in the Irish Free State. Some beggars were very vocal about the starving "childer", while others simply stood there waiting for their donation. There was a mother and daughter, a quaint pair, who made full use of their right to remain silent. Seemingly, in her young days the mother was very beautiful and a wealthy landowner fell in love with her. They married and had one daughter. As things worked out, the marriage was a failure. She did not have what it takes to be a lady, having neither class nor taste. She drove the man to drink and he drove her to drink and there was no hope. They fell into the hands of the money-lenders from whom there was poor hope of escape! By the time the daughter was nine years of age, the big house and the land and everything they once possessed was all gone. The mother and daughter took one road and he took another. The mother reverted to the black shawl but she never dressed the daughter in anything other than a long coat and hat. In summer the daughter always carried her high-button boots around her neck, tied together. They called to the school from time to time but they never said anything, not even a "thank you." I am sure they thought whatever they got was little enough for making their appearance.

Of all our visitors Paddy the Prayers was the most welcome. Paddy grew up on a large farm and his widowed mother was prepared to sacrifice all "to make Paddy into a priest." He spent many years away in college spending her money freely. He had everything: money, brains, wit, you name it – Paddy had it. But, alas, he had no vocation.

Eventually he came home "a spoilt priest", in other words, a good for nothing; entirely too important to start forking farmyard manure or to be seen messing with spuds or pigs. In his view, no well-educated man should be reduced to manual labour. Moreover, a man like himself with a sound knowledge of Latin, was in a much higher category than the very best *cúpla focal* men.

Paddy also fell into the hands of the money-lenders from whom, as I said before, there is little or no hope of escape. He joined the unarmed army of travellers and quickly rose from the ranks. During his round tour of the countryside and when calling to the various pubs, he never missed an opportunity of bringing his knowledge of Latin to the forefront. In one pub he was challenged by a local man. "I think," said the man "you are only making up all that damn Latin!"

"In that case" said Paddy, "let's hear you make up some Latin."

"Right." said the man. "*Moonum shineum throughum key holum dooram.*" From then on Paddy had no love for the jester. Ignorance he could not tolerate.

Entering the school, Paddy would have a broad smile and with arms outspread and ignoring Ban Ní Hackendoosh for the moment, he would start off "*gratiam tuam quaesumus, domine mentibus.*" Ban Ní Hackendoosh was reluctant to cross swords with a spoilt priest. Her knowledge of Latin was very limited. Her power resided in the greatest and most ancient language in the world – namely, the Irish language. In her view, only people of limited intelligence had resort to other languages in order to make themselves understood.

Paddy was of average build but that was the only average thing about him. From a religious point of view he could have walked straight out of the Old Testament. His unkempt and tousled grey beard together with his dishevelled clothing and odd-footwear made him a respectable member of that section of society categorised all down the ages as holy men.

He would bow low to Ban Ní Hackendoosh saying, "Every time I see you, you seem younger and more beautiful. May the good God overwhelm you with blessings and may you be happy in your noble calling." This kind of rhetoric went on for some time, giving Ban Ní Hackendoosh ample time to come up with a suitable subscription.

Then he would come up to our part of the school and again introduce himself with more Latin "*Dominus det nobis suam pacem*" after which the Master would say "*Amen*" proving to us that he also had a good knowledge of classical Latin.

Returning to the vernacular he would turn towards the Master. "My good and holy man, teach the children to knock at heaven's high door. And may your pupils fill all the high places in the land, as doctors and judges and above all may many of them become good and loving teachers like yourself, spending their days cultivating enlightenment and praising our heavenly father and may the good God pardon any relapse into sin."

Turning to us he would say, "My children, how I love you all. May the lord strip you of conceit and pride and give you strength to face the sufferings of this life. I have neither boy nor girl because the good God found them better fathers. *Faciam hujus loci, dieique, meique semper memineris.*"

Again the Master said "*Amen.*"

Jerh D's hand shot up. "Tell us, Sir, what is the meaning of the Latin?" Paddy smiled. "A near enough translation is, don't forget this place this day, or me ... you will be a teacher."

A good subscription from the Master would bring this part of the show to an end. Paddy would look at the silver coins and whisper. "Sure all the big people like yourself like to see me rise."

Were I to repeat verbatim his final blessing of the Master, it would run to several pages. I will therefore confine myself to the more moderate of the aspirations expressed so lovingly as he faced the Master.

"May your family increase and your wealth multiply

And may every day bring you health and happiness and peace

And may you live a long, long life with all your ambitions fulfilled

And may your good works be spoken of all over the world

And on the day of your funeral may your friends from all over the country and from overseas come to mourn

And may there be not one dry eye in the whole firmament
And on that day may the whole world stand and gaze in wonderment
At the magnificence and richness and the amplitude of the great turnout
So dearly and well deserved, above all other men."

Turning again towards us he would say, "May God bless you all my dear children. Pray for me. Please pray for me".

In a moment he was gone and a cloud of the same old rigorous routine would surround the school. The light was gone. We would see him again, perhaps in a year, perhaps never.

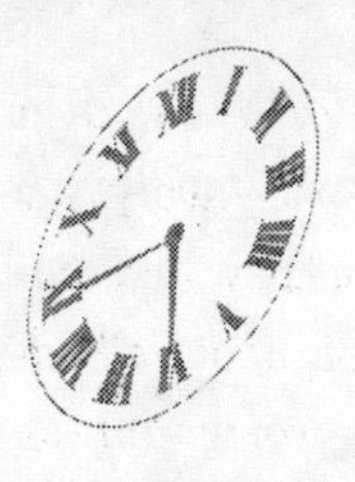

21

THE MATCHMAKER

It was one of those evenings when there was very little on the agenda. We were all sitting around the table, Bill giving out about the Government as usual. Suddenly the back door opened and a stranger stood framed in the doorway.

"I am Finn the matchmaker." said he.

"And what brings you here?" enquired my father.

"I have an account of a match for your housekeeper if you have no objection."

"None, whatever." said my father. "Do the best you can."

Then Bill spoke up. "By the *Croí-an-diabhail*, Sir, whoever you are you left it long enough. And I can tell you no reasonable offer will be refused."

"Bill." said my father. "You must take the black horse to the forge."

After a minute or two Bill and my father went out leaving Mr. Finn and Savage the place to themselves. I was ignored and this was one evening I enjoyed doing my homework. As I sat there listening to the complicated and complex intrigue surrounding matrimony I can safely say the school version fell very short of the real thing.

"Were you talking to my mother?" enquired Savage.

"Be gorra, I was. Where would I be going without a bell on my bike?"

"And what did she say?"

"She knows the man and all belonging to him. She thinks 'tis a great match!"

"Did she tell you I will marry no man who was in jail or no delicate *piesawen?*"

"The man was often in court but never in jail."

"Why was he in court?"

"Belting a few tinkers over trespass and things like that."

"Is he strong and healthy?"

"Healthy! Didn't he pass for the civy-guards, and let me tell you them boys are well-examined by doctors. He'd be stationed above in Dublin by now only he had not one word of the damn Irish."

"I won't fault him for that."

"I don't know what will become of the people if this Irish ever comes in."

The change that came over Savage during the next few weeks was remarkable. She tried to be civil to Bill and she undertook work which up till now she had totally ignored.

During the next few weeks she sent off a letter to her mother almost every day, free of charge. She had a supply of stamps which she had steamed off every letter or old envelope she could lay her hands on. In her view, any stamp that was not completely defaced was a perfectly good stamp. Her mother was also very thrifty and I would not be surprised if some of the stamps used by Savage found their way back again by return post. Neither of them saw any reason why they should enrich the Government by buying new stamps when old stamps did the job equally well. This spate of letter-writing had some connection obviously with the arrival of the matchmaker. Savage had no hesitation in taking his advice. Like Peg Sayers and thousands of women up and down the country, they had a blind faith in the matchmaker and a similar approach and philosophy towards marriage. Perhaps they were wiser than succeeding generations, who laughed at the matchmaker and who subsequently spent their lives writing to agony aunts and going to see marriage counsellors.

When first I saw her make an apron out of a meal bag I knew she had a flair for re-cycling. And let us give credit where credit is due. The re-cycling of postage-stamps seemed a step in the right direction.

Around this time also one could hear her making an attempt to sing and needless to say, she never got any credit for being the inventor of punk rock.

She also declared her intention of leaving the place "*slough-ter*" for the next housekeeper. The use of the word "*slough-ter*" in this context shows she was not opposed to re-cycling the *cúpla focal*. Floors were cleaned and windows attended to. Nothing was neglected. Unfortunately it was all labour in vain.

The range had to be cleaned and on close examination she discovered there was also a chimney which required an overhaul.

Looking up the chimney from the inside, she knew instinctively there was only one man in the area who would be capable of cleaning this previously unknown chimney.

His name was Ned-the-Leg because one leg was shorter than the other. He was born with this handicap. In due course he turned this handicap into an asset – claiming his short leg was the result of an encounter with crown forces during the war of independence.

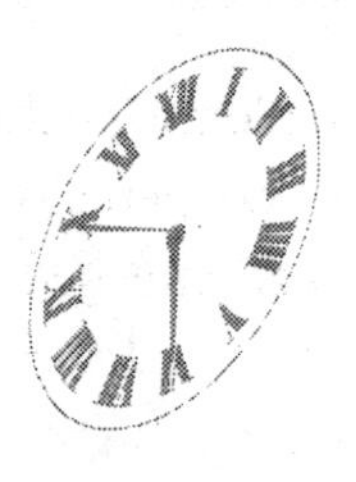

22

THE EXPLOITS OF NED-THE-LEG

In various pubs he made a name for himself, telling of his many exploits during "the troubled times". Ned told stories of ambushes that never took place, in which he played a leading part. But all these encounters were always far away in the foothills of the Dublin mountains or in Kildare where he was chief instructor to a squad of assassins. Collins came regularly to consult Ned about the blowing up of Government property and other matters.

Ned claimed that Kildare was a lively place in them days. The local patriots could stand this blathering no longer. One night one of them told Ned "I have read the books and there was not one single shot fired in County Kildare during the war of independence."

Ned promptly moved all his operations to County Longford, where his time was spent showing the local men how to make land-mines out of mousetraps. Everyone knew his stories were all a pack of lies from beginning to end. But nevertheless enjoyable!

Ned-the-Leg knew exactly where he was Easter Sunday morning 1916. The question "Where were you in 1916?" was one he loved to answer. It gave him an opportunity to open up about his other activities. "I don't think" said Ned "I killed large numbers of the enemy, but by God I put bridges and railways flying. In the field of war the mousetrap land-mine is the most dangerous weapon known to man. I did my best to cripple the country and I ended up crippling myself. *Now* you know what happened the leg."

This was the man Savage engaged to clean the chimney. He came one evening to size up the job. He looked up at the chimney and said to Savage. "You are a smart lady. You asked the right man. Any of them fellows around there would crack their bloody necks before they'd be down out o' there. On top of that I have a new way of cleaning chimneys. I saw them at it down in County Longford the time o' the trouble. There won't be a speck of soot in that chimney when I am finished with it. There are a few things I must get before I go to work."

"No bombs now I hope." said Savage.

"Okay, no bombs. I will use my secret weapon."

A week later Ned arrived ready to go into action. He had a bag over his shoulder which he placed very carefully on the ground. One could see that there was some movement within the bag and Savage looked on it with great suspicion.

"Is that a live bomb you have there?" she asked.

"No," said Ned "that is my secret weapon and tell me how long will himself be at The Ford?"

"He is always home around ten."

"In that case we'd better get to work." said Ned. I was told to bring a long rope from the stables. Needless to say, I did not delay because I wanted to see the new secret weapon.

When I returned with the rope, Ned had the ladder erected and he was placing the roof ladder in position. Savage and Ned went indoors to have a look at things more closely. He ordered all the small shutters to be opened and they both concluded that there was an enormous amount of soot to be removed.

"Ah," said Ned. "I will blow the lot out in no time!"

"May I remind you again," said Savage "this is not a railway bridge!"

Ned put up his hand saying "Now, now, now, you leave everything to me."

The count down was over.

"Right," said he as he went towards the sack which he had brought with him and in which he had his secret weapon. Very carefully he untied the mouth of the sack and pulled from it a huge gander.

"The rope, the rope!" he shouted and I handed him the rope.

"Now" said he as he put the rope around the gander's neck. "there is a very special knot called the Daniel O'Connell knot and without this special knot we would choke the *hure* in no time."

It took some time to make this special knot. Every precaution was taken and Ned said "The vital part of any dangerous job is what they call safety-measures."

With the gander tucked under his arm, Ned went towards the ladder. With his short leg on the first step and holding on to the ladder with his free hand he waited for the all-clear from Savage. Savage looked at him and said, "Are you going to *gup* it?" Ned started to *gup* the ladder, the short leg first all the time. It was dangerous transferring himself and the gander from the upright ladder to the roof ladder but Ned-the-Leg proved himself to be a fearless man. He climbed up on the chimney stack. With a leg on each side he made himself comfortable and now his new and up-to-date method of chimney sweeping was about to be tested.

The wild-eyed gander was allowed to have a good look at the surroundings and then, very much to its surprise, it was lowered slowly into the black hole. One can imagine the screeches of the unfortunate gander and the desperate and frantic flapping of wings – as Ned let the gander sink lower, and lower until finally it reached the widest part of the chimney, just over the range, where there was the soot of decades. After a little while, Ned would start to wind up the rope and once again the desperate fight for life would start. Black soot was driven up and out until a dark cloud covered the townland. In spite of everything, Ned held his position on the chimney and he continued to raise and lower the gander. Conditions were bad outside but indoors things were far worse. No one could foresee what would happen when the storm raised by the gander would blow so much soot out of the chimney that the range would become almost invisible.

Savage was first to see that things were haywire. She rushed out shouting at Ned. “Stop, stop, you bloody fool, stop. Come down you bloody ape, come down!”

Ned continued to raise and lower the gander.

By now things had gone completely out of control. Black soot continued to pour from every opening. Savage was running in and out trying to bring the operation to a halt.

Perched high above the commotion, Ned was engaged in giving the gander a history lesson. “Now, me bould Lie George, how do you like the black hole o’ Calcutta?” Suddenly everything came to a halt. Ned wound up the rope but there was no gander – The Daniel O’Connell knot had failed! The gander was free inside the chimney where it had ample room to walk about above the range. Ned came down to investigate and as he tried to get a view of the gander, Savage warned him, “Don’t get your big empty head caught in that shutter. What are you going to do now you black ape?”

One could see the gander striding around inside. From time to time it would take off in a futile attempt at reaching the outside air; only to collapse again and again, sending streams of soot in every direction.

“What are you going to do?” demanded Savage.

“Theoretically, I see a new empiricism . . .”

Savage cut him short. “That kind of talk is all right for fools like yourself. I want to know what you are going to do now.”

“This is my personal responsibility, leave it to me.”

“I don’t know all about your criminal activities in County Longford but one thing is certain – you returned a lunatic. Himself will be home in an hour and look at the cut of the place!”

“Where is the gun?” demanded Ned.

“The gun?”

“Yes, the gun.”

"Do you mean the gun?" said Savage, now fully convinced that he was mad.

"I could shoot him from above or blow him up from here."

"Who owns the bloody gander?" said Savage, in an effort to change the subject. She did not like talking of guns.

"He belongs to Charlie Daly and I had a hard time trying to capture him not knowing the minute Charlie would arrive with the big double-barrel."

"What a pity he didn't catch you and give you the contents of both barrels between the eyes. You and your ideas from County Longford."

"Down in County Longford . . ."

Again Savage cut him short, "If" said she "I hear County Longford mentioned once more I'll mow the head off you with the brush!"

"Down in Drumlish . . ."

"Forget about Drumlish. I know where it is and you won't fool me with any more tall-tales. I ask you to do a simple job and we end up with the greatest mess I saw."

"Give me the gun and a few cartridges and I will make short-work of him. Then we can rake him out and finish the job. You may say that chimney will not be blocked for a long time. There is a fine job done up along it and if we had that *hure* of a gander out of there we could easily get rid of the soot."

Just then my father arrived home. "What in God's name is going on here?" he asked.

Savage started off giving a long explanation and putting all the blame on Ned.

"I told him a hundred times to stop and he paid no heed. I did not know he was going to hang a live gander in the chimney and lift him up and down. He said he had a secret weapon from County Longford and the secret weapon turns out to be Charlie Daly's gander. Thank God, you are home. I was in danger of getting a stroke."

Turning to Ned, my father said, "You know, or at least you should know that when this is reported you will get a year in jail, six months for stealing a gander and another six months for cruelty to animals!"

"I only took the loan of the gander and you would not call a gander an animal. 'Tis more of a bird kind-of."

"All we can do now is let the court decide on these theoretical matters."

"Look-it here, I don't want to go to jail over a damn gander. Is there something we can do?"

"There is quite a lot you can do, and you'd better do it properly."

My father pointed out a number of little bolts saying to Ned. "Remove this whole plate and you will have access to the chimney. Return the gander to its owner, after which, you can clean up this mess. And if I am satisfied you have cleaned up every speck of dust before morning, I may fail in my duty and not report you."

Next morning he asked Savage how things went during the night. "I stood over him till everything was done and done right. There were times when he hinted he'd commit suicide but I told him 'not 'til you are finished here, you won't'. 'Being mentally defected was no excuse' I told him."

"I am glad you got him to repair the damage."

"And tell me this," said Savage "is it true he did all that blowing up and shooting in County Longford?"

"After last night's episode, you should know that fellow is capable of anything."

And so ended the longest conversation he ever had with Savage.

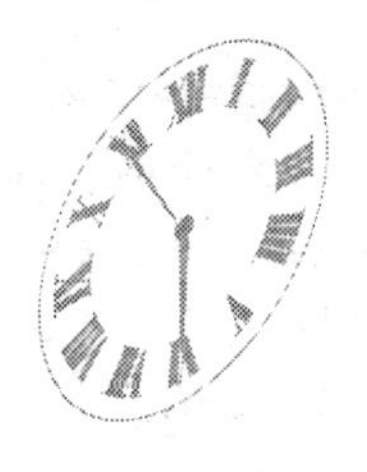

23

HAN THE BISHOP

A week later Finn, the matchmaker, called again and this time he had a pony and trap.

Everything belonging to Savage was loaded up and with her wages intact she sat in and drove off out of our lives. We never saw or heard of her again.

Bill was now installed as cook, a job he did not like. He said, "Kitchen work is women's work."

My father said "If meals are not to your liking you will only have yourself to blame."

"By the *Croí-an-diabhail* I know where there is a right housekeeper, not too young, not too old."

"Who have you in mind?"

"Han the Bishop."

"She must be pension age."

"I am pension age and can you find a better man?"

"We will see what we can do. If all goes well you will soon have your old job back."

Seemingly there was some difficulty in making the bargain. She insisted on milking only four cows and these had to be quiet and easy to milk. And her four cows had to be side by side in a separate house. She also had to be provided with a chair on the grounds that a three-legged stool was undignified and unladylike.

Bill was prepared to do anything to get out of the kitchen but Balla, the boy about the place, was very upset when he heard Han the Bishop was coming. He said she was a big fat useless sour oul' devil going around with a holy bone in her pocket.

Apparently she got this relic of a saint from his lordship the Bishop sometime before he died and everywhere she met school children she made them all kneel down around her and kiss the silver box that contained the powerful relic.

One evening nearing the time when Balla was finishing school she captured five or six boys, including Balla, and ordered them to kneel and kiss the relic.

Balla was terrified of this bone and no way would he do as the others were doing. She gave out wicked! And one word borrowed another. Finally Balla told her what to do with the bone!

It goes without saying, Han had an equally bad opinion of Balla. It is strange that there is often less friction between members of a large staff in a big farm than between the two or three employed on small farms.

Han the Bishop said "I don't know why any man should have that big long useless, badly mannered, wheel-string of a boy around the place."

It is strange that in real life things oscillate from one extreme to the other. Inside the house, things were changed from the careless Savage style to "his lordship the Bishop" style. During meals Han would spend her time attending to everyone, including Balla; filling cups of tea and moving plates and telling us how easy it was to wait on his lordship the Bishop. When everyone was finished she would attend to herself. Her breakfast was very important because every morning she had to have two very brown eggs; and if there were no brown eggs available she would still have two very brown eggs! She had her own teapot and that too was brown. Into this brown teapot went two spoons of tea and two eggs of any colour and last of all she added cold water. When the ingredients came to the boil, it took another three minutes boiling before she was satisfied. Out of that teapot came strong tea and two very brown eggs. She claimed there was very important stuff in the shells of eggs. Sixty years later a famous scientist in America made the same discovery. In fact it was "the stuff in the shells of eggs" that made him famous.

She was an excellent housekeeper and she had cures for many minor ailments. And for the more serious she would produce the silver box. I saw the bone several times and I was not afraid of it, like Balla. It was very like half a match-stick resting on a little pad of red velvet. Unfortunately, her reign was short. The stuff in the egg shells, even though it was good, just simply was not good enough.

Always at milking time Han enthroned herself on her old armchair and when she started milking she started to sing her one and only song. There were four verses in the song; a verse for each cow she had to milk. We could hear her and we now knew "Banks of Brogeen" almost as good as she did. The song was probably composed by some local poet in former times as he walked along the banks of this little stream. There was just enough water in it to turn a small mill-wheel and one could say it was a romantic environment.

One evening she was hammering away at her song and as usual the line "I sat myself down by the banks of Brogeen" ended in a high note and then complete silence.

"Surely," said Balla "she is not finished milking already?"

After a while I decided to take a quick look in and see if she was finished.

I found her sitting on her chair, hands hanging sideways. The bucket had fallen away. "Jack" I shouted "come up here. Han is dead!"

She was a heavy woman but we succeeded in bringing her out of the house. And then we put her back on her armchair in the middle of the yard. Bill and my father had not yet returned from the wood. Balla and myself were in complete charge.

"What are we to do?" I asked Balla.

"I saw my father bring a calf to life by throwing water on it."

"Well," said I "we'd better start throwing water on her." And as luck would have it there was a barrel of rainwater quite near. We gave her bucket after bucket down on the head and all over.

When the barrel was empty Balla said, "start pumping" and after buckets of cold water from the pump she showed some sign of life.

We speeded up the operation and suddenly she sat upright and drawing in a long breath she said "Stop."

Just then I heard a noise of the horse-cart coming into the haggard and I ran off to tell them about the near death of Han and to report on her present unstable condition.

My father said, "Medical opinion on our first-aid may not be wholly united. The best thing to do now is for you to run fast for Elly Sheehan and tell her come as fast as she can!"

I must not have fully explained the position to old Elly because she left a note for her brother explaining how she was gone to "lay-out" Han the Bishop.

In the meantime, my father had brought out the bottle of Paddy an a few cups. He poured out some for Bill and himself. Balla was ignored because of his Confirmation pledge, with the result that Han was handed the bottle and told to "drink some of that". And now Elly arrived eager to take over.

The first thing she did was take the bottle from Han saying "Them as lays them out are more in want of whiskey than them as being laid out."

I thought they would fight over the bottle but my father intervened saying "Get her inside and put her on the sofa. Elly you get some dry clothes and keep an eye on her until the doctor comes. Jack, (my father never called him Balla) you go for the doctor and tell him everything. He won't delay."

Elly was quite confident that Han was on the way out and that she had a full night's work ahead. She explained to my father that in trouble like this, herself should be called in first then when everything was ready the doctor should be sent for and last of all the priest. The sight of the priest with his box and the candles an' all is sure to finish them off.

"I am glad we did not make that fatal mistake." said my father.

The doctor ordered Han the bishop into hospital saying "There is a good chance of a complete recovery – but I'm afraid her working days are over."

We were sorry to see her go. The likes of her were few and far between.

Old Elly felt cheated.

24

The Woman of the Greyhounds

Our next housekeeper was known far and wide as "the woman of the greyhounds". The first morning she came to work she brought six hounds and for some unknown reason hounds require a six-mile walk every day. Therefore, the three miles to work every morning added nothing to her daily mileage. Needless to say the dogs were fed every day and Bill pointed out to my father "That bloody gangster is feeding her hounds with meat and raw eggs. I'm telling you watch her carefully!"

Every morning on her way to work she called to the local pub and grocer's. Everything that would make life easy for her was put down on the book. There was nothing new in this. All previous housekeepers did the same thing. Every evening on her way home she would push her way into the bar and monopolise the conversation, making greyhounds the principal topic. The old-timers resented this intrusion. She was the only woman to stand at the bar and everyone knew that any woman who stood in a bar was in fact *a tinker woman.*

She became very unpopular and every chance the men got they gave one of her "oul' dogs" a kick. There was the occasional misunderstanding. On the home front things were not too bad. All went well until my father went to pay the grocery bill at the end of the month. The figures were away out of line with all previous demands. I think he nearly lost his temper for the first time in his life. I heard him warn her "Mrs Mac," said he "I don't ever again want to see brandy on the shopping-list."

More *skulduggery* came to light when it was found out that she kept a dog, free of charge, for the garda sergeant in town. Seemingly there was an understanding about her dog licences. Some greenhorn of a guard held her up one evening with her six dogs. "Owner's name and address?" said he, book in hand.

"Them is not my dogs." she told him. "That one there, *Avalanche* he calls him, is belonging to Sergeant Buckley in town and this one belongs to the priest. But Sergeant Buckley will tell you everything, he knows all." The book and pencil were put away.

A wise man said *The words of truth are always paradoxical.*

25

LIFE IS A STORY

We were well used to change, having had one contrary housekeeper after another; each of them a law unto themselves. Young ones eloping during the hours of darkness; older ones open to the first offer of marriage; widows partial to dogs and drink, and one who very near died on the job.

Nevertheless!

"*Life is a story in volumes three*

The past, the present and the yet to be".

The "yet to be" came as a great surprise to us. No other boy or girl in school had a stepmother and there was a feeling, often openly expressed, that anyone with a stepmother was cursed for life. Stepmothers were the subject of crude and cruel jokes. There were those who said a stepmother's love was like a winter's chill and Shakespeare, so seldom wrong, said, "*The very name of her sufficeth.*"

Alas! How wrong public opinion can be. Never did there live a woman of kindlier nature than our new stepmother. Her whole life consisted of doing countless unremembered acts of kindness. She never tired of trying to make our home a happy one.

From the beginning we called her Aunt Kate and now my father had less to worry about. He could see we were in good hands. She was born into a farming family and at a young age emigrated to America.

Needless to say, America was a great topic of conversation between my father and herself. However, America meant two different things to them. My father's America was the whole of America. To Aunt Kate it meant working for the Bush family and the Bush family only. Little did she know she had the honour of rocking to sleep a future president of the United States of America.

We have all heard it said in a flippant manner, "'Tis a small world" and in many ways so it is. Anyone familiar with the history of the Indian mutiny will have heard of the blowing-up of the magazine at Derra Dun when the defenders had no hope of survival.

For this act of bravery, Captain Forrest was awarded the Victoria Cross. Side by side with him were two other Irishmen named Buckley and Scully. Aunt Kate's maiden name was Buckley and without going into great detail, let me say they were the same Buckleys.

One of the things Aunt Kate brought with her was a gramophone and once again there was music in the sitting-room.

My mother's piano and harmonica were still there; silent now for years. And from the walls, framed pictures of my grandmother and my uncles from my mother's side looked down unmoved by this new contraption. Unmoved is the right word – for there they stayed exactly where my mother had put them in former happy days.

On one wall there were two large pictures of rough seas and in childhood we were fascinated by them.

One was a picture of Grace Darling in her small boat amid the towering waves and the other was titled *A Lesson on Navigation.* Aunt Kate left them all in place. It was my-stupid-self that moved them in the end.

Aunt Kate made no effort to destroy our childhood memories but this went quite unnoticed then.

It often takes years for the heart and mind to respond to the many kindnesses we receive, as we go unthinking on our way.

She quickly became friends with all the neighbours. Every Sunday after Mass the women would collect near the traps to exchange information of special interest to them such as "who was expecting" and they would measure someone's chances of survival "after an operation" – while their husbands were discussing more weighty matters such as prices and farmyard manure or pig markets and the bad weather.

One Sunday morning a farm worker was boasting about his new Raleigh bicycle to a group of farmers outside the church. "Yesterday I brought home a bag of flour on the handlebars and a hundred-weight of coal on the carrier." One farmer interrupted him "Could you," said the farmer "give me a few days with it drawing dung out of the yard?" "Not a hope." said the bicycle man "Your neighbour asked me first."

He turned an insult into a joke.

The dark days of schoolboy life was slowly but surely nearing an end. Within a few months Billy and I would reach the magic age of fourteen years and in one day, leap from the half-civilised middle-ages to the reality of the present day.

Billy would then be free to stay at home and help his father on the farm. There was however a question-mark hanging over my release. My father was of the opinion that I still had an awful lot to learn. And no doubt he was right as usual.

My brother had to endure the Christian brothers for years and yet he never became a classical scholar. The bits and pieces of dead languages such as Latin and Greek and the *cúpla focal* and the trains overtaking each other and the leaking cistern and the algebra were all swept away in a breath of reality. I was not going to tolerate any more artificial frustration. Stories of the cruelty of the brothers had filtered through and as far as I was concerned, they could keep their dogged grammars and their dictionaries.

On giving this matter of education serious consideration I came to the same conclusion as the wise man who said "You can buy gold too dear". I decided to do without their kind of education.

For the vast majority of pupils in our school their last day in school was the ultimate "achievement"; the *Quixotery* was over. The world was still marvellous.

I told Aunt Kate I would run away from home rather than attend the Christian Brothers College.

I heard no more about it and I am sure she made what they call representations on my behalf.

In spite of all my misgivings with regard to Christian brothers I am duty-bound to say here that in later life the finest and best man I ever came across was a Christian brother. His name C A O'Farrell of CBS Athy. He loved nature. He loved teaching. He loved his fellow man. He alone would redeem the lot. Perhaps there were many like him.

The years teach much that the days never know.

26

Donkey Racing

At last the evening came when we closed up our books for the last time. Bags and books would be flung aside. We were ready to sign a truce with "compulsory education."

After many years of torture our *cúpla focal* died a sudden death. From now on it would be "up the river and o'er the lea for Billy and me."

However, what actually happened was slightly different to our romantic vision of life after school. The multiplicity and variety of jobs on the land was truly amazing.

We started as creamery boys, in other words, donkey-drivers. Then we had to qualify as drovers, mowers of hay, singlers of turnips, shepherds and animal night-watchmen. And in due course elevators of everything heavy such as hay, straw, fodder of all kinds; last but not least farmyard manure and fertiliser.

Our first day from school was a far cry from all this responsibility. We were given the "creamery job" which amounted to the most junior post; the preserve of very old men and schoolboys in summer. The odd servant girl undertook the creamery job and from then on she became known as "boy-girl".

The big change in our status was, we now had the stick and our donkeys learned from us what it was like to attend school in the Irish

Free State. But, unlike some teachers, we were never vindictive.

We had a Spanish donkey and for some unknown reason Spanish donkeys were regarded as the best. Billy's was a plain black Irish donkey and needless to say we would quickly check them out for speed, preferably on a Sunday morning. Everyone was in a great hurry on Sunday mornings because it was a deadly mortal sin to miss Mass and being slightly late was worse because one could not plead ill-health. And so a race to the creamery with ash-plants hopping off the unfortunate donkeys was justified – on religious grounds.

No one could risk hell for all eternity and the sooner the donkeys got that into their thick heads the better for themselves.

Without knowing it, many donkeys suffered a kind of Christian martyrdom on Sunday mornings. However, we better not enter this hypothetical bog. Perhaps there is a place for good donkeys.

Travelling around the country today, you will find abandoned, what were for a long time hives of industry, derelict and dilapidated. I am eluding, of course, to the many small creameries erected many years ago by farmers for farmers. Alas, change came. And few now remember the long line of milk-carts outside every creamery gate.

Arriving at the creamery your first task was to take note of the next driver from the opposite side. In other words, if you came from the east you took note of the next man who joined the rank of those who came from the west. Keeping an account of your turn at the gate is difficult to explain, yet in practice, it was quite simple. Oftentimes, it was easier to identify the horse or the donkey or the "outfit". From time to time there could be a change of driver and knowing the animal was better than knowing the man.

This was brought home to us when a man from the western side said to Billy, "So you are a son of Ned's"

"That is right, Sir. How did you know?"

"Ah, sure, I'd know you out of the old donkey."

This was not a derogatory remark. Nor was it taken as such. The smooth running of these creameries depended very much on voluntary labour. You helped to unload and empty the milk from the cart ahead of you and you did the same thing for the man after you. And in this way there was a constant stream of helpers "on the stand".

A senior member of the staff kept an eye on the weigh-bridge and wrote into a ledger and into your creamery book the amount of milk delivered each day.

The fellow doing the writing would not be a qualified manager, nor would he have kind of extra eligibility. Nevertheless he was regarded as a class of a half-sir.

Many farmers had good grounds for harbouring grave suspicions about the integrity of some of those responsible for the day to day running of some of these creameries.

Needless to say, neither Billy nor myself had any interest in the bad or good running, or the bad or good management.

We were glad to be rid of details for the moment.

Everyone will agree that donkeys as a rule are very stubborn animals; almost unmovable and tenacious. Once a donkey is trained, it will never break the rules of the road.

A donkey will always stick to its own side of the road. Secure in the knowledge that this is the case, drivers would often walk a mile or two while having a talk and a smoke leaving the animals to plod away on the homeward journey.

Billy and myself, being in no great hurry, decided to have a walk, a talk and a smoke.

"Do you remember the evening of the carbide?" said Billy.

"Will I ever forget it." I answered.

It happened like this. Jerh D arrived in school one day with a pocket full of carbide. This was the stuff men used in bicycle lamps and when water was added it turned into gas. One "scientist" suggested putting a lump of carbide into every ink-well so that when the ink would start to bubble up and overflow and turn into gas Ban Ní Hackendoosh and the Master would get a great fright. At the appointed time, a lump of carbide was dropped into every ink-well. Immediately things went out of control. Carbide in water is one thing;

carbide in ink is another. The ink began to bubble and swell. Schoolbags were put down ink-wells. This only made matters worse. Now there were black swellings the size of a pig over every ink-well. Jerh D failed to talk himself out of that. Every one of us paid dearly for that insurgency. Thank God it was all over. Today we would celebrate our freedom. We decided to race the donkeys past the school and we knew from experience that from inside the school all any pupil could see was the bare tops of the twenty gallon milk-churns. The drivers were unseen because of the high-edge which spoiled the view. To us, who wanted to create a lasting impression, the poor fellows were still under control. We had to do something that would be remembered. We decided on maximum speed for the "fly past." With plenty of the stick and when we were getting the last ounce out of the donkeys, we would stand upright on the lids of the churns and shout "*hurrah*" and "*hallelujah*" and wave our sticks over our heads.

We would see all the care-worn faces of the children looking out at us and envy written all over them. We would shout at ould Ban Ní Hackendoosh and the Cutler and the Witch and at the "Grand Mufti" himself – and let them see their dominion over us was at an end.

My donkey being a Spanish donkey would lead and Billy's would gallop along at full speed behind mine. Everything was going according to plan. We had estimated correctly; we were a considerable distance above ground and in full view of everybody. We were going grand shouting "*hurrah*" and "*hallelujah*" when right in front of the school gate the legs were taken from under my Spanish donkey. I was catapulted several yards ahead. Had it happened to anyone else I have no doubt the result would have been fatal. I recovered quickly and when I looked back I could see the donkey's backside was to the front. There was no hope of it regaining its feet without it being released. Billy's donkey was wedged-in under my cart and whatever way it was tangled up, one could know from the sound it was making that it would choke to death within minutes. To make matters worse Billy was spouting blood from a wound on top of his head. To us it was a catastrophe of untold magnitude. No words could describe our feelings as we saw the Master and the new priest come rushing from the school to our aid, followed by the other teachers. We were so humiliated we were almost suicidal. Truly, pride cometh before the fall.

"Oh you poor lad." said the Cutler. "Come inside and I will clean and dress that wound." I saw Billy being taken away for treatment. Truly, the gates of hell are open night and day. We definitely needed help – but help from this quarter was akin to heaping coals of fire on our heads. Believe it or not, I half expected the priest, on account of his great power, simply to raise his hand and start off "*gloria patri*" and that the donkeys would unravel themselves and stand upright. He chose not to use his divine power on this occasion. Instead he went to work like any ordinary man putting his shoulder to one wheel of Billy's cart while the Master put his shoulder to the other wheel. Together they pushed back the cart, allowing the donkey to straighten its neck and breathe freely. In the meantime, Ban Ní Hackendoosh and myself were doing all in our power to free my Spanish ass from its harness and I must admit she was a great woman around a donkey. But then a wit might say she had vast experience.

We had everything almost back in order when the Cutler and Billy rejoined us. Everyone who knows anything about first aid will tell you that the scalp is very difficult to bandage. Nurses will try to explain all about the *capelin* double-headed bandage. One side will form the horizontal bandage; the other will form what is known as the vertical bandage and they will tell exactly how to pass the vertical bandage forwards and backwards alternately. But enough of this. The Cutler found no difficulty in stemming the flow of blood. All she did was wind the bandage over the top of his head and under his jaw in such a way that his mouth was permanently shut leaving me sole spokesman for the survivors. Billy looked very like an arab bandit, with blood seeping through the bandage. Then, to add to our embarrassment, who drove up in his stately model T but captain THM Leader DSO, MC – a black protestant.

Taking the pipe out of his mouth he said to the priest. "Can I help in any way?"

"I think we are fine now." said the priest, "But thank you for your offer of help."

"What about the boy with the head wound? Perhaps I should take him to the hospital . . . you know . . . brain damage and all of that."

The Cutler came forward and I thought she was going to say to Captain Leader not to worry about brain damage because the boy had no brains to damage.

"Sir," she said "it is merely a superficial wound. There is no danger of brain damage and thanks again for your offer of help."

Captain Leader drove away and we stood surveying the mess. Billy looked very forlorn and now Ban Ní Hackendoosh and the Witch decided to check the medical work carried out by the Cutler.

Away back in the dark ages of nursing before hospitals or professionals were thought of, two women became famous. They were the pioneers of nursing and when Ban Ní Hackendoosh and the Witch approached Billy they reminded me of someone or something. It took me years to find out who or what they reminded me of. But perhaps "reminded" is not the right word, so I'd better explain.

The scene remained in my mind for years and years. Billy with his bloodstained bandage being examined by two women who meant well but knew nothing about nursing or first-aid.

Then I came across an article in some magazine about the two pioneers – Sairey Camp and Betsy Prig. "Ah," said I to myself "that is who they reminded me of – Sairey Camp and Betsy Prig."

By now we were surrounded by the school children laughing at us and pointing at the donkeys and generally having great fun at our expense, until the teachers warned them off; promising a good dose of the stick to the more forward brats. There was a wee bit of humanity in them after all. The priest also turned out to be human. And when all is said and done, we learned one great lesson that day. Our education had just begun. Forgiveness was in the air.

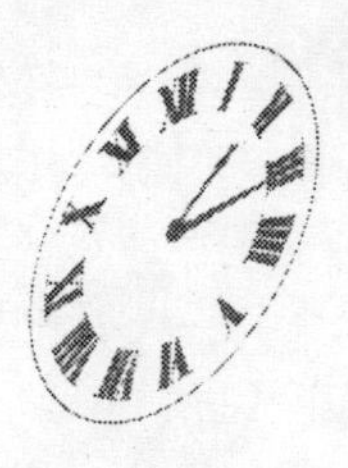

27

At the Crossroads

We now entered what might be described as a transition period in which every effort would be made to facilitate transmutation. The schoolboys of yesterday would become tomorrow's men. And the first step was always into a long trousers, provided, of course, that one was of normal height and build. It also entailed the wearing of a cap on a full time basis.

Hats were worn by older men who were well beyond military age and married. The familiar black bowler hat was the insignia of wealthy farmers, publicans and retired gentlemen. For us this upper class head-gear was a long way off. We were quite happy with the large tweed cap worn on the side of the head and hanging well down over one ear. There was a terrible waste of material when making these caps. Jim Sullivan, a man who could always see the funny side of things had this to say to a young fellow who arrived at the cross one evening wearing one of these large tweed caps – "Jay-zus! Young fellow, where do you think you are going with the *government haybarn?*"

And the more fashion conscious young men began to purchase nice little hats with a wee fancy feather in the hat-band.

Every evening, summer and winter, the crossroads was our meeting place. Here men of every age and from all walks of life came to talk and argue, to discuss everyday problems and voice their opinions on matters about which they knew little. There were, of course, exceptions to the rule. Patsy Sheehan, the head gardener at the Great House and who had unlimited access to Captain Leader's library, was well versed in ancient history. One could say he was on first name terms with all Alexanders' successors; not that first names ever came into the picture.

There was Paddy O'Toole, who long ago had abandoned the practice of attending mass or any religious ceremony. People dismissed his unorthodox opinions under the heading of insanity. Anyone who suggested, as Paddy O'Toole did, that the Pope should get a dose of ground limestone to cure his hiccups was without doubt beyond redemption. He had equally strong views on other matters.

Tomlinson, the spoiled priest, was always ready to iron out any question on theology and science. And we had a few war veterans to deal with military matters. As well as these, we had a young IRA man who was interned by the Cosgrave Government. He was familiar with the inside of the county jail and the Curragh Camp and some Cosgrave supporters were of the opinion that the Free State soldiers would have done a better job if they had given him a few kicks in the behind and sent him home to his mother.

As universities go, we had quite a good university at the crossroads and while the elders did not have the power to confer degrees, judging from the results from other universities this handicap made little or no difference.

Most of the men at the crossroads wore the "*government haybarn*" caps. Patsy Sheehan always wore a respectable brown felt hat plus a collar and tie, even on working days. In any case, Captain Leader would take a poor view of a ragamuffin working in the garden. When Tomlinson made up his mind to quit the seminary he must have brought home a fair supply of black hats and this, together with his long lonesome face, made him look more like an undertaker than a thriving dairy-farmer. Very few crossroads could boast of men of such high calibre. The big difference between our leading men was mostly confined to pronunciation. Other than that, one could say they were "on the one word."

None of them had ever passed an examination which would direct them into the civil service, fit them for the position of shoeblack or perhaps pig-driver. Avoiding years of rigorous paper work they all became "capitalist and independent." Needless to say, we had no tycoons or moguls. Nevertheless every man at the crossroads believed in free enterprise and private ownership. They were profoundly at ease with the world. About this time, Mussolini was starting to make a name for himself in Italy. Patsy always referred to him as *Mus-a-line*. As far as he was concerned *Mus-a-line's* son-in-law was Count Can-o and Czechoslovakia became *Co-so-sal-avac*. This mispronunciation went unnoticed until one evening Tomlinson could stand it no longer. A dispute arose between them about Napoleon and the battle of Quatre Bras. Patsy, who generally had his facts right, was insisting that Napoleon directed the battle of Quatre Bras. At this stage Tomlinson was ungracious enough to remark "Perhaps Patsy, you are thinking of the battle of *Katr Bra*."

"I am glad you are able to help my pronunciation, rather than my history." said Patsy with a touch of sarcasm.

"Cattle were down to nothing today in the fair." said Big Mick.

"I had to bring mine home again." said Dinny O.

The debate on the fair was interrupted, in the same manner as the previous debate, by Jack Pad wanting to know if anyone had started spraying yet.

Every evening the agenda was wide open. All subjects were under review: politics, religion, agriculture, literature, law and wages. We were glad of our emancipation. Looking ahead, things seemed remarkably hazy. It was great. It was youth's soft season. There is an old saying,

"*Rare are the buttons of a Roman's breeches,*
In antiquarian eyes surpassing riches".

We have lots of things to compare with the buttons of a Roman's breeches. Infinitesimal and worthless then, the memories so varied and diverse of the old crossroads are to us who still remember, our riches; – riches we are happy to share with the poor of the television age.

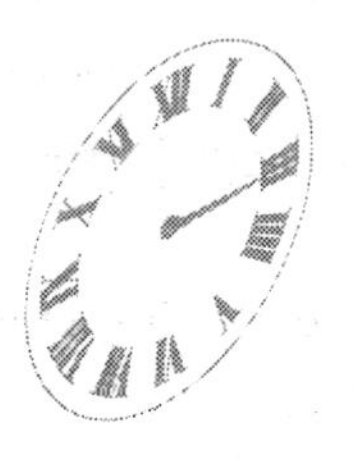

28

The Rambling House

We were of that age group who find it necessary to fill every hour.

"*Ever let thy fancy roam,*

Pleasure never is at home".

This seemed to be our guiding principal. And it so happened one very wet evening we made up our minds to sample Bet Seán's rambling house. It was a rambling house in her father's time and in his father's time. Bet was a very capable person and her house was a great meeting place for older people more interested in the past than in the future. Most of the clientele were of the opinion that there was no future of any account. They preferred to dwell on the past, back in the good times before the trouble started.

Unlike the crossroads there was no room here for muscular activities. Anyone inclined to show off would be told in plain language "This is no *stigatty place*." What exactly she meant by "*stigatty place*" nobody seemed to know, and yet, everybody understood.

The first night, Billy and I ventured into this sanctuary from the sleet and rain. We were a little shame-faced, particularly when Bet heaved herself out of the old home-made rocking-chair in the corner by the bellows and welcomed us by assigning us to two fifty six-pound butter-boxes on the sides of which was clearly stamped ***PRODUCE OF THE IRISH FREE STATE***.

"Keep out of the men's way," she warned "and take no stories out of this house." And then she added as an afterthought "or anything else for that matter."

When she resettled in the rocking-chair Billy whispered "She is a right sour old-dog of a woman."

Needless to say, first impressions are not always correct. People said she was always helpful, extremely honest and a real pleasure when laying out the dead. Under certain circumstances she would lend her American glass candle-sticks. At some poorly-organised wakes she would take it upon herself to give out the rosary, followed by a lengthy litany. Talk about inspiration, truly it was an orgy of imagination. At least that is what some people said.

Old men and women complained of being crippled from kneeling for hours on some stone floor. Bet's litany brought home to them, very forcibly, the true meaning of eternity.

She had many life long friends and Jurry Murphy was one of them. His place at the fire was directly opposite her's at the other side of the fire. And if for some reason Jurry was a little late and his place was taken by someone else, the moment Jurry would appear, Bet, exercising her full authority in her own house, would say to the culprit – "*carthig*", and the culprit would move, quickly as often as not, to an upturned Irish Free State butter-box.

We had never heard the word "*carthig*" in school. Nevertheless, we concluded it had great power like all the *cúpla focal* and the Latin and all.

No matter how high or how low any set-up is, be it the Government or the local creamery committee, there is always an inner-circle. Bet's rambling house was no exception. Bet was a great believer in protocol and the older you were the nearer the fire. All under twenty-five were confined to "the bottom of the kitchen." Here they looked funny with their big *government haybarn* caps all sitting on Free State butter-boxes. These were the days when everyone knew their place and there was no hassle.

Next to Jurry sat Big Mick and he occupied space enough for two people because he had to have the bad hip always turned towards the heat; Paddy Óg came next and next to Bet sat Poteen Judeen. That completed the circle.

There were no fairy stories told in Bet's rambling house. Poteen Judeen would have none of that rot. They were not interested in irrelevant gossip. They liked to shed light onto the dark pages of our recent tangled history. They confined themselves to facts – and facts only.

One whole night was spent discussing the best way to sharpen a cut-throat razor. The *fiddlestick* of a safety-razor was not yet on the market.

Finally, everyone agreed that the blacksmith was the best man to knock the thickness out of a razor. Seemingly, the local blacksmith discovered a stone of the proper texture in the wall of the bridge and he was often seen sharpening a razor on that wall.

Those were the days when men shaved once a week; usually on Saturday nights in preparation for Mass on Sunday morning. For those of us who had as yet no use for a razor it was interesting to watch the men arrive – partly shaved – at the rambling house, some seriously wounded with blood stained bits of *The Cork Examiner* adhering to their faces. And if these little scraps of paper were removed too soon, the blood would start to flow again.

The man who could shave with one of these open razors without drawing blood was rare indeed. Some of these razors were passed on from father to son. Naturally in the course of time, the smooth edge of former days disappeared and everyone knew they were due a visit to the wall of the bridge!

The shape and make of the face had a lot to do with the amount of cuts and bloodshed. In most cases bloodshed could not be avoided. Take for instance Paddy Óg, with his sunken cheeks over which no razor ever made could manoeuvre successfully. And there was Kavanagh, whose cheeks were so far in that a little more would result in his head being turned inside-out.

Public opinion in the Rambling House was very much in favour of the "fair-sized spud in the mouth" to combat the sunken cheek malady. A side to side movement was recommended. Paddy Óg maintained that two spuds were better than one, pointing out that one spud could not combat the elastic force of the skin.

This matter of shaving was discussed with apostolic fervour and it was generally agreed that as the beard got thicker and stronger, one soon found out that the days of yahooing were over.

Dan Joe Emington came one night but he said "Never again! I could not stand them discussing something all night long – like a flock of sheep gnawing at fresh-turned sides of turnips or mangles."

Dan Joe was a man of action. Uncorrupted prejudices and fixed ideas made Dan Joe a man apart. Dan Joe had left school about a year ahead of us and we valued his company and his advice. However, on this occasion he was wrong in his assessment.

Here in the Rambling House were men and women who were not entangled with so-called education. They lived rightly and happily by the tenets and principals of *The Sermon on the Mount*. They hid nothing from each other. The light of experience was freely available and help was offered without having to ask. They spoke of the law with respect and they had little use for printed matter.

Old Jurry Murphy could tell the day of the week simply by rubbing his chin. And Big Mick could foretell any change in the weather by rubbing his painful hip. Their language was unsophisticated and Bet made sure there was no swearing by this or by that. She was quick to intervene telling the offender "simply let your *yes* be *yes* and your *no* be *no*". Grammatical inflection and syntax was unknown rubbish. Instead there were farmer jokes and shepherd jokes, containing the wisdom of the ages.

They were the type of people Virgil wanted to find out about when he went to work for a farmer on the banks of the Tiber. He wished to meet the founders of civilisation, namely the farmer and the shepherd. However, as far as Billy and I were concerned just then, forming an alliance with the "founder members of civilisation" in our area was not on.

We appreciated the shelter and the heat, when out-of-doors would skin the proverbial brass-monkey.

It was always nice to step in from the cold and find Big Mack in the chair, telling a story the truth of which would be hard to prove or disprove.

"Was I ever telling ye about the two farmers who were watering their cattle at the same water hole?"

"No, Mick you never told us that one."

"Well, there they were, the cattle drinking the water, the farmers talking and then one said to the other. 'Them cows of yours are in great condition. What are you giving them to eat'?"

"Yerra, nothing much except a handful of badly-thrashed oaten-straw." said your man.

"Well, that is a terror." said the other fellow. "I am giving mine well-thrashed oaten-straw. Tell me now how is that?"

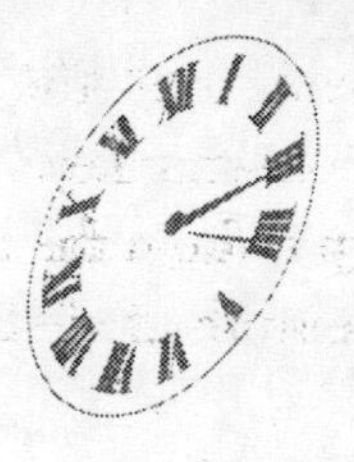

29

The Circus

After our annual visit to Duffy's Circus a new wave of activity would start up. A rope would be tied to a branch of the old elm which stood beside the crossroads. Hand over hand we would climb the rope and hold our positions, hands off. In fact, if we'd had the facilities which they had at the circus we could have performed every act, at least that is what we thought.

This year the acrobat, instead of putting one leg behind his head he put both. The challenge was immediately taken up and the only one coming anyway close to putting both legs behind his head was Paddy Boyo. Time and time again he failed, in spite of all the encouragement we could give him.

"By the Lord God," said he "I will do it tomorrow evening."

Little we know of the heartbreak and hardship endured by champions as they battle for success and supremacy. Many, within grasp of the peak, fail and are flung into the Stygian depths forgotten – as if they never lived. We would not let this happen to our acrobat Paddy Boyo.

Paddy was employed by the widow Kearney as a farm worker. She was a husky, middle-aged, masculine type of woman and many said that working for her was a type of manslaughter.

It so happened that the very next morning she ordered Paddy off to the turnip field saying "Them turnips must be singled this week or they will be gone wild. I want them done as quickly as possible!"

Paddy was delighted. The turnip field was two fields from the house. Knowing that she could not keep him under surveillance all day, he saw an opportunity of getting in some practicc at trying to put both legs behind his head.

As he worked along the first drill he just simply could not get his mind off the problem. And when he was about half way up the first row he decided to have a go. Why, oh why do people so readily forget the words *Lead us not into temptation.*

It was again a case of so near and yet so far. Then it dawned upon him that perhaps it was the tight trousers that was holding him back.

Off came the boots and socks. And off came the trousers in the sure knowledge that no one could see him, for basically he was a shy type of individual.

Now in his new-found freedom he got the first leg into position with far less difficulty than on previous occasions. However, getting leg number two back over number one was still a problem. It was only when he said to himself, "if he can do it, so can I!" that he steeled himself into a superhuman effort; pushing with all his strength and bending himself into a complete hoop he finally locked the second leg behind the first.

Everyone knows the most difficult part of this act is to bring the legs back again to their normal position. One might say that Paddy Boyo was now in a queer dilemma. But things were far worse than that. Paddy had no choice. Every effort to free himself failed. And with agonising cramps in both legs and pains all over his body he decided to call aloud for help, only to find his jawbone pressing so firmly on his chest that he could not open his mouth. All he could do was think. And his thoughts were anything but pleasant.

"I have not long to live and everyone will think I took my own life," were some of his mournful thoughts. Another disturbing idea now entered his head, namely, that several days might elapse before

Mrs Kearney would make the grim discovery. And by then 'rigor mortis' would have set in and no way would he fit into an ordinary coffin. Little did he know about the skilful work carried out by undertakers, wielding the small axe and the meat-saw. He need not have worried about the shape of the coffin. No undertaker would disgrace the firm by burying a man in a sort of low dog house.

In such a deadly predicament most people would turn to prayer as a last resort, but for Paddy even this avenue of escape was closed off.

Brought up as a good God-fearing Roman Catholic, he was of the opinion that God would take a poor view of a man praying with his bare backside cocked up to the sky. He knew the parish priest would not approve, and there was no doubt in his mind that even the priest's housekeeper would be in a state of profound shock were she called upon to help a man in this situation. Slowly and still more slowly the minutes and the hours ticked away. Soon Mrs Kearney would have the midday meal ready.

Paddy heard the farmyard bell on the nearby Leader Estate. It had a different sound to the church bell. It was much more lively and schoolboys always mimicked the sound "*deenderum - downderum, deenderum - downderum!*" This day the *deenderum-downderum* seemed to go on for ever. Other farmers used the humble whistle but Mrs Kearney was far more practical. She simply gave the iron pole of the haybarn a few blows of the hammer. This was always the signal for Paddy to return to the house for his dinner. Alas, today Paddy could not move. He envied the man who, having made up his mind to kill himself, could leisurely go about the job; measuring the length of the rope or changing the cartridge in the gun. He was as the book says "mightily tormented" in mind and body. Mrs Kearney was out again belting the iron pole and this time the local people could be forgiven for thinking she was demolishing the whole structure. The hammering went on and on and Hanny Dick, who lived about half a mile up the road, was on the point of collapse under the tension of not knowing what was wrong down at

Kearney's. Hanny Dick was one woman who wanted to know everything and quickly she tied her boot laces – an unnecessary task on most dates – and she hit the road with a kind of hostile feeling towards Mrs Kearney for not keeping her fully informed. Were I to describe the condition of Paddy Boyo as Hanny Dick trotted down the road in search of information, I am afraid I would have to overlap the bounds of decency. And things were getting worse.

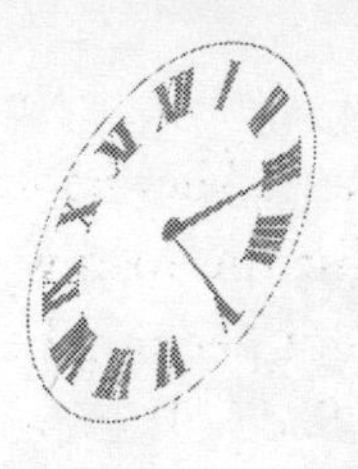

30

Discovery

Hanny Dick rushed in the gate and faced up to Mrs Kearney.

"Mrs Kearney, Mrs Kearney will you stop belting that pole and tell me what is the matter."

"O, 'tis you, is it?"

"Who do you think it is?"

"Well" said Mrs Kearney. "If you have to know, 'tis nothing important. I'm trying to get that young fellow home to his dinner. He must be stone deaf."

"Sound asleep is more like it, as sure as my name is Hanny."

"By God he is in for a rude awakening." said Mrs Kearney as she took hold of her walking-cane.

"I will go with you for the walk." said Hanny Dick. And off they went towards the turnip field.

The first thing that entered Mrs Kearney's mind was the small amount of work done, but Hanny Dick interrupted this line of thought by asking, "What is that white thing above in the middle of the field?"

They started walking towards the white thing. They were both flabbergasted when they saw Paddy Boyo naked and tied up in a knot!

"*Holy Mother of Divine God.*" said Mrs Kearney.

"That we may be made worthy of the promises of Christ." said Hanny Dick.

"Stop your praying, *he is still alive*." said Mrs Kearney.

"'Tis the work of the devil." said Hanny. "We can't go near him without the *Holy Water*."

Mrs Kearney returned in haste to the house to procure some *Holy Water*, leaving Hanny Dick to watch over Paddy. And you may be sure she scrutinised every inch of him. Mrs Kearney, being a practical woman, was ashamed to admit she had no *Holy Water* in the house. She procured what she considered was the next best thing, namely a half-gallon of rainwater from the barrel.

She lost no time getting back to the turnip field and Hanny Dick was handed an ample supply of what she understood to be *Holy Water*. Now with renewed courage she sprinkled plenty of it on Paddy and on the surrounding ground, to defy Satan and his pack of devils. Mrs Kearney suggested that the rest of the *Holy Water* should be "rubbed in" and while Hanny was rubbing in the so-called *Holy Water*, she swore she saw the devil coming out of Paddy's eyes. And I am sure she did. When she had it all well rubbed in, to use her own words, "I tore him apart, straightened out his legs and put him standing. I was a match for ten devils, so I was."

Paddy made a quick recovery. That evening he went to an agent who lived down the Mallow road, who for the sum of ten shillings would supply would-be emigrants with the names and addresses of several building constructors in England who were always ready to employ good workers.

Paddy knew that Hanny Dick would be holding a "press conference" at the Post Office when she went for her old age pension. He knew she would be questioned in great detail and that she would reply in even greater detail.

Sooner or later the story would reach the parish priest via the housekeeper and the fact that there were two women involved with a naked man in the middle of a field would merit a good sermon from the altar. "Nothing like this should ever again take place in a Catholic country".

Paddy would not be around to hear the condemnation and reproach. He was one man who sailed for foreign parts devoid of egotism. Within a few years five young men from the surrounding area found work with Paddy Boyo in Romford and letters with the postmark "Romford" were eagerly looked forward to.

Destiny is not a matter of chance, or is it?

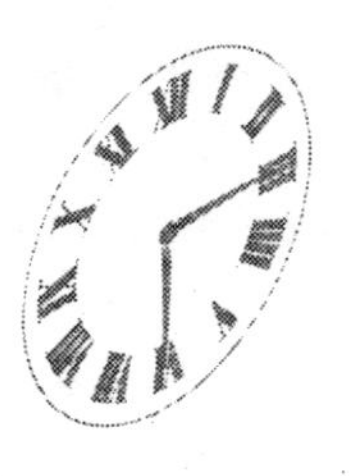

31

PATSY EXPLAINS

We all know that truth is not always evidence, nor is evidence always truth. Nevertheless there was agreement at the crossroads that Paddy Boyo succeeded in putting both his legs behind his head and this gave rise to an inquest rather than an inquiry. Patsy Sheehan fancied himself as an expert on most matters not fully understood, especially "human relationships" and "inter-relationship".

He was of the opinion that climbing rocks and ropes and twisting our limbs and jumping about proved beyond doubt our close relationship with apes and monkeys, of all sorts. Our closest relation in his view was the orang-utan.

"Yes, yes, I say." said Patsy. "The orang-utan always adopts the legs behind the head position when sleeping or resting." He went on to explain. "Generally its resting place was on a large branch about ten feet out from the tree trunk where minor branches would form a base for its bed, mostly composed of broken twigs; the end result being more like an armchair than a bed. When the orang-utan was satisfied that all was in order it would sit down and place its legs behind its head, always making sure its backside was towards the tree trunk."

"Why always towards the tree trunk?" demanded Tomlinson.

"Yes, yes, I say. In this position it was fully protected like a man with his pistol under his pillow. No enemy could approach except along the branch and the moment anything touched its backside all the orang-utan had to do was tilt its head forward and the two powerful legs, when released in this manner, acted like a catapult the force of which would dash any enemy against the tree trunk; usually with fatal results."

"I don't believe there is any such thing as an orang-utan." said Jack Pad.

And Vaughan said "You are right there, there isn't."

Patsy went on to explain. "As regards nature and physics . . ."

"We all know about physics." said Vaughan. "In the Curragh Camp they gave us what they called purgative laxative every week."

Patsy ignored this intrusion, putting it all down to Vaughan's dismal education. Patsy went on "Elementary science and physical science . . ."

Jamsey Ben could stand this kind of talk no longer. "I never heard such rubbish. Them ole books they do be reading is all *gibberage!* I don't believe we are related to monkeys. Monkeys is people in themselves!"

And Vaughan said "What about a game of pitch and toss?" And most of the men joined Vaughan in the game.

Again ignoring the remarks of the unlearned, Patsy turned to Tomlinson. "We don't have to go back to the egg and the ovum but we must pay attention to the shape of the skull and the position of the eye ball and to all the scientific measurements carried out: all prove beyond doubt that man's stature and dignity is firmly based on his big toe."

"Big toe?" said one old timer. "I won't say what is in my mind."

"You are right, Patsy." said Tomlinson. "It all comes back to me now. The word is on the tip of my tongue." And pushing his black hat more to the rear. "The word is quadrumana. Fair dues to you Patsy. You know your stuff."

"And what is the meaning of this quadrumana?" inquired James Ben.

"It means," said Tomlinson "four handed. In other words, apes and monkeys have everything we have except big toes."

All during the inquest into his behaviour and subsequent disappearance, Paddy Boyo was sitting in a lonely bed-sitter on the outskirts of Romford after his first day on a building site. Before him was an almost blank sheet of paper. His new address was easy enough. Then the words "*Dear Mother . . .*" At long last he got it right and quickly wrote. "*I had to leave. I am glad I came. Don't worry. Next week I will send you all I can. Your affectionate son, Paddy.*"

The jury at the crossroads had reached a verdict. "He was one right bad lazy scoundrel to leave the poor widow woman at a very busy time. Now she had no one to do the turnips. May God help people depending on Paddy Boyo and the likes o' him".

32

Tinkers and Trouble

Lingering in the far background of my memory is the vivid picture of a family of itinerants standing around the remains of their caravan, which they intentionally and deliberately set on fire. Bits and pieces, not fully consumed, were picked up and thrown into the hot centre of the fire. Nothing was saved or taken away. Only the iron bands remained. Like their former owner, they too had reached the end of the road.

The burning of the caravan was the final stage in a type of religious ceremony performed in memory of the head of the clan. Old men of the settled community were familiar with this "madness". They knew it was part of the old funeral rite and part of the secret tinker religion. I heard one old man say, "'Tis the devil of a queer religion."

Queer religion it may well be, but we must remember all religions have one thing in common: self-denial and self-imposed austerities. Christian doctrine teaches, "*it is by fasting, self-sacrifice and penance man is drawn closer to God.*"

Faith and trust in God is clearly shown by the itinerants, and they see God as the great provider. Their faith is firm and earnest.

Who has ever seen a Catholic or a protestant display such conviction by setting fire to their inheritance, be it a farmyard or supermarket and start again from square one. Therefore we must admit, from a religious point of view, itinerants are very much better than their reputation.

Sadhuism, a religion which was hoary with antiquity when Alexander was marching over the plains of the Punjab, is perhaps as close as we can get to the secret religion of the tinkers. Like the sadhu and Faquir of India and the east, the gipsies of Europe all have something in common.

However, when it came to the share-out of supernatural powers, the Irish tinker did poorly. All they were given was the "*evil eye*" and from this narrow base they extended their influence all over the country, and many feared them. Old tinker women were respected in the same way as one would respect a mother alligator when crossing the Nile.

Young mothers dreaded the "*evil eye*" above all else. Farmers were intimidated and superstition lingered on.

A time came when caravans were better built and itinerants were reluctant to set them on fire. And like all religions they too had the right to change the rules, and all except the very "*flat-earthers*" were happy to leave the caravan unoccupied for a period of six months or more. In other words, the caravan was placed in quarantine. Ordinary people became familiar with the change in an ill-defined fashion, which lacked trust of any kind.

Abandoned caravans became objects of fear and distress in some localities. A few miles west of the crossroads there was an old oak wood and the mighty oaks stood well away from each other. It was part of the Leader Estate and an ideal place to "quarantine" a caravan. It was a place of great serenity.

For the benefit of those who were not superstitious, the old widow would call to a few neighbouring houses seeking sympathy and support on the death of her husband and without giving any hint about the religious aspect of the abandonment of the caravan, she would give several good reasons why young and old should avoid going next or near it.

"Ah, Missus that caravan requires a good airing out. Poor Jack, he suffered terrible with the German train-mange. 'Tis *taking* too, and there's no cure for the German train-mange. And sure Missus, the van is ate with the vermin. They sucked his blood, they did. Poor Jack won't know himself in his clean bed in heaven. 'Twas the consumption-purge that swept him in the end. He didn't have time to get worse!"

Naturally the story would be told and re-told and the health-conscious and the timid would keep well away from any caravan in quarantine. The seeds of fear were well and truly planted.

But, the time had not yet come:

"*when the wolf shall dwell with the lamb. The weaned child was about to place his hand on the adder's den*".

We decided it would be a great joke to bring the caravan from the wood and let it roll down into Ned Harmon's back yard, from where it would be almost impossible to retrieve it. Harmon was a law-abiding citizen, unsociable, unfriendly, and to make matters worse he was the "summons server" in the area. He was never known to laugh.

We wondered what his reaction would be when he found himself in possession of a large tinkers' caravan with no hope of getting rid of it. No one would help him haul it out. It would be the joke of the century.

The "A" team were as follows:

Eddie Tarrant and his brother Billy, both now dead RIP

Jerh Emington and his brother Dan Joe, both now dead RIP

Tom Drake and his brother Jack, both now dead RIP

Jim Sullivan and Sean Murphy, both now dead RIP

Billy George, the youngest of the team and the first to die, RIP

I am the sole survivor. Talk about the curse of Tutankhamun's tomb and the curse of Rameses II! It seems that given time every curse will materialise.

Came the appointed evening and we all marched off in the direction of the oak wood. We were in no hurry. Around midnight was zero hour.

Tentatively we stood looking at the monster with all its built-in dangers: German train-mange, consumption purge and vermin.

It was a big caravan and it was full of rubbish.

"Let's face her to the road." said Dan Joe and the pushing and shoving began immediately.

Had Laurence Sterne's uncle Toby been anywhere in the background he would have had good cause to repeat "*Our armies swore terribly in France and Flanders but nothing to this*".

Finally, after much pushing and pulling and swearing, we got it to the roadside and luckily the road sloped away in both directions. We turned it to the right. And now that we were all still alive our courage grew. To young men "*the frontier-grave is always far away*".

Tarrant and Dan Joe displayed great courage by going inside and lighting an oil lamp which created more shadow than light. Nevertheless, they continued to hand down instructions from the bridge and presently we were ready for blast-off.

Imperceptibly, we gained speed. Things were going great. Soon we would be manoeuvering the caravan into its final position before sending it on a nosedive down into the summons server's back yard. Let him explain to the tinkers how it came to be there. It was now a case of holding it back. And then we saw old Mrs O'Donoghue coming towards us on her way home. She was no ordinary woman. Her daughter was married to the local garda sergeant and, without wishing trouble on anybody, this matter of the caravan was bound to come up.

We dived for cover, leaving the caravan to career wildly down the road completely out of control. Would it run over the old lady, killing her instantly? Or worse, would she be severely injured and die a lingering death? These thoughts were uppermost in our minds as we lay under cover inside the fence. It was a toss-up between jail for life or the hangman. And at this time there was an occasional hanging. Unfortunately for the hangman, his clients never made a return visit and I could almost see the gleam in his eye as he anticipated the money for a dozen jobs the one day.

Our only hope was that before the fatal day we would all be swept away by the German train-mange or the consumption purge and thus in some small way preserve whatever was left of the family honour.

Faintly we heard *click, click, click* and then it grew louder. *Click,*

click, click. The miracle had happened. She had escaped! Never before and never again will the sound of stiletto heels bring such relief to men in trouble.

When the footsteps died away we left our hiding place and we took off after the caravan as fast as we could go, expecting to find Tarrant and Dan Joe dead amid the wreckage. It held the road for almost half a mile, increasing speed all the time until it struck the wall near the castle gate. The whole super-structure went straight over the wall. The four wheels and the base, plus a pile of rubbish remained on the roadside and, without we knowing it, a second miracle had taken place. Tarrant and Dan Joe were uninjured, but very unthankful to those of us who had abandoned ship. There was a bit of recrimination and bad language, but common-sense prevailed; sworn alibis were concocted. Weeks and months of misery followed.

Tinkers came in droves. Guards were cycling around non-stop. There was a rush for dog licences and bicycle lamps. Suddenly the whole area became law-abiding. There was always the fear that one of us would go down with some terrible disease like the German train-mange or worse.

It took over a year for things to quieten down. By then it was taken for granted that the destruction was caused by another tinker family because of a vendetta that had gone on for generations.

Then there was the murder of a tinker in Galway whose name was familiar. The man charged pleaded "not guilty" on the grounds that he had often given the murdered man a much greater belting with little or no results. He claimed he had no bad intentions.

The doctor involved in the inquest testified that the dead man had over eighty old head wounds and skull injuries, any of which would be sufficient to cause the death of an ordinary person. The charge was reduced to manslaughter. Never again, under any circumstances, would we ever again lay a hand on a tinker's caravan. From now on, they would have complete freedom of worship as well as plenty of alcohol and tobacco together with many unknown diseases. We wished them well.

This was the sunset of our boyish pranks. In future, we would be much more careful.

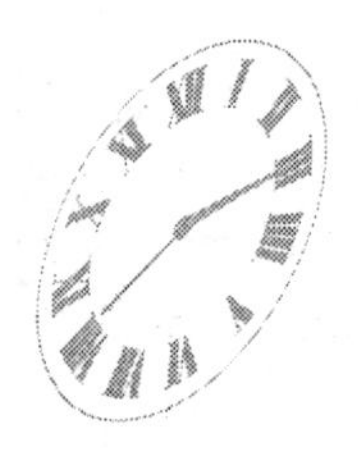

33

THE ONE EYE

We know from experience that there is no definite design of life. "*Que sera, sera*", whatever will be, will be.

In ancient times, Plato forbid children under the age of eighteen to drink wine. And anyone under forty, found drunk, ran the risk of being beheaded or boiled in oil or suffering whatever form of cruel death was popular at that time. For those over forty, drink was more or less recommended because "*drink bestowth cheerfulness upon men and youth upon the aged*".

A year ago we looked forward to freedom from the "school cum torture chamber". Were we now to wait till the grand old age of forty before bringing any cheerfulness into our humdrum existence? – an existence stereotyped in every hole and corner of the Irish Free State, where the only running water was in rivers, radio was almost unheard of and television was not even a glint in someone's eye.

Sitting on a swaying and broken stile was considered amusement enough for teenage youngsters. Grown men, on the other hand, could look forward to the occasional wake, where free drink, tobacco and clay pipes were distributed every half-hour to a chorus, "May God increase you'es" or "the Lord God ha' mercy on the dead". All very fine for those qualified to attend.

Is it any wonder we had little interest in maintaining the status quo. Occasionally we would walk away from the crossroads on some devilment of our own, weary of listening to the wisdom of the ancients. We might block a chimney, by placing a wet sack across it and smoke them out, or hop stones off the iron roofs of some local houses.

Collecting a few village dogs and tying tin cans to their tails was great fun. But on a summer evening there is no better sport than "crusting" a good nest of wasps.

With the air thick with angry wasps the idea was to rush in close and give them another bang. More often than not the wasps won the fight. One sting was always enough.

After the *tinker's van* affair we would now try to foresee the logical consequences of our sporting schedule. Time would tell if we were capable of doing so.

Bill, the friend of our young days, had now retired from farm work and his place was taken by Dan Nolan, a talkative Kerryman, who married a nice girl who had a nice cottage of her own, not far from our place. He was a good family man, a good worker and liked by everyone.

Like those who were home from foreign parts or soldiers home from the war he brought with him some new expressions, which inevitably found their way into everyday conversation.

These were the days when families of nine or ten were the norm, sixteen was no great surprise and I knew of a family of twenty-one boys, most of whom went to America where they joined the Massachusetts light infantry bringing honour to the regiment in the fight against the Ku Klux Clan. However, to return to matters nearer home, an only child was a rare phenomenon and Dan Nolan's name for an only child was "a one eye". The father's name was changed to "the father of the one eye"; the mother's name was changed to "the mother of the one eye"; and collectively the parents became "the pair with the one eye".

Most people think that an only child is always pampered. The parents submit to its every whim. Side by side with this individual treatment "the one eye" always got more presents and more pocket money than other children who had numerous brothers and sisters. But, as nothing stands still in nature the good times pass quickly, when an only child starts to grow up, over protective parents make its life a misery.

The only child is forbidden to ride a donkey, forbidden to ride a bike or play with other children nor can it be out of sight for more than five minutes.

Old Doyle, the father of "the one eye", was true to form. And worse still, people said he was as headstrong as a barrow pig. Envy is now a thing of the past. We sympathise with the solitary child; now we see a prisoner.

Young Jimmy Doyle was indeed a prisoner. Every time he crossed the threshold required an explanation and old Doyle had a hard time inventing reasons why young Jimmy should stay indoors and well away from his school friends during holiday time. His final word was "I'm for your good Jimmy, my boy. I'm for your good."

One evening in the dim twilight a terrible thing happened to young Jimmy Doyle. And to make matters worse, it happened under the watchful eye of old Doyle himself.

We had no intention of injuring young Doyle and yet, one could hardly describe what happened as an accident.

After walking from our own crossroads to the next, on the look out for something to happen, when nothing happened we decided to take a different road home and this was mostly a private road on the Leader Estate. With woods on either side it was like a green tunnel.

Here and there along the road were a few workmen's houses.

Unfortunately, the Doyle family lived in one of these houses. As we came close to Doyle's we spotted a huge hedgehog crossing the road and there was a rush towards it. The poor thing lost its nerve and made itself into a round ball as hedgehogs do when danger threatens.

With its head and legs neatly folded inside, thousands and

thousands of prickly boney spikes faced in every direction. Here indeed was nature's masterpiece of defence.

Nature however did not foresee the advent of the GAA or the scarcity of footballs. There was about eight of us in the gang and Billy George was first to give the old *parkapine* an almighty kick which lifted it a few feet off the ground. "O, my leg." he cried. "'Tis one right heavy hure of a *parkapine*." I would like to point out here that the word *hure* when used in the context and spelled in this manner is not offensive or derogatory. It simply means out of the ordinary.

While the hedgehog is a fairish substitute for a football it does not lend itself to the finer points of Gaelic. There can be no picking up or hand passing. Therefore a match played with a hedgehog looks very like a world cup contest, with everyone dribbling the ball along, waiting for an opportunity of having a good swipe at it.

We, in our time, played many world cup matches but our day never came.

The road widened slightly at Doyle's house and here we decided to play a match. It was almost dark but as there would be long distance kicks the match should go ahead without any difficulty. Needless to say we had no bishop or archbishop to throw in the ball. Instead Billy George gave the *parkapine* another almighty kick and the match was on.

No sooner on than old Doyle opened the door. "Get out of here ye pack o' hures. Ye pack o' hures, do ye want to wake the child?"

The child was a twelve year old hardy young lad. We continued to dribble the ball about and the man became more violent. "Get home ye pack of bastards before I get the pike."

I am sorry but I must omit most of the details of his great oration from the doorstep. Had I the courage to give it in full, nobody would ever again waste time reading Mark Anthony's funeral oration!

Young Jimmy, on hearing the commotion, rushed out of bed wearing nothing but his nightshirt. And before anyone could warn him, on seeing the ball rolling towards him he gave it a right kick with his bare foot. He gave a loud cry and sank to the ground in a dead faint with his foot super-glued to the hedgehog by a thousand inch-and-a-half dreadful spikes.

We ran for home feeling we could not be properly identified. After all, if a young fellow with good sight could not distinguish between a ball and a hedgehog . . .!"

We could not ask questions about the "one eye" least we betray our involvement. All our information was second hand and none of it was good.

Seemingly old Doyle ran at high speed, forgetting about his heart condition and other ailments, to the great house to ask Captain Leader for help. Explaining in full what happened, he mentioned again and again "the pack of hures."

"Let us call them Mohawks." said Captain Leader as they both sat into the Model T.

He was wise to enlist the Captain's help. He being the only man in the area with experience of wounded men. And as well as that he was the only car owner within miles.

In the meantime, the lamentations of Mrs Doyle were out of this world in more ways than one.

"Great God forgive us all. Going for a protestant before going for the priest. There is no hope for us now and my only child dying" were some of her thoughts.

Captain Leader took the family to Mallow hospital as quickly as possible. The mother spent her time in the back seat muttering about a priest, and the father spent his time muttering about "the pack o' hures" and "after all my care."

"Accidents can happen in the best-regulated families." said the Captain.

"It was no accident." said Doyle.

News from the hospital was very skimpy and then one morning at breakfast, Dan Nolan announced in his usual loud voice "I hear the leg must come off the "one eye." Thankfully, this story was unfounded. Nevertheless, with winged speed everyone had it.

A few days later, when Captain Leader again took the father and mother to the hospital, young Jimmy was in great form and Captain Leader told him "You put up a jolly good show lad. A jolly good show indeed."

In spite of everything Jimmy grew up to be a fine man.

What happened to the hedgehog we will never know.

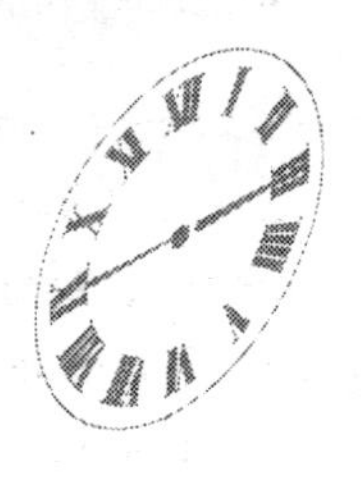

34

A Fair Morning

Many great writers have tried to describe the Pyramids of Egypt. All of them, without exception, admit failure. They failed because certain things defy description and to be truthful, I think a fair morning in the early days of the Irish Free State is another one of those things that defies description. Others have tried it but perhaps they did not have first-hand experience.

Let us take a line at random from one of the poets:

"*And she stepped away from me*
And she moved through the fair"

We get the impression that she moved gracefully and elegantly. Alas, my friend, she did not. It simply could not be done, in view of the fact that the whole town had become a shallow lake of green slurry. One would require instructions on how to perform the sword dance. So one would need to be able to walk the tight rope and a few lessons on skiing would be very useful. Thus prepared she *might*, and only might move through the fair, without getting plastered with the same colouring material that discolours the lower half of shop windows and forms "no go" areas in every street.

At the cattle fair money changed hands. Bits and pieces required on the farm were bought and paid for. Small accounts were settled.

Some towns had the luxury of a fair field but, by and large, most cattle fairs were held in the town centre and adjoining streets. Many shopkeepers and publicans regretted the demise of the time-honoured cattle fair. In many towns, meetings were held to protest against the establishment of cattle marts. Store keepers forecast lean times and others, more vocal, had no doubt that in a short few years we would have ghost towns with foxes and wild animals roaming the streets.

For a brief moment we will consider the modern cattle marts which superseded the old romantic melodramatic rip-roaring fair days.

Today the cattle are loaded into lorries in the farmyard. Someone might ask, "Have you the cards?" and that ends the matter until the cattle are offered for sale by the auctioneer. In less than five minutes the whole thing is over and the farmer emerges from the seller's box, flushed and glad the whole thing is over. And were he put on oath he could not tell you exactly how much his cattle made. No money changed hands. Not even a *lucky penny*. A week later he receives a cheque, and you can imagine all the excitement as he reads all about fees and levies and costs of transport and subscriptions to farmer's organisations etc. So ends the story of the modern cattle marts. We return to the never to be forgotten fair in the town centre, and how we got there.

To understand fully the tumult and aggravation connected with a cattle fair we must return to the farm. Step by step we will try to unravel the bedlam.

On the evening prior to the fair the farmer would point out the animals he was offering for sale so that the man responsible for driving them would recognise the required animals in the early hours next morning.

No marks of any kind could be put on the animals, as this might mislead buyers into thinking they were already sold. Or worse, some people might think the animals were "*thrown-up*".

Every buyer had his own private mark, and this, and this alone should be on the animals, to facilitate loading onto the train. Animals with a K were put into Kellihers wagons, and those with a red daub on the right flank went into Ryan's wagons, and those with a blue X went into Farrell's wagons and so on. And all this would take a lot of sorting out later, as there were many different buyers. However, it would be later afternoon before we reached the loading platform.

The one and only advantage a farmer's son had over other pupils in school was that from time to time he would be kept at home from school to help drive some cattle to the fair. And this entailed "run before them," "run behind them," "run beside them," "get beyond them," and "why do you think you were kept at home from school?"

You might well ask why cattle intended for the fair were not separated from the other cattle and held in readiness for the fair. Alas, my friend, things were not that simple. Cattle separated from their companions would spend the night bellowing. And next morning, they would look poor and empty and few buyers wanted hungry cattle. No man wanted to stand over a hungry lot and be forced to take a greatly reduced price.

We must also remember that these animals would see neither bite nor sup until they reached Kildare or Meath or perhaps the six counties. The reader, no doubt, is familiar with the propaganda surrounding city marathons and the imaginary black wall encountered by runners as they drop out of the race. Alas, for the schoolboy kept at home from school there was no dropping out, and by the time the animals were on the train he would have run at least two city marathons, not along nice level streets, but over ditches and hedges, into pools and ponds in the blind dark. Another hazard often encountered were snares placed all around fields to catch rabbits, hares, foxes and badgers.

Were a man to get his foot caught in one of these snares while running as fast as possible after a truculent bullock, his head would hit the ground at the speed of sound; enough to put any of today's so-called men into the intensive care unit of some city hospital for several weeks. Our men in the old days would rise quickly, muttering something about 'a hure of a snare.'

There would be no law case, no compo, no messing. It was all part of the job. These men were no cry-babies. We would see men like these no more, no more.

Anticipating a whole day free from school and its hateful pitfalls and hazards, the boy being kept at home to help with the sorting out of the cattle spends most of the night awake and just as he drops off to sleep, the "alarmer" goes off.

The Boss is out of bed in seconds. He wakes the servant boy up and the lad being kept at home from school. Merciful God, this is it. This is the fair morning.

The boss puts on the kettle for a supposed breakfast. No one has any appetite. The foreboding and apprehension is too much.

The door opens and Dan Nolan, the workman, arrives. His first salute is. "'Tis one hure of a bad wet morning. Dark as pitch and by the looks of things the day will be no better."

"Well, Dan, one can expect bad weather in November."

We move out into the field above the house. We can barely see each other. The battery lamp with its on/off switch had not yet reached the market. The oil lamp was useless and the trap-lamp with its butt of a candle was equally worthless.

"Dan, you try the Mock field and the Middle field. Jack, you try the Knob field and the Quarry field. We will try the Kiln field and the Barley field and whoever finds them give a whistle."

Half an hour later an ear-splitting whistle from the Knob field; the wild confusion is about to begin.

Dan gives a shout. "Strawberry and Dan Hayes is here." Believe it or not *Dan Hayes* is an old milking cow bought many years ago at Millstreet fair from a man named Dan Hayes. Strawberry was a great big cow but her best days were over. Farming is a pitiless doleful business as every good cow will find out in due course.

"Right, Dan. Try and wheel them around towards the house." And then a sudden call for help. "I want someone here. That hure, Dan Hayes, is gone on me." Strawberry makes a dash for freedom after Dan Hayes. She gets a clout of a stick that puts a hump on her and she increases speed in the wrong direction.

An hour or more is spent rushing hither and thither using very uncomplimentary language, which the boss pretends not to hear, before the cattle – two old cows and six bullocks – are finally out on the road.

This is merely the end of the beginning. It is now the trouble really starts!

We know every farm gate between here and Kanturk. And we know the gates usually left open at night. And we know every long laneway and boreen as well as where the roadside fences are poor. And we are well aware of the fact that Dan Hayes and Strawberry will avail of every opportunity to turn for home at an unstopable gallop. And we are also well aware that there is often a difference of opinion among bullocks. While some might leap over the fence on one side the others could opt for the side opposite.

By now the reader will have some idea of the various dilemmas one might encounter on the road to the fair. Nevertheless, people will always underestimate the difficulties which can and usually do crop up.

Two men go ahead of the animals. Their job is to block every gateway and laneway and, above all, every boreen. If your cattle got into a boreen they could end up three farms in from the road after being hunted by three separate batches of mongrel hounds and dogs. And as one man put it "all this frightening would make rags of 'um."

As we draw near every cottage along the way there is a fresh batch of dogs. All very upsetting, to put it mildly.

There is also the probability we will encounter a camp of tinkers which some animals refuse to pass without soreful persuasion. Fires from the previous night are smouldering, babies screaming, highly coloured rags on every bush and a smell far more penetrating than poisoned gas. However, a man has got to do what a man has got to do.

As we draw near the town we find cattle ahead of us with their noisy drovers. And behind us there are more cattle and their minders. Behind them there are more and more and as far as we can see, so on, *ad infinitum*.

Day is breaking. And we see the town in the valley with its few dim lights growing dimmer as the eastern sky grows brighter.

We thank God. We think the worst is over.

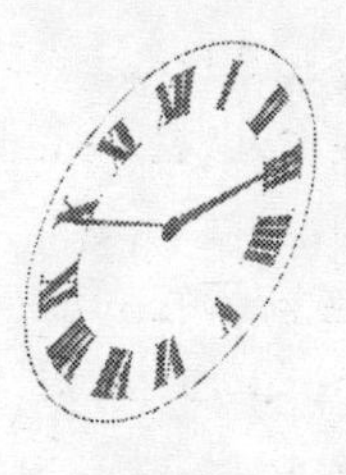

35

A Fair Day

We now, as we come closer to the town, encounter a new and bigger nuisance – *"blockers and tanglers"*. Every road into town has its quota of professional bums whose job it is to examine and find fault with every animal. These men are specially picked and paid by the buyers to harass and badger the farmers, offering ridiculous prices. It is their job to discourage the seller in every way possible. They preach pauperism, saying "No one will make an offer for the like o' them". And then they might ask more or less, as an afterthought. "What are you asking?"

"Five pound a head."

"You must be joking or insane or both. I will make you a right good offer. I will give you two pounds for the two best. I would not take the rest if you gave them to me for nothing."

This softening up process paid dividends as some easily swayed farmers lowered their prices, to the detriment of the whole fair.

Blockers and tanglers used every trick, like passing remarks between themselves, which were meant to be overheard, such as "There are only a small few wagons at the station. There won't be much buying today."

The irony of the situation was that the more *blockers and tanglers* there were, the better. It was well known that the day you failed to meet a large number of these impostors would turn out to be a bad day with very few buyers.

The next big problem is to find a stand as near the town square as possible. Directly in front of a public house would be ideal.

Once in place, you can expect a buyer almost immediately. But one thing is certain, no deal will be made on the first.

"That is my final offer. Take it or leave it."

"No. I won't take it."

"Please yourself." And the buyer walks off in a great hurry.

A few minutes later his assistant arrives. "What are you asking there?" As if he did not already know.

On being told the price he laughs aloud and offering a much lower price he goes to the trouble of pointing out one or two animals he will not take because they are of no use to anyone.

"You are wasting your time. They go together."

"No Sir. 'Tis you are wasting your time. Standing there expecting a fool to come along and give you money for them." And he walks off in a bigger hurry than the first fellow.

There was one farmer by the name of Denis Murphy and he made a name for himself in several towns for telling off buyers. At the very first offer his temper was up.

"J . . . C . . . Almighty! Your mother was a queer H . . . to have the likes of you. Be off before I split your empty skull. But wait till I tell you where to put your offer." And Denis uncompromisingly said where to put his offer.

In spite of this forthright and candid exchange Denis always sold his cattle, but never below their market value.

Later in the day Denis and Rocky Healy would confront each other on the loading platform and another candid exchange of views would take place, leaving an indelible mark on the rising generation and adding greatly to their vocabulary. All sorts of vulgarity was acceptable on the loading platform. One thing was certain, delicacy would get you nowhere.

At times the loading platform resembled a battlefield where all leaders were dead, leaving the combatants to sort things out for themselves.

Talk about abuse, talk about blood, with insults flying in all directions while farmers and their helpers battled it out. Some trying to load their cattle into Ryan's wagons, others trying to force their way with their cattle towards Farrell's wagons. This confusion was bound to develop where there were so many different lots, all mixed up together.

Rocky Healy was nominally in charge of the loading but his efforts to maintain order were mostly ignored; there were people who said Rocky and his crew accepted bribes from farmers who wished to have their cattle loaded quickly.

One could see cattle being forced forward by men with sticks while other men tried to force them back to await their proper turn. Men lost their temper and cattle lost horns and eyes. Sometimes men received blows intended for cattle and sometimes blows not so intended.

Let us pretend we have our cattle in the right wagons and the ticket signed by the aforesaid Rocky Healy, whose duty it was to make sure your animals were in the correct wagon.

The boss would later produce this ticket duly signed, when receiving payment outside the bank or in some pub. We were now free to spend our few shillings pocket money. As soon as the streets were reasonably free of cattle the ballad singers and the *faugs* would appear from nowhere. Tinker women with droves of children would also arrive. All of them on the prowl for easy money.

Travelling salesmen would erect their standings, selling all kinds of everything. But important people, who fancied themselves as pillars of church and state would not be seen dead near these salesmen and their reduced prices.

There was always a good crowd around the standings, even the stand where they sold spectacles and where a newspaper was provided so that you could test yourself.

Fine, well made spectacles they were and when you found a pair that improved your vision, you bought them for two shillings and six pence. In other words, you could buy eight pairs for one pound. Now you can buy one pair, which may be of little or no use to you, for fifty pounds.

Across the street, a ballad singer is ogling "*Kevin Barry gave his young life* . . . Thank you Sir, thank you Mam, . . . *for the cause of Liber . . . tee.*"

The three-card trick man is up to his old tricks outside Lehane's Pub. "Oxo" Carver, tired of trying to sell a lone cow, ties her to a pole and joins his many friends inside. The cow, an animal well used to fair days, lies down beside the pole and starts to chew the cud, having once more escaped the factory and the humane killer. However, there are always men on the look-out for a bargain and such a man now sidles up to Oxo. "I made you a good offer for that old frame Mr. Carver, are you going to sell or not?"

They both go to the door for another look at the cow.

"What did you offer me?" enquires Oxo.

"I bid you two pounds." says the potential buyer.

"My dear man," says Oxo "I would not wake her up for that." and they return to the bar. The old cow has another narrow escape.

The patriotic ballad singer whose pathetic rendering of "Kevin Barry" leaves a lot to be desired, has gone off for refreshments and his place is taken by another songster of the romantic school. Unfortunately, he is years ahead of his time. Thin and wretched-looking with long hair and showing signs of being in great pain, he starts to sing:

"*Outside your car-a-van . . . your campfire bright*
I'll be your vagabond . . . just for tonight."

Those of you old enough to remember will agree – it was a romantic song, and one old lady, instead of giving some support, tells him "You should be ashamed of yourself."

Inside another pub we can hear the untrained voice of some farmer singing more or less for his own amusement, his song goes something like this.

"*For the one that got rich by mining*
I saw . . . there were hundred grew poor.
I made up my mind to try farming
the only . . . pursuit that is sure."

It is easy to conjure up the shaking of many wise old heads when they heard about "*the only pursuit that is sure*."

Roll on, the next fair-day.

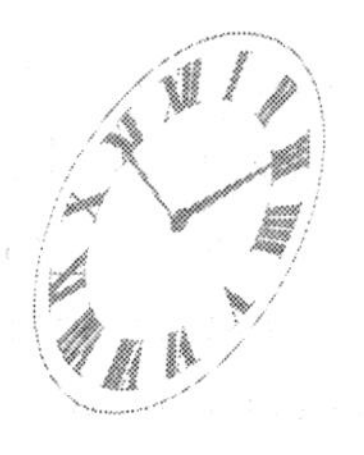

36

The Blessed Well

In the early days of the Irish Free State it was a poor, and one might say, almost pagan parish that did not boast of at least one holy well.

The day set aside for honouring this unofficial saint was called Pattern Day and everyone, especially the young teenagers, looked forward to a great day. On this day, everybody downed tools; shops closed; schools remained closed because not one pupil would attend.

It was an unofficial holiday, but a holiday just the same and the unofficial saint was a saint just as good as the rest of them. Without demands by trade unions or facilitating acts of Parliament, the "well day" became an idle day for some, a day of prayer for others. For many it was a day of pilgrimage, and for many more it was a day of merriment, sing-songs and drinking.

People came in their thousands and whenever it fell on a Sunday, churches were almost empty. Few people attended Mass and for this reason there was no love lost between the local clergy and the saint of the well.

One priest caused consternation one Sunday morning when addressing the congregation. He began by saying that all those who had gone to the well, without first attending Mass, were scandal givers "turning their backs on the church and the tabernacle to pay homage to a so-called saint whose name is neither in book or paper."

I found myself in agreement with all he said. I belonged to an age group who found it difficult enough to believe all the things we were bound to believe, without the additional trouble of bringing so-called saints, together with their dubious performances, on board.

Needless to say, the younger you were the better you enjoyed the totally bizarre exhibition of such profound faith by so many, as they prayed going round and round the well "paying rounds". Others, who came within yards of the well, were quite unconvinced. Perhaps they were right. Perhaps they were wrong. Who knows?

The local priest had no doubts whatsoever as to his own views. The clergy seldom express doubts of any kind.

Prior to the day of celebration, the graves in the nearby graveyard got an unmerciful grubbing or face lift. All the weeds and trash had to be dumped somewhere and where better than on some old chieftain's granite tomb. If the old chieftain's tomb was too far away people usually found some graves surrounded by three foot high heavy iron railings belonging to some "once upon a time" rich family. It was quite safe to use this forgotten grave space as a dump. In any case, rich families were a thing of the past in the Irish Free State. One would think that the futility of trying to make graves look nice would have dawned on people by now. Alas, they will continue to grub their own and dump on others, forgetting the march of time.

While everyone else gave up work on the "well day" publicans were duty-bound to erect huge marquees all along the wall fronting the graveyard. The wall added stability to the specially erected shanty-town. Hundreds of cases of all kinds of alcohol lined the wall and the poles of the open-fronted tents stood firmly in no man's land, but as close to the roadside as possible. Opposite the porter tents, on the other side of the road, dozens of tables were erected by old hags and "coal-quay" women from the city; most of them were unscrupulous thieving hawkers, especially the one with the handful of envelopes shouting "All a penny a draw and a prize every time." Her stand was littered with different coloured articles such as penknifes. And indeed there was the old half-crown to tempt the unwary. Under the impression that they could win one of these, boys and girls paid their pennies and drew an envelope which they handed to the old hag in charge. She would turn back the flap and read out the prize "Oh, a lovely rosette." Several times she would call out at the top of her voice "A lovely rosette." These rosettes were useless. One could get a hundred of them for a penny. On every envelope in her hand there was one word, the word "rosette."

One could hardly see the end of the line of stands, all loaded with sweets and cakes. And at every stand stood a "coal-quay" woman shouting "All the cakes, apples and oranges and ripe bananas, all a penny each." For kids it was the next thing to paradise. But across the road in the porter tents the real paradise did exist.

"Here, Paddy. Drink that. For all we know 'tis inside the wall we could be this time next year."

"A truer word was never spoken, Mick."

"There is many a man inside the wall would like a drink today Paddy, if they could get it."

"They had their chance, Mick. They had their chance. God forgive them."

Here in the porter tents there were farmers and farm workers, shopkeepers, tradesmen, council workers and ex-soldiers who served in the Boer War, the Great War, the Tan War and the Civil War. They all came to the well to drink and get drunk, to talk about old times and to keep up the friendship.

Young men with romantic ideas had to avoid the porter tents if they wished to meet up with a nice girl at the dance that night. Young ladies at that time had a horror of drink. Today, alas, they cannot get enough of it. How times change.

We can hear a fairly good attempt at "Faith of our Fathers" coming from one tent and we know the GAA are in a majority there. In another tent the IRA supporters are doing the best they can with "The Felons of our Land" and nearby a group of Oregon men are in great form, many of them displaying the hallmark of *The Wild West*, namely one or two gold teeth. "All together now lads!"

"As I walked out in the streets of la-re-do
As I walked out in Laredo one day
I spied a young cowboy wrapped up in white linen
wrapped up in white linen as cold as the clay."

They were good. In spirits they were back again in *The Wild West*. Back again in "The Black Hills of Dakota". But none of these singing groups could match the energy behind the lines of "Tipperary" and "Pack up your Troubles".

In this tent the veterans of many wars, melancholy ghosts no longer receiving the world's applause. Many of them had small pensions which, if the truth were told, the world begrudged them. Between songs, the Boer War veterans were back again at the battle of the Modder River and here standing side by side were Bill Seck and Sergeant McCabe, who made history when they captured two Vicker-Maxim guns during the battle. Now they spoke with feelings of nostalgia. Longing for the past they recalled stories of "Babs" and Pole-Carew.

Beside them former Irish Guardsman Batt MacSweeney and Munster fusileer Jim Flur Sullivan were discussing the retreat from Mons. But they were overshadowed by half a dozen ex-Royal Navy men. There was Dan Twomey who spent four years on mine-sweepers off the south coast and big David White, wounded several times in many naval battles. But the only one of them to make real history was John Connolly, by, in his own words "taking a destroyer up the bastard yellow river farther than anyone did before." Jack fell silent about China when Jim Flur agreed to sing. Jim was an outstanding singer. One of the very best. He began . . .

"Upon the hill he turned
To take a last fond look
Upon the village and village church,
And the cottage by the brook.
He listened to the sounds
So familiar to his ear
And the soldier leaned upon his sword
And wiped away a tear."

The singing and the exchange of memories went on and on.

In the meantime most of the women had spent the day at the Holy Well, going round and round as they prayed for everyone and everything and tying tokens like beads and bandages to the thorn bushes nearby. They filled bottles with water which in due course would go into competition with the real thing, helping to cure all sorts of ailments. Like many, I was sceptical and perhaps hypocritical. But I admit of one outstanding miracle. Year after year in spite of the overcrowding, I never heard an angry word.

37

BREAKING THE PLEDGE

One of the principal drawbacks in farming is the constant doubt about everything; doubt about prices, and above all, doubt about the weather, on which so much depends. Those of us about to be sucked into this farming quicksand-cum-quagmire had few options. Many young men had no choice. The day they left the local national school they went to work on some local farm.

Some of us had, if we obeyed our parents, the opportunity of attending the Christian Brothers and being submitted to beatings. And with plenty of the leather, being brainwashed into believing that suffering was equally good for body and soul and vice versa.

Rebellious by nature, being beaten by what some people called "The Pope's Armoured Brigade" into good civil service material, with a great love for the Irish language, a great hatred of the British and a tendency to genuflect whenever 1916 was mentioned, was not for me. Long ago in an unguarded moment my Grandad said to me "If you learn to read you can find out all you want to know." But! We must return to important matters.

The harvest is a very busy time on all farms. Co-operation becomes vital. But back in the early days of the Irish Free State it was even more so, because mechanisation was far from being fully hatched-out.

Very few farmers owned "reapers and binders". As the name suggests, these machines cut the corn and bound it into sheaves. Every time one of these machines went into action someone was bound to remark "Begorra and all, the man that thought of the knotter had a queer head, by the hokey".

There still remained a lot of hard work: hauling home the many loads of sheaves and building them into ricks in the haggard in a position to suit the thrashing-machine, allowing space for the straw rick, and many other details looked into, and problems resolved.

During harvest time one heavy shower of rain could upset the best laid plans. A whole wet day would hold up all progress for a week or more. And when we thought about it, we had little sympathy with the city man, who even today will lose his temper at the traffic lights.

The moment the latest sheaf was in from the fields the thrashing-machine was on its way from farm to farm and everything was going well. An average of thirty men was required if sufficient numbers were to take their place, on the rick, at the straw, on the machine, at the bags, on the left and the most useless man in the place would get the job of keeping back the chaff.

As a rule, the farmer himself would take on the job of distributing the stout and lemonade at regular intervals. For days before the event the farmer's mind was fully occupied with the logistics and sexagestimal arithmetic as regards the amount of food and drink required for a successful operation.

At the end of a hard day, at the noisy dusty smutty mouth of the mill, or forking sheaves and straw non-stop, one could see the difference between the "stout" men and the "lemonade" men. The former had maintained their strength and good humour while the latter were spun out and as weak as water.

When the basket of bottles came round one needed little encouragement to sample the bitter sweet taste of the stout or porter or whatever was in the black bottles. It was now or never. A long farewell to the clear glass of the child's bottle with its bright label, showing oranges ripening in the sunshine in Spain or the Holy Land. All kid's stuff without any doubt.

The fact that breaking our confirmation pledge was a mortal sin scarcely cost us a thought. Like cutting the head off the wrong man in Baghdad, it was all over and done with and that was the end of it.

During the run up period there was much manoeuvering as to where the thrashing would be on Friday, because on Fridays it was a mortal sin to eat meat. Therefore catering for a large crowd would be less expensive and far less trouble. This mortal sin was one with which I was in complete agreement. On the other hand, those who loved large helpings of hairy bacon suffered greatly.

A "tea-dinner" was a welcome break after a long week of bacon and drumhead cabbage, Aran Banners, Kerr Pinks and British Queens, with second helpings for all. No doubt it is difficult to please everybody. One day I sat beside a man at table and when he saw the huge amount of bacon and cabbage with which he was confronted, he folded up his sleeves, took hold of his knife and fork and turning to me he said "Give me anything, anything but the barefooted tay."

I felt like saying "You are a better man than me '*gunga din*'".

Howard was a man who understood human nature perfectly, and most people would agree that he was probably the best farmer in the area. He maintained that human nature was very unreliable and for this reason he was most careful never to offend other people's feelings. One might say etiquette was one of his strong points. But this year a problem arose that Howard, with all his etiquette, could not solve. Everyone knows there is such a thing as protocol involving customs and standards but under the following circumstances it is hard to tell how any one of us would proceed.

His house and farmyard were only yards away from the home of Mrs Molloy and all down the years they had the greatest respect for each other. Early in the harvest word got round that the old lady was not well and as the days went by the story got worse. One of her daughters gave up her job in Dublin to look after her and she was soon joined by her sister who came home from London to assist. Things were serious, and all this time Howard went on with the harvesting, calling in regularly to see the old lady and trying to figure out how long she would survive.

The doctors had ruled out any hope of recovery and every time Howard saw her he came to the conclusion that she was no better or no worse.

Now the thrashing-machine was in the townland and the owner let it be known that the machine was off to Limerick on Sunday, where there were many big farmers waiting on him. For Howard it was make up your mind time. He could get finished with the whole thing on Saturday or wait until after Christmas, by which time the mice and rats "would have him eaten out of house and home".

The big question was, would it be right to thrash if his next door neighbour died the night before. With this in mind he decided to have another look at her. He came to the conclusion that Mrs Molloy had no intention of dying for another week.

He gave the all-clear, but took the precaution of getting in much more extra stout and lemonade than would normally be required.

He would keep the workforce well supplied and in good form. No one would find fault with him even if the worst happened. There would be no dull ingratitude when every man had his belly full of the best food and drink.

It looked like rain on Friday evening but Howard said "God is good. The weather will hold." He was right about the weather but for Mrs Molloy *in articulo mortis* came at four a.m. The die was cast. He had reached the point of no return. Normally a very level-headed man when dealing with a crisis, on this occasion he took the view that her dying when she did was a malicious act against himself and now, dead or not dead the thrashing would go ahead.

The first man to arrive was Ned-the-Leg. "I thought Mr Howard," said he "you would postpone the thrashing until after the death, the death like."

"Don't worry Ned. We will all die sometime. Life still goes on. I am putting you in charge of the chaff."

It was a lovely day. Solitary leaves drifted down. The sound of the thrashing-machine could be heard miles away. Like a lament becoming a wail or a keen as the pressure on the drum rose and fell.

Every time a round of drink was distributed, which was often, the men made the sign of the cross and "*May the Lord ha' mercy on the dead*" was repeated over and over. Bottles were raised, drained and cast aside.

It was almost nightfall when work ended, and Howard remarked that things were not as tidy as things should, ought to be. And worse still, props had to be put to the straw rick when Paddy Lehane, the holy sailor, pointed out it was leaning too much to starboard.

Quietly the older men went home to wash and shave and don collars and ties before calling next door to pray for the dead and offer condolences. There was however, a younger group. Some of us had not yet any good reason to stand close to a razor nor had we attended a wake so we took the opportunity of attaching ourselves to a slightly older group who saw no good reason for spoiling good drinking time on superficial and unnecessary sartorial endeavour.

Jack-the-sickener went forward as spokesman for the group. And whatever else he lacked it certainly was not what is commonly called "neck". We were met at the hall door by a smart-looking young woman, presumably a daughter of the deceased.

"We are sorry for your troubles Misus." began Jack and the handshake that went in tandem with the expression of sympathy had the air of a general election about it. She moved back a few paces and this was the signal for the whole delegation to follow. Unfortunately, Jack had too much drink taken and he failed to notice the step. And as one fellow put it, "Jack was put standing on his head in his full length inside the door". This was embarrassing enough but he made matters worse making profuse apologies and placing all the blame "on the bloody hure of a step . . . " It was a rough beginning but worse was to follow.

"Come this way." said the young woman and we followed sheepishly into a large well furnished room where we had every comfort. There was a good fire and a box full of coal, about a dozen chairs and, by the far wall, a large old fashioned sofa. Before we were properly settled down the young woman and a helper returned. Between them they had a case of stout which was much too heavy for them. Nevertheless, they nicely put it to one side. Then she handed a corkscrew to one of the men saying

"Help yourselves, I will be back later."

The man with the corkscrew went to work immediately.

"'Tis a wonder," said one idiot to the idiot beside him, "'tis a wonder we were not taken to view the corpse." Receiving no answer he repeated the question and someone said "Because in your condition you are much safer on the ground floor." That seemed to satisfy the questioner and the matter did not arise again.

We had Long Carty with us. He was called Long Carty because he was very tall and thin. He was pale faced and in poor health and always complaining about a pain "that was doing him no good".

Always after a few drinks he would change colour from pale white to green yellow and promptly drop off to sleep. This day however the excitement of the thrashing and prospect of another good night at the wake kept him going far too long and this resulted in a sudden and complete collapse. He was breathing very poorly and every now and again he would draw a long breath as if at long last it was all over. We decided to place him on the sofa for safety sake and we covered him with a rug, a kind of Persian carpet which seemed to be serving no useful purpose on the floor. Someone remarked he looked very like old Mrs Molloy before she died.

In Mrs Molloy's hat box we found a nice black hat and when this was put on Long Carty's head his resemblance to her was greatly enhanced. The final touch however was when her big black prayer book was placed under his chin, something that was always done to keep the mouth shut until *rigor mortis* set in. In this case, it also served to cover his rather prominent Adam's Apple. Mrs Molloy had many friends who came in droves to pay their respects and some who were not familiar with the layout of the house instead of going upstairs turned to the right and into the room where we were. On seeing the "corpse" they went on one knee, said a few prayers, each making the sign of the cross and departed quickly, least they should find themselves caught up in an extended version of the Rosary.

We had forgotten that the lady said she would return. And return she did, bringing a couple of bottles of Paddy. She looked around and saw "the outfit" on the sofa and instead of ordering us out of the house, she asked "Is everybody comfortable?" She knew how to deal with people. Kipling must have been describing someone like her when he wrote:

"*if you can talk with crowds and keep your virtue . . .*"

It was late next morning when Long Carty came out of the coma. People said he made a great recovery. Howard's thrashing was over. Mrs Molloy's wake was over. We had broken our Confirmation pledge. Already we were up to our eyes and forehead in the worst kind of mortal sin . . . that is, if all they tell us is true.

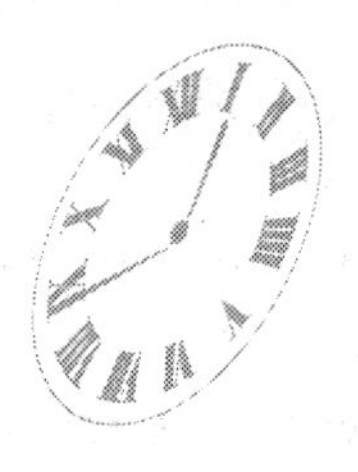

38

TRIPTOLEMUS ! INVENTOR OF THE PLOUGH

Shelling galvanised houses, wrecking tinker's vans and attending wakes was all very well, but these activities put ne'er a shilling in the pocket.

As a rule we worked a twelve hour day, from six in the morning until six in the evening. Milking a herd of cows after six was not regarded as work in the true sense of the word. Milking machines were non-existent. Every member of the household plus male and female staff were each allotted five or six cows to milk and a fair divide was always worked out. No one got all the difficult ones nor did anyone get all the easy ones and there was no messing about. One milked the same five or six cows during the whole lactation period.

Everybody hated milking and every excuse was put forward to avoid having to take part. A very sore finger was no excuse. A broken arm might merit some consideration. Come what may, it was taken for granted that the cows had to be milked and that was the end of it.

Ploughing, sowing, reaping and mowing as well as hauling and spreading farmyard manure, cutting hedges, repairing fences and opening drains were operations always regarded as men's work. But in times of difficulty the women had no hesitation in joining the field force.

In the winter and spring one was often up at night attending to cows, horses, sows and sheep as a new generation of farm animals began to make their appearance.

Facilities were not great. There was no electric light on farms nor would there be for decades.

We had what was known as a storm-lantern which went out at the first puff of wind, usually at a critical moment. From our point of view we had enough work already, when our "*macnoon*" Government decided to establish the sugarbeet industry. Triptolemus! You have a lot to answer for. A sugar factory was built in Carlow. But this was the thin end of the wedge. Soon we would have one in Mallow, one in Thurles and another in Tuam. Farmers were brainwashed into growing sugar- beet while overlooking all the slavery connected with this particular crop. All during the growing period every spare moment was spent singling, scuffling, weeding, applying special fertiliser at stated intervals and putting fresh earth around each plant. This last operation was called rising to the beet.

I can say without fear of contradiction, this new industry drove many young men off the land and on to the emigrant ship. Worst of all, the harvesting of this crop coincided with the worst months of winter. I never did understand nor will I ever understand the willingness of farmers to lap up free advice. Over two thousand years ago, Virgil went to work for a farmer so as to learn all about husbandry and nature. This enabled him to understand country life. Otherwise none of us would have the pleasure of reading the *Georgics of Virgil*. Other writers more ancient, were of the opinion that tillage and civilisation came together. In other words when man learned to till the soil there was no need for him to continue as a nomad moving from place to place with the seasons. Tillage, we are told, enabled man to reach his full potential. There is, in my view, plenty of room for doubt. I strongly believe tillage put an end to whatever civilisation there was. All history, since the advent of tillage, is simply a never-ending story of cruelty and war because now the criminally-minded, the wicked, the scientific, the unprincipled and the unscrupulous were all fed and clothed without having to go to fend for themselves. Indeed, I could claim that Virgil shared my point of view when he wrote:

> *"Ere Jove had reign'd no swains subdued the ground*
> *Unknown was poverty, unjust the mound*
> *At will they rov'd! And earth spontaneous bore*
> *Unasked and uncompelled, a bounteous store."*

The farmer for whom Virgil went to work had "strong" land by the banks of the Tiber and having survived a plane crash when our plane ploughed into a cornfield outside Rome some years ago, I know exactly what the poet meant by "strong" land. And when I say the land by the Tiber is very like our own land by the Blackwater I am in a strong position to do so.

Eventually Virgil became tired of this "strong" land and the hardship which accompanied it. He complains:

> *"Tillage grew toilsome, and harvests died*
> *Caltrops, wild oats, and chick-weed assail*
> *Hide the fair tilt, and o'er the crops prevail*
> *Unless with harrows' unremitted toil*
> *Thou break, subdue, and pulverise the soil."*

What a pity beet crops were unknown in those far off day. Had we been warned we could have avoided much hardship. Virgil goes on to say:

> *"Much too he helps, his laboured land, who breaks*
> *The tumbling clods, with harrows, drags and rakes*
> *Who ploughs across, and back, with ceaseless toil*
> *Subdues to dust, and triumphs o'er the soil."*

All this ceaseless toil was in preparation for corn crops which, in comparison to root crops, is relatively easy. We know from a complaint made to Pope Clement XI that corn crops were the principal if not the only crops grown in Italy and especially in that area surrounding Rome all down the years since the dawn of "civilisation".

Rome was now a city full of sophisticated well-fed idlers who objected to the smoke from burning straw and stubble at harvest time, as farmers, or swains as they were called in those days, set fire to the stubble in an effort to clean the fields.

The Pope was about to forbid the practice and make it a mortal sin to burn stubble. It could be said that perhaps he had no wish to see smoke from straw for a long time.

It so happened that a Cardinal drew the Pope's attention to a passage from Virgil. On reading it the Pope changed his mind and rejected the demands of the people of Rome. Had the people of our area spent some time reading the *Georgics of Virgil* instead of *The Cork Weekly Examiner* and the *Christmas Number* they might have done like the Pope and rejected the propaganda. Alas! Few heard the footsteps of the elephant. By and large we took on the growing of beet.

Slavery became firmly established in the Irish Free State. "*It must be understood,*" says one ancient writer "*from the beginning of the rainy season, which was itself unfit for work and which took up most of December and January. Slaves, who at other times were kept busy, were allowed liberties and spent their free time in mirth and joviality. This was turned into a holiday period called Saturnalia*".

From now on we would spend the winter months working in the beet fields exposed to cold bitter wind and rain, snow, frost, storm and hail. Always cold, always wet. Thinking of the good old days when there was no brutal, bloody sugar beet. Comparing our situation with that of the slaves of Greece and Rome one must admit that the slaves had "the life of Reilly".

The agricultural instructors, or more appropriately the well paid confidence tricksters, who went about enticing farmers to grow beet always referred to it as a "cash" crop. And the promise of cash in the middle of winter had its appeal. The price offered was thirty shillings per ton of washed beet, provided the sugar content was up to a certain standard. By the time the various deductions were made for labour and transport etc., the farmer received the price of five Silk Cut cigarettes in today's money. And this, we were told, was a cash crop! Teenagers found it hard to make ends meet in the Irish Free State. Where was the promised Utopia?

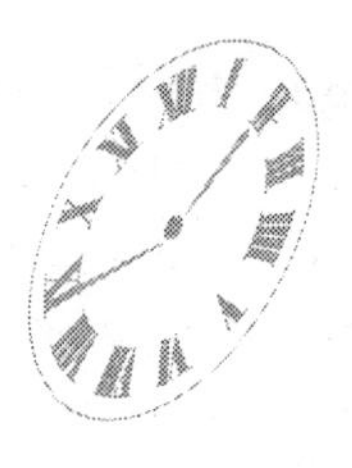

39

The Beet Loading Agent

The appointment of a beet loading agent was a highly important political matter and once appointed he assumed the attitude and power of a kind of high court judge. There was this air of supremacy and domination typical of this new bogus ascendancy now taking root in the Irish Free State. The agent's job was to regulate and ensure a constant supply of beet to the factory during the manufacturing season. The farmer was bound to send off a lorry load of beet when ordered to do so by the agent and needless to say, there were misunderstandings and accusations of bribery and political pull. As a rule the farmer received a week's notice and come hell or high water the load of beet had to be delivered on the day appointed.

Previous to all this, farmers and farm workers spent the winter months looking after cattle and sheep, mostly under cover and sheltered from the icy wind and lashing rain. Now all these chores took second place and any man who spent extra time around the farmyard fell under suspicion of the rest of the labour force.

Come with us to the beet fields. There are four of us and we stand for a moment looking at five acres of grey frost. The beetleaves are frozen stiff, the ground is rock hard. It looks like rain and hopefully it will rain and soften the ground.

Each of us takes on five drills and we start pulling. You grab a beet by the frozen leaves with both hands and with all your strength you get one beet out of the ground. Then again, using all your strength, you pull another and now you strike both beetroots one against the other until all the adhering soil is removed. When you have twenty or more out of the ground you place them in a small circle, root in, leaves out, to shed the rain. You continue to build a round clamp about four feet high and shaped like an old-fashioned bee-hive or skep. Day after day you labour in the open wintry fields until everyone is satisfied that we have a good lorry load.

Now we start all over again and once again we must deal with every beet separately. Now we start crowning. We have our moveable stands, usually an empty tar-barrel with a short piece of plank on top. The stand is put as close as possible to the beet clamp. As each beet is picked from the clamp it gets another belting on the plank to remove the last traces of soil and then with one blow of your beet knife, while holding the beet across the plank, you "crown" the beet. Almost half the beet is waste and with the leaves it has to be carted away for animal feed. And remember no matter how carefully you clean and crown the beet, the mandarins at the factory will find an excuse to reduce your price.

The know-alls, or if you like the agricultural instructors, told us everything depended on deep ploughing and rocks hidden beneath the sod since the ice age were rutted. Quins or whippings as they were sometimes called, were broken into flitters and carpenters worked hard making replacements. Blacksmiths worked hard trying to re-align bent plough beams. Ploughmen along the Blackwater Valley had more bones broken and dislocated than all the crusaders put together. When catastrophe struck, old experienced ploughmen did not fly into a rage using four letter words. Instead, one could see the ploughman take off his cap and make the sign of the cross, and one could almost hear him pray "Dear God, don't let me be driven to the lunatic asylum by this damned deep ploughing. Dear God, prevent me from taking my own life or the life of whoever is responsible for this outbreak of insanity".

The beet loading agent feels he is defrauded of his rightful pay. Everyone knows that everything depends on the loading agent. Without the agent, on his Pierce bicycle with his docket-book and pencil stub and large Player, regulating the supply of beet to the factory Comhairle Suicre Eireann would grind to a halt. And the beet loading agent knows he is not the only one being defrauded.

As a matter of fact he came upon an oul book one time and in it was written:

"Where sacred order, fraud and force confound
And every various vice and crime is crown'd
Dishonour lies the plough"

'Twas a bad wet evening and he had a slow puncture. Every few hundred yards he had to dismount and pump up his leaking tube. A bad evening for poetry, so it was.

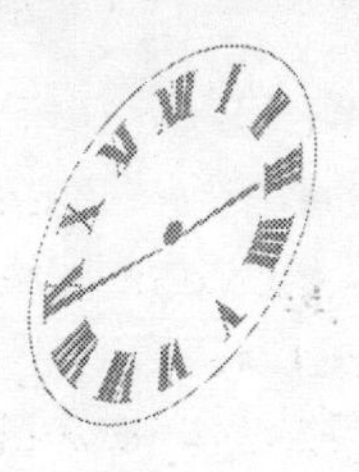

40

DIFFERENT OPINIONS

It was dark and dreary. The crossroads were uninviting and if I decided to go up to Betty Seán Bán's rambling house I would have to spend the night sitting on one of her Irish Free State butter-boxes listening to people who had no vigour in mind or body or conviction. Disputes often arose as to whether a certain thing happened forty or fifty years ago. The majority usually supporting the longer-term ancestral voices, of little interest to our age group.

I was having a quiet look at '*The Paper*' in other words *The Cork Examiner* and there was quite a lot in it about the Army Comrades Association. At first this organisation was composed of ex-Free State soldiers but now it was open to anybody who was more or less opposed to the IRA.

I took it for granted that this was for older men who understood all about politics and I was taken by surprise when David came downstairs and said to me "Tarrant and myself are going to join the Blueshirts tonight," I had little interest in politics as yet. However, joining the Blueshirts was a romantic idea and wearing the blue shirt to parades and public meetings was even more romantic.

Tarrant was the eldest of the Tarrant brothers. My friend Billy Tarrant would never be called *Tarrant*. He would remain Billy. I probably suffered the same handicap but we took no notice of it.

Feeling a bit peeved that elder brothers had the first of everything I decided then and there to break new ground. I would pay my first visit to the local pub. I would keep a low profile and my mouth shut. Teenage drinking was not a problem in those days. We did not have cars to endanger life nor enough money to completely change our life style. Bridie, the barmaid, understood the mechanics of the trade perfectly and while a new customer was made very welcome the fact that it was your first drink at the bar was ignored.

The lighting at The Ford was unique. The far end of the bar was almost in total darkness. A feature sadly lacking in today's ultra-modern lounge bars. Here at The Ford one did not have to wear the dark glasses of the terrorist to hide the physiognomy and here, in the dark recesses, old timers discussed politics and related matters. The voices rose and fell, depending on whether they wished to be overheard or not.

This night the two men in the dark corner were hard at it. Their theme was the high cost of Irish Freedom. Jack Tom had no inhibitions whatsoever about being overheard. "After all the murdering, intimidation, assassination and looting and every kind of atrocious crime for the good of the cause, the hures come and reduce my old age pension by ten percent."

"Ah, don't we all know." chimed in his companion. "This freedom is all a hoax. But some of them did well out of it."

"There is no doubt that the Englishman and that American dago brought great misfortune on the people." declared Jack Tom.

"What Englishman?"

"That Pearse fellow. His father was English. I worked with him in Dublin. A decent man. 'Twas them Christian Brothers made a republican out of the young fellow. Better for him he'd never met them, the poor fellow and the brother too. God help us."

"And the other fellow, de Valera?"

"The whole cause of the civil war they say. People are often fooled. Them two foreigners put the whole Irish nation fighting between themselves for years."

"And mark my words, 'tis not over yet. Come on Jack we'd better go home. We are here all day."

"Good night, Bridie." from both of them as they moved unsteadily towards the door.

I came to the conclusion that Jack Tom and his friend had a very poor opinion of the IRA and the Irish Government.

The ten percent cut in the old age pension was an unkind cut indeed.

As Jack Tom and his friend went out two others came in. I knew them well and it was obvious they'd been elsewhere before arriving at The Ford. They made their way to the dark end of the bar.

The new men in the dark end made no attempt to cloak what they had to say. The conversation was more or less a series of questions and answers relating to the civil war and internment. It was a case of do you remember this or do you remember that? And, of course, they remembered.

After a while a young man, who had married a local girl, came in. After a few words with Bridie and myself he drifted away to the dark end where the two civil war heroes were delighted to absorb him into their company. Now they would have a captive audience. Now they could recall the great turning points of history in which they played a noble part.

They began by telling the young man how they were both under sentence of death at one time. But the young man was not impressed. "Do you know," said the young man "that in my part of the country I was always the man picked out to carry out the death sentence on traitors. I don't know exactly how many I shot." This information was not required and worse still, as the night progressed, every time any of the two republicans came up with a first hand account of a good ambush from which they barely escaped, the young man would tell of how the roads in his part of the country were constantly littered with the dead bodies of Free State soldiers and said he with great emphasis, "*Everyone knows who was responsible.*"

Finally, "Captain" Murphy could stand it no longer.

"Who the bloody hell do you think you are codding. The Civil War was over before you were bloody well born." And I got the feeling from his tone of voice that Murphy was about to lose his temper.

"Hold it. Hold it now, old timer." said the young man. "The Civil War went on a lot longer in my part of the country than it did around here. We did not hand ourselves up to the Free Staters like youse did." Just in time, a few strangers came in and the argument was over for the time being.

This history did not tally with what we were told in school.

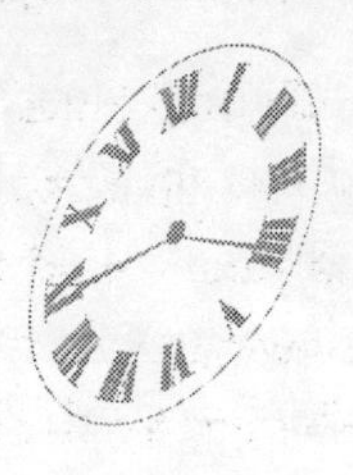

41

From Bad to Worse

Seemingly the majority of people of Ireland welcomed the treaty. They wanted the gunmen off their backs. They were fed up with armed gangs taking over their homesteads after dark, taking over the food supply, and the beds, while the men of the house were ordered outside to keep watch and ward over the men "on the run."

History books will supply you with day and dates regarding many of the things that happened while scrupulously avoiding anything that might take from the honour and glory of the cause – *saoirse* and the *cúpla focal.* It is true to say that many young men were genuine in their belief that *El Dorado* would automatically accompany freedom from British rule. It is equally true to say that the vast majority were under no such illusion: many firmly believed that revolutionary factions always and ever brought nothing but poverty and misery upon the ordinary peace loving population.

We are not unduly concerned with those who won positions of power and affluence as a result of the upheaval which took place. However, we cannot avoid mentioning some of them from time to time. The "vote early and vote often" election held in 1918 was regarded by many as the greatest hoax of all time. The Home Rule party was reduced from seventy-eight members to six. And Sinn Féin increased their numbers from seven to seventy-three!

Intimidation was so widespread many feared to cast their votes. John McCabe, a highly respected member of the farming community in our area, told me the inside story of the 1918 General Election. On the evening prior to the election a group of armed Sinn Féiners called to his house and warned him to remain at home next day. They told him "We will do the voting for you."

Next morning early, John made his way through the woods to the polling station.

He took them by surprise. However, most people obeyed orders and Sinn Féiners did the voting.

The result of the next General Election showed that in spite of all the propaganda, preaching and panegyrics a vast number of people voted "A *plague on both your houses*". By now Sinn Féin was no longer united and with both sides keeping watch on each other there was far less intimidation and impersonation, resulting in: sixteen independents, fifteen farmers and fourteen labour candidates all elected to the Dáil. The people who voted Farmer, Labourer and Independent were more concerned about unemployment and bread on the table than the hocus-pocus and mumbo-jumbo of politicians. We will, as the local chemist said, "Leave them to God".

In 1926 de Valera parted with Sinn Féin, more or less on friendly terms, forming a new party known as Fianna Fáil. And the new party promised everything, including a United Ireland "*abracadabra*" fashion: the restoration of the Irish language, freedom for all political prisoners, the removal of the oath, an end to emigration, the return of the shilling to old age pensioners. Keeping the good wine till last, Fianna Fáil would enable every Irish citizen to live a noble and Christian life when the land of Ireland would be re-distributed, by breaking up the large farms and estates so that the greatest possible number of Irish families would be "rooted in the soil of Ireland". Landless men would become land owners and small farmers would become larger farmers. Poor old Bill Cosgrave and his party, who had the job of rebuilding bridges and hospitals etc, after the "trouble" had no hope of retaining power. In 1932 there came a change of Government and another outbreak of nationalism-cum-patriotism. Land owned by protestants and supporters of the Cosgrave party was targeted by local Fianna Fáil clubs for immediate division. Needless to say, all the high hopes were not always fulfilled. Imagination and wishful thinking made many small farmers happy, fantasising in their own minds as to what it would be like when they became big farmers. Alas! They did not know what was in store for all farmers both large and small. Little did they think that in a few short years de Valera and his Government would bring about a situation in which all land and cattle would become valueless and unsaleable. Let me elucidate: de Valera got great honour and many votes for his promise to "retain" the land annuities which were due to the British Government as a result of the various land acts, which had enabled many tenant farmers to purchase their farms.

Most farmers were under the impression that this would be the end of paying rent to the Land Commission. Alas! Again they were taken for a ride! Now the Irish Government would collect and "retain" what was legally due to the British Government. The British Government responded by putting a tax on all Irish cattle entering the British market. And de Valera responded to this by placing a tax on all British goods entering the Irish market and so began the Economic War.

In the meantime, local Fianna Fáil branches continued to divide and sub-divide large farms and small estates, to their own satisfaction. And headquarters let it be known that in places such as the west of Ireland, where good land was unavailable, anyone willing to let his small holding go to a neighbour would automatically be granted a thirty acre farm in Kildare or Meath, where some large estates had been broken up and on which, it was hoped, entire *cúpla focal* communities would be established. It was not all plain sailing. It was not easy to hand over one's home and bit of land to some neighbour with whom you and your family had been on bad terms for generations. Nevertheless, many got over their scruples and were willing to move.

This was a rough time for Cumann na Gael speakers. Many were hunted from their platforms, but these attacks were of little importance and soon forgotten. On the other hand, anyone who was around at that time will never forget the Fianna Fáil victory celebrations. Barrels of tar were set alight in every town and village; torchlight processions all over the place and every fursey hill and glen became an inferno. Pubs were full of glee-men full of hope and once again "Phil the Fluter's Ball" rang out:

"*Och! We'll shoot and we'll loot*
and with bullets we will riddle o
We'll keep the whole land sizzling
Like a herring on a griddle o."

It came as a big surprise to some of his followers that de Valera would only tolerate a certain amount of this "Phil the Fluter's Ball" business.

In describing the years that followed and the lunatic Economic War, I will avoid making any prejudicial, sweeping generalisation.

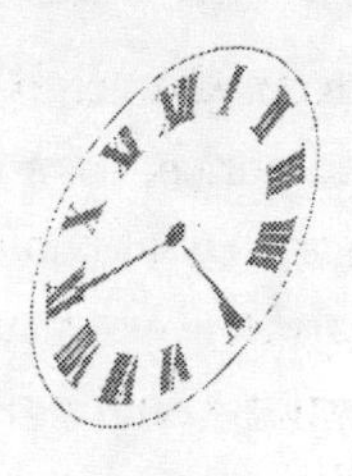

42

DeV Miscalculates

The keynotes of de Valera's policy was 'national self-sufficiency'. Not a very mystifying term. Yet very few understood exactly what self-sufficiency entailed. Perhaps if he'd fully understood all about it he would not have been crazy enough to embark upon it. It is easy to produce facts and figures to prove how disastrous this policy actually was.

At the crossroads, our expert on all complicated matters was old Patsy Sheehan, a man familiar with ancient history, the rise and fall of Rome, and the fickleness of human nature. Patsy could quote from all those ancient writers, but his special favourite was Michael Lord of Montaigne and seemingly Michael said, "The true genius and characteristical turn of men's minds are best to be gathered from the small and seemingly inconsiderable particulars of their lives and fortunes." Who am I to dare dispute with men like Patsy and Michael Lord of Montaigne. Therefore I will abandon statistics and recall some minor events in the lives and fortunes of people who, like myself, lived through that very sad period. Men and women of every age will feel the lack of money but teenagers feel the loss more keenly than all others. With very little money in our pockets, nowhere to go, and no prospects nor freedom, the *cúpla focal* amounted to very little.

Every Sunday evening there was what was called a "hop" in the local dance hall. It took place between the hours of eight and midnight and the entry fee was four old pence, or one penny in today's money.

To find the four pence entry fee was quite a problem for many, and the man who could "pay for her in" was a man of some standing. They say money speaks all languages but it is especially fluent in the language of love.

I remember one Sunday evening when a group of us decided to venture into pastures new. The hall we intended to patronise was seven or eight miles away and going that far was a risky undertaking considering we were all mounted on cannibalised bicycles. The danger of having to return on foot, lugging your broken-down bicycle had to be borne in mind. And the idea of having to walk home alone past two graveyards and the Protestant Church, where the devil himself was often seen in the form of a black dog knocking sparks off the gate with his long tail, was enough to put the heart crossways in most of us. Having to walk past the Catholic graveyard was worse because there was the ghost of a woman who had taken a false oath and whose tongue was hanging down to her knees. If she laid eyes on you she would follow you home and no matter how fast you ran she was always only a few feet behind! It was a terrible risk to take for the sake of a dance, but to young men "*the frontier grave is always far away*". We were ready for anything.

Luckily we were still all air-borne on arrival. In other words none of us were riding on the rim.

We entered the hall without delay so as to get good value for our money. There were few inside and the crowd were very slow in coming in. In actual fact, they didn't come in at all! And after half an hour or so Billy Brien, the leader of the well-known Millstreet Rovers band announced that owing to the poor attendance they had no alternative but to down tools unless the owner of the hall came up with the money immediately. Needless to say, this did not happen.

No one ever saw musical instruments packed away so quickly. This was one evening we did not have to stand facing the music as the band belted out "*Amhrán na bFiann.*" No money, no anthem.

The midday sun of the market place shines equally strong at night. Sentiment dissolves when money is scarce! Romantic Ireland was taking to its sick bed and unfortunately de Valera's remedy was "more of the same".

"*Anois mar bharr air gach mí greann*" – and I weep as I pen the sad story.

The withholding of the land annuities made little difference to the British Government. The duties imposed on Irish cattle entering the British market more than made up for the loss. In the meantime, the Irish Government continued to collect land annuities from farmers. Farmers had now to pay far more than they had done previously and many of them found themselves in great financial difficulty as the price of farm produce continued to fall.

It is impossible to reconcile what happened next with the actions of sane men. Gone were the days when crowds of "*blockers and tanglers*" were active on the roads leading to cattle fairs. Prime cattle became almost unsaleable and de Valera took the opportunity of announcing, "The British market is gone for ever. Thank God". Steps were taken immediately to stop the supply of cheap Irish cattle to Britain and this gave rise to what was known as "the free beef". Under a Government scheme free beef was distributed all over the country and needless to say, most of it went to Fianna Fáil supporters.

There are people today who will try to advance their political standing by saying "I was born into Fianna Fáil." But search where you will, you will not find one man ready to admit eating plenty of free beef during the Economic War. But, as one Cosgrave supporter put it "Ah, the devils ate plenty of it".

Some farmers who failed to find a buyer were forced to murder their own cattle and hawk the cut up carcass from pub to pub, in an effort to find a few shillings. This is not hearsay. I saw this happening with my own two eyes.

Time and time again, I have heard people speak of the Economic War and the degradation of farmers. Never did I hear it put more succinctly than by the late Jimmy Doyle.

At that time Jimmy was a schoolboy, and like every schoolboy that ever was he hated school. These were the days when all school-work was done through the medium of Irish. In other words, the *cúpla focal* added to the misery.

Jimmy was delighted when a neighbouring farmer required his help to drive some fine cattle to Dunlavin Fair. Paddy Byrne was a good farmer and his cattle were always top class. And one morning at four a.m. Paddy and his young helper started out for Dunlavin, a town eight miles away, in the very heart of some of the best cattle and sheep producing districts in Ireland. Young Jimmy was glad to be free for a day. Old Paddy was not too hopeful. He had heard stories of how things were getting worse. However, having good animals he was not completely without hope.

The town was overflowing with cattle and sheep and men stood near every lot hoping that a buyer might come along. Alas! They waited in vain. Hour after hour they waited; growing more hungry and tired as the weary day wore on. They were lucky it was a dry day because the weather can be bad around Dunlavin at times.

At long last when all hope of meeting a buyer was gone Paddy said, "We'd better start for home while we have a spark of daylight."

Silently they drove the animals home. It was up to Paddy to make conversation but he remained silent until within sight of home.

"Young Doyle," said he "do you know what I am going to tell you? – I am going to tell you that it will never again be worth raising your boot to give them cattle a kick in the arse, as long as that hure de Valera is in power."

Next day Jimmy was back at the *cúpla focal* and it was a worse day than the day at the fair.

Pockets full of money became a thing of the past in the Irish Free State. Farmers could remember that only a few short years before they could ask for and receive twenty pounds for an old cow.

43

HUMILIATION

When things go wrong in this country one can expect a fresh outbreak of patriotism and superstition, with the powers that be calling for fresh sacrifices. It is hard to believe that people were capable of such madness.

Seemingly, de Valera was of the opinion that without Irish beef and farm produce the population of Britain would be reduced to starvation and the British Government would have to submit to all his demands. The daubers were out again painting. "Starve John Bull" was a favourite slogan. De Valera was now about to accomplish what the French had failed to do, what the Spanish had failed to do, what the Dutch failed to do and indeed what the great German armies had failed to do a few short years before. A new and better Napoleon, a new and better Bismark was about to deliver the *coup de grace* to the ancient enemy.

Having completely destroyed the cattle trade he now set about eliminating all young calves which might at some date be offered for sale and in some roundabout way reach the British market and give sustenance to the people of that island. From now on a bounty of nine shillings and sixpence would be on every calf-skin, provided it was whole and complete and without what they called a "*nick.*" A "*nick*" was always the result of a slip of the knife by an unskilled operator. Such a slip would cost a farm worker his week's wages. I can tell you, they soon developed skills and dexterity which would be the envy of any college of surgeons in the world, had they known such skilfulness existed.

From one year to the next, slight changes were made to the scheme, making it more machiavellian. For instance, one year, half the two front legs, or if you like, from the knees down, had to go with the skin. Another year it was the lower lip; to sever this from the jaw bone was some job and many a bounty was lost in this area.

Every time no bounty was paid was a win for the Government. After all, the calf was dead and there was now no danger of it ever reaching the British market. Farmers were now at the mercy of the calf-skin agent. On arrival at the agent's private house which also served as a collection centre, every calf-skin had to be opened out for inspection and the discovery of the faintest "nick" resulted in immediate disqualification. The farmer would receive no bounty and needless to say, he abandoned the skin. Human nature being what it is, it is hard to tell whether the said skin qualified later when the agent made up his account. Perhaps the Government had to pay in the end.

The true story of the Economic War will never be written because the stupefied mentality of the people can never be explained.

Before the Economic War, 750,000 cattle were exported every year to Britain and de Valera figured that if 750,000 calves were put to death every year there would be no more need of the British market. In other words, we would be independent.

He also figured that the number of bounties to go out would be around 750,000, give or take a few hundred. Needless to say he didn't have a clue as to how things worked down on the farm . . . he completely overlooked the fact that from twenty to twenty five percent of all calves died within the first few weeks from one disease or another.

Now, things being the way they were farmers had no hesitation in skinning every calf they could lay their hands on be they dead or alive; still-born or premature, they all suffered the same fate. De Valera, the mathematician, did not understand the mathematics of agriculture. Official figures showed that many calves had two or more skins.

Now that people were well into the skinning culture, all dead animals were skinned.

On a farm near ours, the owner went out one morning to find one of his cows dead, for no apparent reason. He suggested to his two teenage sons that they should skin the cow before burial. They could then sell the hide to some "*knacker*" and make a few shillings for themselves.

When the hide was removed he decided to carry out a post-mortem. He fancied himself as a bit of a cow-doctor. He failed to find the cause of death, but his sons discovered two fully mature calves which would have made their appearance in a few days.

The boys went to work and with the utmost skill and carefulness they skinned both calves and drew the bounty on each.

It would be grossly unfair to immortalize any one farmer or farm worker by saying he was the best skinner in the locality. Suffice to say, the clumsy soon became professional.

Around this time many estate owners became disillusioned. The captains and the majors and the brigadiers, all intelligent men who had money to spend on the upkeep of their estates, saw no future in a country where bunny rabbits were of equal value to prime bullocks. They flung their land to the land commission for small recompense and left before coming completely impoverished. They were not the type of people who would walk down the road to the calf-skin agent with a calf-skin around their necks and the two front feet dangling from it. These estates were now broken up into twenty and thirty acre plots and given to land-hungry small farmers. Alas, they were given "dead sea fruit." Land had become valueless and changed hands for as little as five, six, and seven pounds per acre.

To fully understand what conditions were like during the Economic War we must go down to the country and visit a farmyard. Conditions in the farm "surgery" were primitive, blue-bottles fill the air, and no matter how many cats and dogs in the area, no way could they cope with the supply of calf carcasses presented to them. Grey crows feasted so heavily they had difficulty taking to the air. Water rats abandoned the river to help their brown cousins at the mopping-up operations. Digging holes in the ground was just simply not on, the heap of farmyard manure became the temporary resting place for all the skinned calves. Talk about additional calcium, this was the calves' Blenheim.

> "It *was a summer's evening*
> *Old Kasper's work was done,*
> *And he before his cottage door*
> *Was sitting in the sun!"* . . .
> Giving his penknife another "dose of edge"; tomorrow would be another day of killing and skinning."

Neglect and disease did most of the killing. No effort whatsoever was made to combat the deadly "white scour." In some farms, starvation took its toll to avoid bloodshed. The healthy calf that survived these conditions was dragged out into the bright sunshine and its throat cut. Sometimes it was throttled with a rope. Sometimes it was killed by a number of blows. There was no cruelty to animals or people in those days; or else they kept a very low profile. To fully describe the nauseating stink which surrounds all calves that succumb to the "white scour" disease is beyond me. However, there are a few words in the Irish language full of meaning for when the occasion arises. Let us suppose, for a moment, one familiar with the Irish language suddenly came face to face with the stinking remains of a calf that died of this terrible disease. Without a moment's hesitation that person would turn away uttering the words, "*Ow* . . . *oo* . . . *whadda*" with a short pause between the words for greater effect.

Is it not strange that with all the hardship and all the flogging and beatings connected with the teaching of compulsory Irish we never heard the words, "*Ow* . . . *oo* . . . *whadda*". We must give credit where credit is due. The Irish language described something the English language was incapable of doing. Were it possible to do so, many would turn away from the whole country with the "*Ow* . . . *oo* . . . *whadda*" feeling. Plans for wholesale emigration were being teased out at every crossroads.

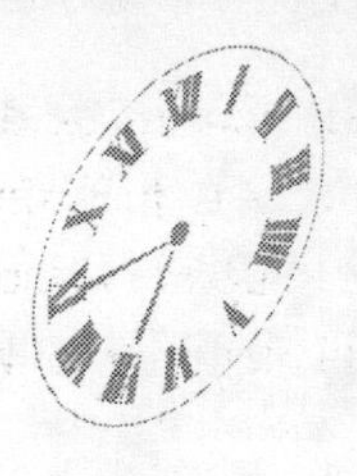

44

THE EUCHARISTIC CONGRESS 1932

The Eucharistic Congress of 1932 was held in Dublin shortly after de Valera came to power. It provided him with an opportunity to show his loyalty and devotion to the Catholic church . . . in spite of the fact that a few short years previously a very prominent Catholic bishop had declared that "hell was not deep enough nor hot enough" for the IRA and its supporters.

De Valera's conversion to Christian principles on the road to Leinster House was more dramatic than St. Paul's conversion on the road to Damascus.

It soon became obvious to everybody that the Irish hierarchy and the new Government had found a solution to all problems. From now on both parties would present a united front and one could say a marriage of convenience had taken place and for decades afterwards may God help the politician who suggested any form of separation.

In the months and weeks preceding it, the clergy made every effort to bring home to the people the importance of the Eucharistic Congress. People were exhorted to attend if at all possible. They were reminded that the least they might do was to have every member of the family wear suitable holy medals and badges in honour of the occasion. It was of the utmost importance that every household should display at least one papal flag side by side with the national flag. Villages and towns were well decorated and there was much co-operation between people in built-up areas.

People living along the road in rural areas had to fend for themselves as regards papal and national flags.

These were the days of the travelling saleswomen. Day after day they went from house to house crying out "*U-cress Con-gress medals . . . U-cress Con-gress medals . . . U-cress Con-gress medals.*" Every time one opened the door one was confronted by a tinker woman selling *u-cress con-gress* medals and the fact that she was retailing "de holy medals" gave her the right of way to the kitchen table for display purposes. "Ah, sure de childer love de holy medals". Well! Rather than risk the evil eye, the unfortunate mother would collect the last remaining pennies so that every child was decorated and the child in the pram looked like a war veteran home from the Crimea. One by one the houses along the country roads began to display papal flags. Some were quite small, others large and somehow the size of your papal flag and your national flag flying side by side was an indication of your standing in the community.

The parish priest had the biggest flags on proper flag poles but there were those who said he got the lot free from parish funds. Seemingly, we will always have some begrudgers. To most people the display of flags outside the presbytery looked very nice.

The parish clerk and Ned-the-Leg went to great trouble erecting two very high poles. However, when it came to the crunch, Ned had second thoughts about venturing too far up the poles with the result that the flags were flown at half mast all during the run up to the Congress.

Jack Connolly, an ex-royal Navy man noticed the flags at half mast as he made his way to The Ford and he caused consternation at the bar when he announced "The b. . . Pope must have kicked the bucket. All flags are at half mast up at the presbytery."

Even when the matter was fully explained Ned-the-Leg let it be known that he hadn't the least intention of committing suicide by taking the papal flag to the top of the pole "and as for the national flag he never saw it any other way except at half mast."

Mick Reardon was a good few years older than his wife and with only a few days work in the week he found some difficulty in providing for their growing family. To him, any amusement such as a football matche or sports meeting was "just another silly carry-on" and as far as he was concerned, papal and national flags were not a top priority. None of his hard earned money would be spent on indoor or outdoor displays. Public opinion was the least of his problems. Peggy was thus thrown back on her own resources and all she had was one empty flour bag. And the empty flour bag of those days was a very valuable and universal article almost in line with the empty tar barrel. Empty flour bags were opened out and made into pillow cases or stitched up together and made into bed sheets or articles of underwear. Therefore, let us not underestimate the sacrifice made by Mrs Reardon. She set aside half a flour bag, which she, to the best of her ability, would make into a papal flag of which she and her family might well be proud. She squared out her material and began to stitch in cross keys and triple crowns with great care. However, it soon became obvious that the Congress would be over before her flag became air-borne if she continued with this embroidery. Undaunted, she decided to finish off the flag with some spare mahogany paint which remained unused for years on top of the dresser. And those of us who have strolled around various art galleries in different capital cities are well aware that great things can be done with paint. Michaelangelo, Picasso and others spring to mind. But we must remember these gentlemen had all the proper equipment: different brushes, different paints and chemicals of all sorts. Mrs Reardon had only the remains of a brush and the remains of a tin of paint, now rock hard. Necessity being the mother of invention, she discovered that by adding an eggcup of Jeyes fluid and bringing the whole lot to the boil, she brought the mixture to what she considered was the right consistency.

The base and the background and the materials were not the best but when it was ready for hanging one could scarcely take their eyes off it. One casual observer said it was "a holy terror to the Lord God".

Ned-the-Leg, having made a name for himself with the papal flags, volunteered to nail it to the gable end of the house nearest the road. A small crowd assembled when they saw Ned erecting his ladder. One rather forward youngfellow looked at the flag and said it was "the colour of sick".

Were I as wise then as I am now I would have, by some means or another, taken possession of that flag. It was the first and by far the finest piece of modern art I ever came across. On account of my great ignorance of modern art at that time I have lived a lifetime of regret. Let us suppose for a moment I could now produce that flag, the art galleries around the world would run into financial difficulties out-bidding each other for this unique and matchless specimen. It fulfilled every criterion by which modern art is judged. First, no one could make head or tail of it, nor would they in their wildest dreams associate it with the Vatican. And on being told it was a papal flag the immediate reaction would be one of disbelief. Its authenticity would thus be easily established.

As Ned-the-Leg drove home the final nail, one old man remarked "'Tis a grand flag entirely, so it is, Mrs Reardon."

"Who knows," said she "I might have a priest in the family yet."

"Well," said Tomlinson, as he pushed his priestly black hat to the back of his head and gave a sarcastic look up at the flag, "if you do have a priest in the family you will have no difficulty in getting stuff for the collar."

Many people believe that the Congress brought about the end of the travelling road-shows because they could not afford the additional cost of flags and medals. As well as that, many people were saving every penny so that they could travel to Dublin for the great event.

The road-shows were mostly family run outfits such as Hutchins and Turners. Year after year crowds would attend to see the same show over and over again.

Murder in the Red Barn was probably the most popular. There was one old actor who had the required courage to tell some bawdy jokes such as the following:

"Ah, may God be with the good old days . . . how things have changed . . . in the old days a girl would be courting a fella for years before she would dare bring him home to the house. Then after a year or two the parents would slip away to bed leaving the pair by the kitchen fire chatting to each other. Over the fire there was the big eight-day clock saying: tick, tock, tick tock, tick, tock, tick, tock, tick, . . .take . . . your . . . time . . . take . . . your . . . time . . . take . . . your . . . time.

Ah how things have changed. Now they all have these new alarm clocks saying: Get-at-it Get-at-it Get-at-it Get-at-it Get-at-it. Is it any wonder things have gone to the bad."

People did away with alarm clocks for safety sake.

45

CATTLE SEIZURES

As a direct result of the Economic War more and more farmers became impoverished and many of them failed to make ends meet. They now decided to resist some of the demands made upon them by the Government and this gave rise to the "pay no land annuities" campaign.

The Government retaliated by carrying out cattle seizures. The cattle were then taken to central depots and sold at give-away prices to unscrupulous buyers. At these so-called public auctions, newspapers told us *"the principal buyer was again Mr Smith."*

The Blueshirts became very active trying to prevent seizures and the subsequent sale of seized cattle. Needless to say Billy Tarrant and myself followed the example of our older brothers. And we now joined the Blueshirts. By this time de Valera and his Government had declared the organisation illegal.

At around this time a young Blueshirt by the name of Patrick Lynch was shot dead at a sales-yard in Cork while taking part in a public protest. Also at this time the newly set up "military tribunal" was in operation and any Blueshirt brought before the tribunal could look forward to a long term in jail.

Times were rough and tough but from our point of view exciting.

Our "secret" service was very poor and often acting on unreliable information; all the roads leading to a certain farm would be blocked by fallen trees and all telephone wires cut, only to find out later that a seizure had taken place a few miles away without the least trouble. Council workers were always called upon to clear away the fallen trees while the gardaí and de Valera's special police, known as "Broy Harriers" were busy taking statements and arresting well known Blueshirts.

The men arrested were always charged before the military tribunal. There were people who said General O'Duffy and his Blueshirts were like Hitler and his Brownshirts or Mussolini and his Blackshirts; forgetting the Blueshirts were unarmed, their only weapons being a short cudgel sometimes called a baton and on rare occasions the humble knuckle-duster. The Blueshirts had no love for Hitler or Mussolini and in the fullness of time this was proved without any doubt. We will not go too deeply into these matters here because this is simply the story of how ordinary people had to cope and struggle at that time.

For our monthly branch meetings we assembled at the post office and when our officers arrived on bicycles we moved up the Castle Boreen or if you like, the back entrance to the castle. Where we halted depended on the wind and rain. We picked a sheltered spot and I can guarantee there was no reading of the minutes or other nonsense. Our head man was known to us as Captain Tim O'Connor, an ex-National Army man from Cork. However, the opposition party and the republicans always referred to him as "Timmeen Connors from Derry". It was obvious they had no love for Captain Tim O'Connor. Everyone stood in a close knot around our officers as instructions were given out relating to: national collections, dances in aid of the party, public meetings, and as time grew, tough collections for the purchase of cartons of cigarettes for Blueshirt prisoners in Arbour Hill jail.

We were on stand-by at all times in case a seizure might be attempted in our area and truth to tell we were looking forward to the excitement.

As far as I can remember, members of our branch were called out only once. And as was often the case it proved to be a false alarm. Nevertheless, trees had been felled across all roads leading to Kanturk and telephone lines chopped into various lengths.

Cutting telephone lines was regarded as child's play. Billy and myself and a few others did a splendid job on the wires with a view to upsetting all enemy communications. Tom Drew and my brother were seconded to the Kanturk branch, where help was needed to cut down trees, thereby cutting off all access to a certain farm. Next morning, I asked David "What did yourself and Drew do last night?"

"Almost nothing." was his answer. But as I said before, he was never one to exaggerate.

Needless to say, this outbreak of lawlessness was followed up by an intense and vehement police investigation resulting in the arrest of several Blueshirts, including Tom Drew. How my brother escaped arrest I will never know. They were all brought before the military tribunal and sentenced to long terms of imprisonment.

It was immediately decided to hold a monster protest meeting in Kanturk and preparations for this began all over the country and beyond.

For meetings and dances we had a highly developed transport system. We avoided travelling on bikes as far as possible, being under the impression that horse-transport was more aristocratic and upper-class – in spite of the fact that both horse and trap were more or less stolen for the occasion.

Had my father had any suspicion that we were taking Van Dyck on regular outings he would have been very upset. And had Ned Tarrant had the faintest idea that his trap was out of home so often he would have been even more upset!

Great things were expected of Van Dyck in his early days but as a yearling he suffered a serious set-back. And when it became clear to the original owner that with Van Dyck his hopes of winning the Grand National would never be fulfilled, Van Dyck was sold to the tinkers.

In a moment of weakness and magnanimity my father bought the failed racehorse, saving it from a life of hardship and hunger.

Long after the time of the Blueshirts stories were told about our adventures with the great-hearted Van Dyck and Tarrant's trap.

As a rule we never had much difficulty getting the horse and trap on the road. However, on this day, of all days, we had a major problem. Every Sunday after Mass Ned Tarrant and a few other farmers of that age group went without fail to The Ford for a few drinks. And no one could tell how long the session would last. It could be an hour or two hours or indeed as it often happened it might well be nightfall before the assembly would break up. There was the danger that as we drove down the road we would meet the owner of the trap returning from The Ford; if this happened the fat would definitely be in the fire because the road was too narrow for a quick u-turn.

On the understanding that the worst never happens we all sat in and started off for town. This was not our lucky day. As we drove along the narrowest part of the road we saw him coming towards us. David, who was driving, said, "Don't panic!"

He stood in off the road with his arm raised to bring us to a halt. "Glory be to God, boys. I see ye are off to the meeting."

"We are, Sir." "Yes, Sir." "That is right, Sir." He could be forgiven for thinking he was already knighted! He failed to recognise his own trap but continued to ask questions. "Will there be trouble?" "Will Duffy himself be there?" "Glory be to God, boys. I'd go myself but there is no room."

Finally he turned to his two sons and said "Whatever happens, I'm warning the two of you to be home to milk the cows. Whatever about the country the cows must be milked."

As a matter of fact this warning applied to all of us. Milking cows in the evenings was the bane of our lives.

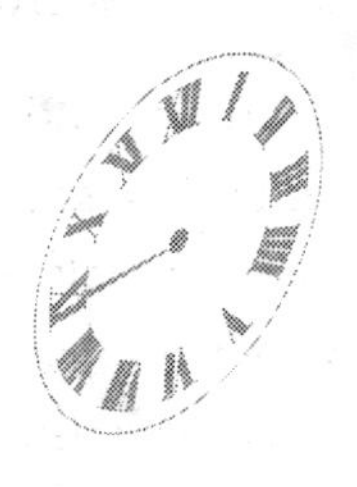

46

THE PROTEST MEETING

Once again the drop of alcohol saved our bacon as it so often did during our school days. We drove at top speed into town and Van Dyck automatically turned into Danny Ford's backyard, this being the place where he was always parked on market and fair days. Training is a wonderful thing. Our horse was always at ease when tied to a pole here and for safety sake we unyoked him from the trap.

With everything in order we started out for Strand Street. Whoever built Strand Street must have done so with the EEC in mind; it is so wide and spacious; few Irish towns can boast of anything even remotely like it, with its large stores, magnificent Clock House and its well-appointed and gratifying range of public houses. Other towns may look at Strand Street and despair.

Thousands of people, most of them wearing blue shirts, had already assembled. There was not room for another person between the Clock House and the far end of the street.

We stayed together more or less on the outskirts of the crowd and we were just in time to see the speakers mount the platform. As this was a protest meeting one could take it for granted that there would be some hard hitting speeches. Today was not a day for the *cúpla focal.* The men on the platform were not *cúpla focal* men anyway. Soon the crowd was fairly well worked up as speaker after speaker gave litany after litany of our woes and wrongs under the "present tyrannical Government". I knew most of the men on the platform but now, after the passage of over half a century, I can not say for certain which of them delivered the punch line. I saw him raise his hand and point towards the Clock House. "Over here." said he. "We have a bunch of Broy Harriers (special police). They are well paid. They are well dressed, but are they respectable?"

The crowd roared as crowds do and there was a rush or surge of Blueshirts towards the six or seven Broy Harriers, who had been standing at the rear of the meeting. The Broys ran up the street one of them carrying a Blueshirt on his back. Quick as lightening the uniformed guards tried to form a cordon across the street by holding hands and this might well have contained the angry crowds were it not for the shot that was fired by the Broy with the violent Blueshirt on his back.

There was now a mad rush of Blueshirts after the Broys. Bending down, I dashed out between two guards. Not that I wanted to lead the attack. I just wanted to see what was happening. The cordon of guards was swept aside as thousands surged forward. I could see the Broys were losing ground with the mob closing in on them. Suddenly they turned and with guns blazing they brought the mob to a halt. It was obvious this situation could not hold as pressure built up at the back. The Broys made another dash for the safety of the garda station and this time they succeeded in turning the corner. But on the bridge, the mob was once again on their heels. Again they turned and opened fire. Again there was a short halt, and this time they got half way up O'Brien's Street before again repeating the manoeuvre. Then, in one final dash, they reached the garda station and once inside they closed and bolted the door. The crowd surrounded the building thumping the door with batons, and climbing on to railings, shouting threats and abuse.

Opposite the garda station there was a wall and many Blueshirts by standing on this wall had a bird's-eye view of all the commotion. I shouted up to Dan Joe Emington, who was on the wall, "How are things going?" "Very well." said Dan Joe. "This man here says the right thing to do is burn them out of it."

While all this was going on, senior Blueshirt officers were doing all in their power to cool the situation and trying to call off the attack on the police station. Reluctantly the rank and file withdrew and when all the excitement was over I started to walk back to Danny Ford's backyard where we had left Van Dyck and where I would meet my companions.

On my way back I met a former Irish Guardsman, Jack Sheehan, who was a great war veteran having taken part in many battles such as Festubert, Loose, Cambria, the first battle of the Somme and the retreat from Mons. Jack had spent the day drinking rather than listening to political speeches. "Do you know," said he. "Today reminded me of old times and the smell of cordite." To me it was a new smell but it was not objectionable.

When I reached Danny Ford's backyard the trap was there but Van Dyck was gone. Everybody knows that sudden gunfire will frighten animals and there was no way a highly spirted animal like Van Dyck would remain tethered to a pole while bullets ricocheted off buildings all around him. My brother wanted to know what we would do about Van Dyck and the Tarrant brothers wanted to know what would be done about the trap. "Jasses lads," said Dan Joe "the only thing we can do is emigrate!"

"I know what I'll do." said I. "Where can I get a bike? I will overtake Van Dyck." They told me I hadn't a hope in hell. "And while I'm away," said I "be wheeling the trap down the town. Every yard counts." In a matter of minutes I was mounted and travelling faster than any man before or since. I was almost home when I found my animal tied firmly to Johnny Ryan's gate. In a matter of seconds, I was on my way back into town, Van Dyck trotting along beside me. In the meantime the boys had wheeled the trap to the end of the town and seemingly they were the butt of many jokes.

As they pushed the trap down Strand Street, fellow Blueshirts shouted. "Hey! This is Kanturk, not bloody Hong Kong!"

"You. Who Flung Dung. How muchy ride in rickshaw?"

"Me! I Foo Ling. Not takit Blueshirt inny rickshaw."

Then Dan Joe told someone, knowing the story would spread all over town. "Our horse was struck by a stray bullet. He is dead above in Danny Ford's backyard." And to confirm the story Tarrant said, "We have sent home for another horse."

When I arrived with Van Dyck the crowd around the trap took it for granted that this was a replacement. As we tackled-up Van Dyck for the road home one old lady pushed her way to the front. "'Tis terrible times" said she. "A young man with bullet wounds and now a poor innocent horse dead. I'm telling you that man de Valera will have a lot to answer for."

I learned a great lot that day. I saw the uncontrolable power of the mob. And I must give credit where credit is due: the Broy Harriers, in spite of immense provocation and outnumbered by a thousand to one, kept their cool.

Were I being set-upon by a mob of any kind I would be sorely tempted to "et them have it!"

Had they fired into the crowd instead of into the air the Civil War might well have started all over again.

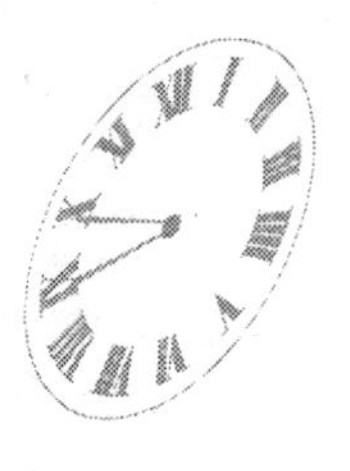

47

LIFE AT SEA

When young men see no great future for themselves in their homeland it is only natural that they consider emigration. In schools we were led to believe, "She is a rich and rare land. This native land of mine". However, a few weeks in the wet and frosty beet-fields and after a few visits to the calf-skin agent, making sure you had the calf's puss in perfect order and that the two front legs were firmly attached to the smelly white-scoury skin, one would quickly change their mind about "this native land of mine".

There was no need to remind us of all we suffered trying to become proficient in the use of Irish as the ash-plant raised blisters from the tops of our bare heads to the soles of our bare feet.

All the hyperbole about the rebirth and the onward march of the nation was without any doubt hyperbole brought to supersaturation.

It was obvious we would never see "a glad confident morning" while we remained here in this mismanaged country. We sat down to consider all these matters and needless to say we did not consult parents or anyone who might be in a position to advise us. Like all young people we knew all the answers.

"I hear," said Tarrant "they are mad looking for men in Jersey."

"And what would they have us doing there?" I asked.

"Picking tomatoes." said Dan Joe.

"Count me out." I said. "I have had enough back-breaking work. We would come back from there with bigger humps than we have already."

"Well," said Tarrant "what do you propose?"

I had just finished reading a story in *The Wide World* magazine. It was all about whale hunting in the Antarctic. The pay was good and there was the promise of a bonus amounting on average to nine hundred pounds at the end of the season. I had visions of Tarrant and Dan Joe and myself returning in less than a year and buying our own farm; or better still clubbing together and buying our own ship. Personally, I would go for the ship. The outlook for farming was never worse. However, there would be plenty of time to talk them into buying the ship.

"I propose" said I "that we strike off next Sunday morning to Cork and that we look for jobs on board some ship, preferably a tramp steamer on which we could circumnavigate the globe."

"A flaming great idea." said Dan Joe. I knew I could depend on Dan Joe for moral support. I did not explain to them that when our tramp steamer eventually arrived in Port Elizabeth we would jump ship and sign on for a season on board a whaling vessel.

Little did any one of us know of what actually lay ahead.

In view of what we had in mind we dressed up neatly that Sunday morning in what was then the height of fashion, light grey sports-jackets and almost-white seaside pants and would you believe it, light blue smart looking felt hats. A far cry from the usual country cap or if you like, *government haybarn.* We looked smart alright, especially when mounted on our bikes; bicycle clips in position showing off our pointed, toney-red shoes all well polished, one could say we were fairly well turned out. Our bicycles were not the best, but I will say this, the long thirty-five mile cycle to the city was enjoyable. I had been to Cork several times with my father and I had a good idea of where to find the ships and tramp steamers. We arrived in good order and in good time and we decided to examine the ships from some distance, wondering if we'd dump the bikes in the harbour or leave them till later. As we wheeled our bikes along the deserted quays to take a closer look a small group of fellows of our own age had us under observation and one said to another. "Look lads, here come the three stooges." Tarrant gave them a sour look and that was the end of that.

We found no ship displaying a "*men wanting*" notice. We did, however, find a ship that fulfilled all our requirements. Even Dan Joe and Tarrant could see that this ship was sea-worthy. We parked our bikes beside the gangway and went on board. There was no door at which we could knock because all doors were open as far as we could see. We proceeded to make a tour of inspection in the hope that the Captain would come along and ask us our business. That would give us the opportunity of offering our services. Ordinary seamen ignored us and we ignored them.

Over every door there was a long brass plate polished to a state of dazzling brightness and each carried a message in large bold print.

One read "*A place for everything and everything in its place*".

Another proclaimed "*Never put off until tomorrow what you can do today*". Over a small shutter there was a plate with the words "*Nothing for nothing*".

Every time we read one of these, our high hopes and expectations about life on the ocean wave dropped a notch or two. But it was when we read "*Delays are dangerous*" that we made up our minds to disembark.

"Talk about rules and regulations." said Dan Joe.

"Feck the ships!" said Tarrant.

"And feck the sea too!" said Dan Joe.

I had the feeling that my leadership was being called into question. However, I was reluctant to admit defeat. I would entice them to give life at sea one more chance. And soon we were on board another ship. This one looked like and actually *was* a tramp steamer.

Tarrant remarked that *The Beowulf* was a right rusty-looking forsaken-looking devil of a ship.

On board we were confronted by a small foreign-looking fellow who apparently could speak very little English. Needless to say, I did not know at that time that this apparent lack of English is one of the oldest and best-paying tricks known to man. You cannot find fault with them because they "No understand". More than likely, these people who say "I no understand" can speak four or five languages.

"*Whata cana I ado a fora youa?*" he began.

"We would like to take a look at your ship if you have no objection."

"*Plicemen very a welcome, brother my he big pliceman. Karachi, him big one.*" Keeping up this nonsensical chatter he led us all around the ship and finally back to where we began. Well, my friend, we were very far back in the ways of the world. When all failed and he was forced to put out his hand, we thought it was for a farewell handshake. We had never heard of "buck-seech" or "tips" or anything like that. But like a flash he understood the position.

"My *vera gooda frens, youa hava seena nothing ayeta. Followa me!*" And we followed him to where an iron ladder led straight down to the bowels of the ship. To give us courage he led the way. The ladder was none too clean and as we went down it got steadily worse. The lower half of it was thickly coated with oil and coal dust and because the ladder was perpendicular there was no way we could protect our Sunday best. Our up-to-date sports-jackets and seaside pants underwent a complete change of colour, full of oil streaks and tinges and our fancy Christy hats became a write-off in a matter of minutes; our hands and faces were equally black and matched those of our guide, to perfection. On top of all this he insisted on showing us how the furnace was fed by shoveling in more coal, creating an almost complete black out. Were we worth a curse we would have taken hold of him and pushed him head foremost into the furnace, slammed the big iron door shut and quit the ship. I am sure his shipmates would have been glad to be rid of him, and the matter would have ended there without any of the usual misgivings or fuss.

After all this hassle Tarrant was in favour of joining the RAF but Dan Joe put a damper on this saying that the only crowd that would take us in our present condition was the French Foreign Legion. One good outcome from our adventure was now we knew a great deal about ships.

We also learned that the best time to run away from home is early in the morning because if things go wrong, as they usually do, one can return home before night without loss of face. I always had a ready-made excuse – just another visit to my uncle Conor who owned a farm near Mallow. As regards Tarrant, I firmly believe he would be gone from home for six months before his father would start to worry. Old Tarrant was an easy-going man and he knew exactly where the boys were at any given time. The mother asked where Eddy or Billy were. “Doing the fool somewhere instead of being here at home doing something” was the usual answer. And he was usually right.

As regards Dan Joe, his father was dead a long number of years and not in a position to ask questions and his mother was the kind of person who saw no reason why anyone should tell a lie. She was a fine person and if any member of her family was out of home for any length of time she assumed they were helping somebody. She was usually right.

It was a good thing we hadn’t flung our bikes into the harbour as we were tempted to do earlier in the day. We were not in the best of form leaving the city after a truly disastrous day and we were only a few miles out when a pedal left its moorings on Dan Joe’s bike, slowing us down greatly. We were within a few miles of Mallow, or to put it another way, we were about twenty miles from home when the heavens opened. It was now nightfall and the thunder and lightning was out of this world. The rain came down in bucketfulls.

48

A Dreadful Night

We stood for a while under a large sycamore, but things got worse. We could not go on nor could we go back nor could we remain where we were.

Well! Everybody knows "a man has got to do what a man has got to do". And I knew what we had to do if we were to survive this awful night.

"What in hell are we going to do?" said Tarrant.

Once again I had to take the initiative. I pointed to a farmyard a little way down the road. "Perhaps," said I "we could get in there to an out-building for the night. It would be better than standing here in this deluge."

"Right." said Dan Joe. "Come on quick!" I could always depend on Dan Joe.

"I won't go in there without the owner's permission." said Tarrant. As we drew near the farmyard we could see the farmer had built himself a new dwelling house on the opposite side of the road. The old dwelling house was still standing and very hospitable it looked between the claps of thunder and lightning flashes which outlined it in the darkness.

"Right." said I. "I will ask the owner for permission to take shelter. And while I'm up at the house you go down and size up the situation."

I turned towards the new house and went up the short driveway; not that I had the least intention of disturbing the farmer and depriving him of his night's sleep. Were I to risk doing so he might well feel duty bound to see us off the premises and not alone that, he might well take into his head to stand sentry all night in case the three dirty good-for-nothing bums would return and set fire to his place. I could not risk a refusal. It was one of those nights when, as Shakespeare said, "you would not put your worst enemy's dog from the fire".

Taking a look in the back window I saw the farmer and his wife sitting by the fire. I saw no children nor did I encounter the inevitable unavoidable farmyard cattle dog. A dog could have upset our plans. In all probability the wretch was off for the night killing sheep; it being the ideal night for the job, dark as pitch and miserable with not a sinner out. What more could a dog ask for.

After a suitable delay I returned to the road to find my two friends still standing in the rain.

"What did he say?" inquired Tarrant.

"He said to make ourselves at home and we were welcome to the old house."

"A decent man." said Tarrant.

"If he was a decent man," said Dan Joe "he would invite us up to the house. It would serve him right if he found three dead bodies here in the morning."

We went down to the old dwelling house to investigate and found that some Robinson Crusoe had carried out alterations. The end room had a side knocked out and here the trap was heeled up. The next compartment was now a grain store and one could smell the rats and mice. The third compartment was now converted into a stable for two horses, one section was occupied; the other section was vacant and here we decided to make up our beds. In the trap we found a rug and two cushions and a lamp. The two boys saw no harm in lighting the lamp and setting it up in a suitable place. I could not help thinking about what the owner would do if he looked out and saw the old home lit up. Was he the kind of man who believed in ghosts or was he the type of fellow who would murder people in their beds? I alone had to bear this additional undisclosed torment. It is hard to believe but there were times during the night when I felt I could welcome any man who would take us out of our misery with a carefully laid aim. Just one final bang and it would be all over and done with.

We had no such luck. Tarrant insisted he should sleep in the middle because he was afraid of rats. Dan Joe said he would like to be a bit away from the horse.

The more silent we became in our efforts to fall asleep the horse was munching hay and pushing it about in the manger and every once in a while, when the old mare had a big mouthful of well masticated hay full of saliva, she would put her head over the barrier and shake her head up and down, spewing the wet trash over the three of us. As a rule I got the most of it. After the first few swirls of this puke you knew it was going to happen again and again at regular intervals. At times the old mare would stop chewing as if to listen to the rain hammering on the roof. On top of this there was a hen hatching in the manger only a few inches from our heads and all night long she was *cluck-clucking* and turning about, turning her clutch of eggs. Not for a moment did she rest. Listening to this was like having a hole bored into one's brain.

The torture inflicted on us by our nearest neighbours was bad and very bad but it was nothing compared to the neverending bedlam in the grain store.

In spite of the fact that there was plenty of food for all, the army of rats spent the night fighting eating each other and squealing as if they were being torn to pieces or made into pulp.

I thought, "will this night ever end?"

It was raining non-stop. The confounded old mare was munching and spewing and doing other things as well. The hen was letting us know all about the incubation of chickens and the rats behaved very much like the human race. When they had everything they could wish for they still found it necessary to fight over something or over nothing.

At long last the rain stopped. We rose from our beds of suffering and a little before dawn we emerged, each of us, looking worse than Lazarus after his four days in the tomb. It was far worse than the night I spent with the five Savage women.

Somehow we survived and in due course we got home with well prepared excuses. After a day or two things were back to normal. Then Tarrant received a letter from Paddy Boyo inviting him to Romford. Seemingly Tarrant had no regrets. He found a good job with Paddy and worked with him for many years before going to America.

Fifty years came and went before I saw him again and his first words were, "Do you remember the night . . .?" And before he could finish I cut in "Will you ever forget?"

To any young fellow reading this, my earnest advice is, "if you possibly can, avoid tramp steamers and don't believe all the good stories you read in *The Wide World* magazine."

49

WE DRIVE THE CATTLE HOME

For some unknown reason quite a few of us were under the impression we would meet more nice girls at the dances in Mallow than anywhere else on earth.

Every Sunday evening a gang of us would strike out for Mallow town hall, a distance of sixteen miles, disregarding dance halls much nearer home. Perhaps it was a case of the other fellow's grass being always greener or perhaps because so many clubs such as the tennis club or gun clubs from surrounding areas always held their dances there. The fact that there was always a good crowd and a good band such as Pat Callahan's, added to the attractions. In any case, it was always an enjoyable place to be. And with some of us, romance of the right kind was making considerable progress.

One Sunday night a proposition was put to us that changed everything. For the time being, at any rate for some. For others the "walk out" was never forgiven. It happened like this. I saw him standing in the crowd at the end of the hall. He was far too old for dancing and in any case he was a happily married man with a fine farm and everyone knew he had plenty of money. He was never seen at a dance. As a rule, wealthy dairy farmers are not dancing men. He had "a thing" about dairy cattle, pure bred, registered and that kind of caper, ignored by ordinary farmers.

When he caught my eye he put up his finger in much the same way as a fellow would book the next dance with a girl across the hall. I went to speak to him, and his first words were "I have found out where my cows are and I want the help of a few Blueshirts to bring them home."

I knew nothing about his cattle or the seizure that had taken place, which meant he had to tell me the whole story. Seemingly, he was out of home one day and the "bums", as he called them took away eight of his milking cows which were later sold in Cork, all because he failed to pay his annuities. "'Tis not the money I am worried about." said he. "There is a principle involved here, and I will not act the scab. All I want is a few Blueshirts to come with me to Cork and drive home the animals."

"You could not have come at a worse time or to a worse place." said I. "It will be hard to get them away from the women."

"Look." said he. "There is a fiver in it for every man."

I consulted Dan Joe and another friend Ned Healy and after much soul-searching thought we decided we could not let the man down nor could we refuse his offer. We decided to start immediately. The plan as outlined to us was simple. A few miles out the Cork road a van would pick us up. Dolan himself would be in the van. He would show us the cattle and together we would drive them home. All very straightforward and simple.

"How sound is your information?" I asked.

"Sound as a bell." said he. "I have it from the horse's mouth. The "cabbage" that has my cattle out-bid the usual "bum" and then he contacted me, giving me chapter and verse of the whole transaction. You see when rogues fall out honest men get their own back." I said to myself if all goes well we will have a story to tell: how we played a noble part in the Blueshirt movement. And our footprints in the sands of time would be recognised by other Blueshirts.

We were travelling along nicely towards Cork when a van belonging to Cade's Bottling Company pulled in ahead of us. We ran the bikes into a farmyard for safety and in a matter of minutes we were on our way. Dolan sat in front beside the driver. We found room in the back and in what seemed a short time, we were in the city centre. Here we had to take to "shanks mare". The van disappeared around a corner. "Follow me," said Dolan "and don't draw attention to ourselves. We could be made account for our movements."

"As sure as God," said Dan Joe "we will be arrested for mopery."

"From now on let me do the talking," said Dolan and he took over the leadership. We followed him to the outskirts of the city on the northern side and every footfall had its echo. We were glad to reach the open countryside. After tramping about two miles we came to a halt and he pointed out a large farm complex in the distance. "Over there the "bum" lives and all the land from here to the other road is his. All we have to do is identify my cattle."

"You are a hard man." said Healy.

"Here we go," said Dolan as we leaped off the fence. We followed. Unfortunately, we found ourselves in a field of wheat, fully grown but still green and dripping with dew. After about twenty yards we were drenched to the skin and our dancing shoes filled with water. Our clothes from the waist down clung to us like wet wall paper. The next field was another field of tall green wheat. However, there was now no turning back. Dolan went in front, receiving most of the water as we followed in single file. At last we reached a grazing area and we found ourselves in middle of a large herd of dairy cattle.

"There is one of them," shouted Dolan. "And here is another — Dromdowney Princess herself." He went over and placed his hand on her back saying "I had your mother and your grandmother and here you are now, my Dromdowney Princess."

"We will take you home, Kathleen," said Dan Joe by way of a joke to lessen the tension.

Dolan now disclosed more details of his well thought-out plan. "Now that we know the facts . . . we will go to the house and let him know we are taking the cattle. I see no reason why I should steal my own cattle."

Obedient to the last, we went with him to the house. It was a very fine house which I could describe down to the last detail but I will refrain from doing so lest I embarrass the present owner. There was a large gravelled area in front of the main door, which was painted green. On it was one of those old-time knockers, which delivered hammer blows which would, as the man said, "wake the dead".

Dolan gave it several good thumps but there was no reply.

"We will take a walk around the yard," said Dolan. "No doubt the "bum" is still in bed."

From what we saw of the farmyard we concluded he was in the liquid milk business, delivering milk to the city every morning. And the curious thing was, Dolan was also in the liquid milk business delivering milk to Mallow town. Dairy cows were of the utmost importance to both of them. At this stage cigarettes were getting scarce and tension was mounting. Back once more at the front door we saw about half a dozen spent cartridges strewn about. "He is letting us know our lives are in danger," said Dan Joe.

Dolan gave the door another thump; before he had time to give it another the door opened and we were confronted by a tall stern-looking man, holding a double barrel gun in the ready-to-fire position.

"State your damn business around my house in the middle of the night," said he. "Quickly, before I level the four of you."

"Easy now, easy now," said Dolan. "One mistake is bad enough. Don't make a worse mistake. I have arrangements with a man from *The Paper*." Dolan looked at his big pocket watch. "He should be here any minute now and I can tell you he will have a fine story for the people of Cork city. What will the people of Cork think when they find out they are drinking the milk of seized cattle? I will be calling for a boycott of all milk supplied from this farm if my cattle are not handed over nicely and quietly."

We could see an immediate change of attitude. The gun was put aside. Dolan had hit him where he was most vulnerable.

"Look here," said he. "Where would your cattle be now if I had not bid for them. They would be hanging from hooks in some factory. Farmers are a pack of fools allowing one man the privilege of buying up all seized cattle without opposition."

"I am saying no more," said Dolan. "I am here for my cattle."

One could see when it came to an argument Dolan was a genius. Just then two workmen arrived and our man went to speak with them.

Dan Joe asked, "What do you think they are up to now?"

When the so-called "bum" returned he told Dolan "You can have your cattle. The lads will help you get them to the road. I want no trouble but I will never understand what profit there is in this campaign. The Government is the Government and farmers should encourage men like myself to bid against the one or two bums who have the benefit and pleasure of having the place to themselves.

"I did not come here to discuss politics. I know if you had not bought my cows, someone else would. And if I found my cattle on the hook, the "bum" would be in his grave by now. You can say to yourself you saved a lot of lives but you are not getting your money back."

"I don't want my money back. All I want is no publicity."

Dolan indicated he wished us to follow the cattle to the road with the other two men and when I looked back I saw them shaking hands. I said to myself "the worst is over." How foolish can one be.

Twenty five miles is one hell of a long tramp after cattle. Not a very pleasant prospect after a sleepless night and rough morning – and not a fag between us.

It is only the heavy smoker attempting to break the habit who can, in some small measure, understand the misery, the longing, the privation and the feeling of destitution that comes over the smoker. And I can tell you from bitter experience there is no worse occupation in the world than driving cattle along the road without a smoke to lessen the hunger and thirst or break the pedestrian routine of step after step in wet clothes, wet shoes and socks; plus the possibility and probability that the soles of our dancing shoes would depart from the body before journey's end.

Deprived and dehydrated, we thought we saw a village in the distance. It turned out to be real. It was the village of Carrignavar. The young man Michael Patrick Lynch, who was shot dead at a sale of seized cattle a few weeks previous to this, was from this area and this added to our melancholy feelings.

The hope of getting some cigarettes in the village kept us going. Alas! Carrignavar was no different to other villages in rural Ireland. At six am not a soul, man woman or child were to be seen and putting two and two together we knew it would be close to midday before any shop or pub would be open. Did we, after all this hardship, have to pass through this village as if it did not exist? It was not an optical illusion. Yet as far as we were concerned it proved to be a mirage. Once again, Dolan solved the problem. He was indeed a man capable of taking charge under trying circumstances. "One of you remain here until the first shop opens," said he. And I volunteered to remain behind. He handed me a ten shilling note saying "Get ten packets of twenty and catch up with us as quickly as possible. We will be on ahead."

I walked around looking for some sign of life and as I went past the garda station I saw a bare electric bulb glowing even now in full day light. "To hell with it," I said to myself. "We have committed no crime. I will go in and find out the lay of the land."

In what they are pleased to call the day-room there was a lone guard with one foot on a chair polishing his boot. "Good morning," said he. "What can we do for you?" He must have noticed my distressed condition. Perhaps he thought I was handing myself up or reporting some serious crime. One could detect eagerness in his voice.

"Will it be long before the shops open? I want a few fags."

"You are in luck. I am on my way out to get some myself. Night duty and card playing gives rise to a lot of smoke."

When he was properly dressed he said "Come along."

A few minutes later we were outside a pub. He looked up and down the empty street and taking a coin from his pocket tapped out a series of taps which I took for granted was a secret code used by policemen to warn friendly publicans. I found out a few years later it was nothing more than the plain old SOS . . . SOS . . . SOS.

We were admitted without delay. He asked for "twenty Players" and I asked for "ten twenties" as carelessly as possible, as if that was my normal quota for the day.

"Will you have a drink?" said the guard.

"Ah, sure I might as well," said I and I at death's door in the want of it.

"I hope you people don't have too much trouble with the cattle."

"Yerra, cattle are no trouble early in the morning." said I, as non-committal as possible, knowing that in all probability he had observed our progress through the village.

"It might surprise you to hear we had a phone call this morning from a farmer telling us if we saw any cattle being moved under suspicious circumstances not to worry as the whole thing was above board. A bit of a mix-up he said, but now the matter was settled."

"Mix-up is right," I said. "You know, one farmer will never allow another farmer get the better of him." I knew the guard had the full story and I was surprised to find out just how much the man who bought the seized cattle feared bad publicity.

The guard looked at his watch saying "'Tis honest bed time for a man who was up all night." We went out. He was on his way to bed. I had to catch up with the others.

My arrival with plenty of smokes gave a great lift to morale. We now moved on quickly for a few hours. Dolan falling further and further behind complaining that his "bastarding ankles" were red from his "bastarding boots." Healy was also complaining about how his toes were in shreds from trying to walk in his fancy pointed shoes – a type of shoe commonly called winkle-pickers. Dan Joe said his "tabs" were in a bad state and "the fiver" was the hardest earned money he ever got in his life. In short we were all fairly crippled . . .

"The spirit is willing but the flesh is weak". Whoever said that must have walked a long way. Dolan was a good talker but a bad walker. He was now a long way behind, making great efforts to keep us in sight. Finally, we found ourselves much closer to Mallow and suddenly our luck changed.

We saw a nine or ten year old boy sitting on a gate and he seemed to take an interest in us by hopping off the gate and trotting along beside us. He was not handicapped by shoes or boots and hopefully he would never know how lucky he was. There were places where he might have to pick his steps but every single step was not painful as was the case with us. Just then I saw the house where we had put our bikes.

"Do you know who lives in that house?" I asked the boy.

"It is my house," he replied with a broad smile.

"Did you find three bicycles in the yard this morning?"

"Yes. And my father said the owners would come for them." He was still laughing and smiling. He seemed quite happy and I said to myself if we were all happy and in high spirits I would not have noticed.

"Now," said I "will you run down home and tell your mother that her cousins are coming down the road and that they would drop in for a cup of tea."

"Honest?" – The almost forgotten boyish question.

"Honest." I replied.

How we envied that boy as he ran down the road darting in and out of the grass margin making the journey as long as possible like a butterfly, and yet not delaying.

"What are you up to now?" Healy inquired.

"Never mind," said I. "If I am offered tea I will not refuse."

"Nor will I," said Dan Joe.

As we drew near the house the boy and his mother came out and standing before the cows they turned them into the backyard. The woman said "They will be fine there! Come in. The tea is ready."

"Your cousin will be here in a minute," said I and I pointed towards Dolan who was making poor enough progress towards us.

She told her son to remain on the road and "make sure the man comes in. The cup of tea will do him good after the road."

When we finished the meal, Dolan included, the woman said, "I should be ashamed of myself but I just can't make out which cousins I have." Before things went to the bad I thought it best to make a proper confession explaining as best I could the reasons for our duplicity. Then Dolan butted in. "Look Missus, don't ever again pay any attention to any cock and bull story like you were told this morning. My name is Michael Dolan of Dromdowney and I will pay you well for your trouble and generosity today. We were on the point of collapse when you opened your door to us."

"Did I hear you say Michael Dolan?"

"Indeed you did. That's my name."

"Well in that case we are related after all. My sister is married to a cousin of yours in Glens Falls, New York."

Just then a lorry drove into the yard. Seemingly her husband had a lorry for hire and when he came in there was a great laugh about the whole thing.

"I am a de Valera man myself." said the husband. "But that will not stop me running them cattle of yours home this evening. It will only take half an hour and it will save you the trouble of driving them through the town."

"Good man," said Dolan. "Blood is thicker than water."

The three of us surely said a genuine mental "Thanks be to God." On our way through the town we put our bikes around the corner and entered Tarrant's Pub where an apology would be in order for our abrupt departure from the dance the night before if the right lady was behind the bar. She treated us as she would treat total strangers. The man who said that women were unpredictable was not too far wrong.

Sadly we mounted our bikes for the last lap of our journey. We spent some time to fine-tune our excuses.

God alone knows what parents have to put up with. Not knowing half of what is going on is a great help to them.

50

The Annual Shoot

From early morning until late afternoon continuous gunfire could be heard and this went on for three whole days, during which all farm work on the estate was suspended.

It was the annual shoot on the Leader Estate, an event eagerly looked forward to by all members of the staff both indoor and outdoor, male and female.

There would be extra money in circulation by way of tips and rewards. The senior members of the outdoor staff would act as bag carriers for their "own" gentlemen, year after year. And the younger workers would act as beaters, rousing the game birds and turning them towards the line-of-fire.

This annual shoot was duplicated in almost all the big estates throughout the country and it was always a great get-together for that section of the community usually referred to as the gentry. Local farmers would remark on all the commotion with a very dismissive "The Lord knows 'tis busy they are. Is it any wonder the half of them are going broke".

I remember the specially built little stacks of corn deep in the woods put there in the harvest time so that no bird, big or small, would be short of food during the long harsh months of winter. The stacks were built in such a manner that the birds had more or less to earn their own living as they scratched and clawed to get at the hidden grain.

The only bit of excitement in Micky Sheehan's life was the annual shoot and his gentleman was the Mac Gillycuddy of the Reeks. Micky shortened this rather long title to "the Maclecuddy, the decentest man of them all". Every day he would give him the finishing of the second bottle of brandy.

The curious thing was the same was said about Lord Fermoy, the Knight of Glyn, Lord Castleross, Viscount De Vesci, the O'Mahoney, Brigadier JOE Vandeleur, (Joe to his friends) and his cousin GAM, Major John L. Bowen, our neighbour Major Grehan and a host of others.

During the Second World War the shoot was a lacklustre affair as most of those involved rejoined the ranks, many returning to their old regiments. But when the war ended in victory, as they all knew it would, it was back again to business as usual. There might well be over a hundred guests at the great house during the shoot. Many of the men had their wives and families with them and this added to the gaiety, and the house would be a hive of industry with extra staff employed.

After every shoot, when all the entertainment was over, it always took two men two whole days to dig a hole in the woods big enough to bury the empty bottles. May God be with the immortal days and nights, so soon to become a thing of the past. It was hard to foresee that within a few short years the great house would be demolished, the estate broken up and the beautiful gardens utterly destroyed, the pink stone pavements torn up, ponds filled up with rubbish, stone fountains smashed, tier after tier of flowering shrubs yanked out and burned. Now nature's robe of green covers all.

Let us return to memory lane and the great days of old.

When the rigours of the day were past, the workmen would go home, wash and shave, and collect at The Ford for a few drinks.

Several of the gentlemen would make a point of attending so as to attend to the helpers and beaters and the only distinction between them was the privilege allowed the gentlemen of . . . paying for all!

Soon all would be merry and bright, former days recalled, and battles of the Great War fought all over again.

Jim Flur Sullivan was head gamekeeper at Leader's. He was known and liked by all the gentry. He served with the Munster Fusileers in Mespotamia (The Mespot) and other outlandish places. But he was generally more fluent when recalling the Hindenberg and the Retreat from Mons. He was a fine singer and he was always called upon. "Give us a verse, Jim" from one was never enough. Only when everyone shouted "Go on, Jim. Give us a verse!" would he oblige. Tonight he was in great form and well oiled. It was a never to be forgotten experience to hear Jim deliver:

"*And I hear the shades tumultuous*
Of the ancient Irish bards
Crying! Sláinte! Mick O'Leary
Of King George's Irish Guards"

Some nights Jim would monopolize the conversation sticking rigidly to "The Mespot" or the "Retreat from Mons". Tonight Lord Castleross was determined to throw Jim off the beaten track.

"Tell me James. Did you ever serve in Afghanistan?"

"No. I am afraid not."

"Jalalabad?"

"Never heard of it." admitted Jim. And Major Bowen cut in "Preshawar?" or "Kabul?"

"No." said Jim. "I did not soldier in any of them places. But I did soldier in a place none of you gentlemen ever heard of and if you don't believe me, tomorrow morning Captain Leader will confirm that I soldiered many a hot day around a place called *Tobar-a-Cuirc*.

The gentry went into close session trying to figure out where this place *Tobar-a-Cuirc* was. All the locals were well aware of its location. It was a small well, from which a couple of families drew their water supply, a few hundred yards from The Ford.

It was obvious the gentry had no knowledge of the *cúpla focal* and

Jim became the hero of the hour. He, and he alone, had borne the burden and the heat of the day while soldiering in that far flung corner of the empire, that lonely outpost of civilisation known to so few as *Tobar-a-Cuirc*.

By degrees the conversation veered around to the fuzzy-wuzzy and his 'ome in the Sudan and here the Gentry found themselves on much firmer ground.

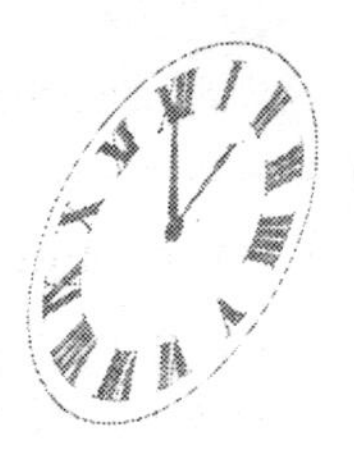

51

THE KING'S FAREWELL

How it became known as "a wireless" will for ever remain a mystery. It was in fact the greatest tangle of wires imaginable. Very few now remember what "a wireless" looked like and perhaps a short description would not be out of place.

Anyone thinking of getting in "the wireless" should have a large table in readiness inside a window because it was much easier to make a hole in the lower part of the window frame than making a hole in the wall. This hole was for the earth wire. There was also a wire from the set connecting it to the aerial. The aerial being another wire strung between two poles at a considerable height from the ground and a reasonable distance from the house. The hole for this connecting wire was made in the top part of the window frame thus avoiding making a hole through the wall, an operation which might rock the whole house to its very foundation.

We are taking it for granted that agreement has been reached as to the exact position of the outside poles required to support the aerial. Some cowboy operators let it be known that an inch one way or the other would make a difference in the "reception". These fellows assumed a status far above the humble water-diviner. They could see the air waves and distinguish between the long and the short waves. The ordinary layman was delighted there were so many gifted men around the country.

The set itself was not very large. One man could move it about easily before it was connected up. When connected up, two wires led to what was called "the wet battery" and two more led to the "dry battery" and another two wires led to what they called "the grid battery". Here again the ordinary lay-man was sorely puzzled. There were wires that were live and wires that were not and to cap it all, there were some wires that were positive and others that were negative. Is it any wonder Ned-the-Leg described the whole thing in the following terms? "The boxeen itself is just a fakeleorum. 'Tis the poles that count". Ned, having built up a name for himself putting up poles for papal flags during the run up to the Eucharistic Congress, now took on the responsibility of erecting "wireless" poles, a job that had to be done with unerring accuracy to intercept the long and the short waves. Atmospherics had also to be taken into account. Ned-the-Leg considered all these important points publicly. But privately, the most important thing was to find a place where it would be easy to dig.

We were lucky in our area because there was one man who understood all about electricity and broadcasting. His name was Charlie Daly and people depended on him for help and advice. He became involved in the radio business in the early days of the BBC. Years before radio became popular, he had built his own receiving set.

He did his best to dispel all traces of mystery and superstition from radio and broadcasting, which was a difficult task in those days. Let me tell you about the first "wireless" he installed.

Old Patrick O'Callaghan, farmer and shopkeeper, a man who travelled widely in his young days and who now spent much of his time reading, decided to take the plunge and get in the "wireless".

There was a proper "official opening" at Patrick's the night of the switch on. People came from far and near and the seating arrangements proved to be totally inadequate. Patrick himself had to surrender his chair to an old lady who came to see what all the talk was about.

Local dignitaries such as managers and sub-managers of local creameries, principal teachers, county councillors and very large farmers were shown into the "throne room" where they sat in silence looking at the box with awe and reverence as if it were the black stone in the mosque at Mecca. There was a small hallway leading from the shop to the "throne room" and this was filled with lesser dignitaries such as the Chairman of the GAA club, the local members of the creamery committee and an auctioneer who did little business. These all more or less stood in line and were well-behaved as befitted the great occasion.

The vast majority stood around the shop, the lucky ones finding seats on the counter. Ned-the-Leg, who was responsible for erecting the two outside poles, was duly honoured by being given a seat on a barrel of pigs' heads.

Patrick was extra careful that no young gurrier would get near the set and perhaps try his hand at turning it on. Patrick was extremely careful of this sensitive apparatus and Charlie Daly had to come every night for three weeks to switch it on and return before midnight to switch it off.

Without knowing it at the time this was a good thing for Charlie because after viewing the switch-on and switch-off, for three weeks, most of his potential customers were more or less trained operators. Had this not happened, he would have had to leave home every evening going from house to house switching on, and returning a few hours later switching off.

He did his best to take the mystery and ambivalence out of radio and television. He was a man ahead of his time;

"taking him for all in all, we shall not look upon his like again".

We all know the old adage!

"Be not the first on whom the new is tried. Be not the last to lay the old aside!"

My father would have fitted comfortably into every category and we did not have very long to wait for our own "wireless". By this time there were few townlands that did not have at least one "wireless" and the number of people collecting around the various fires to hear "the news" had greatly declined. A few old timers would collect at our place if there was the least hint of something important coming up.

The abdication of King Edward VIII gave rise to a lot of talk and speculation. Pad Jack or Dick Dundon or indeed Big Mick, who were far from romantic, believed love stories had little to do with life as far as they were concerned. Nevertheless, as the fateful hour of the King's speech drew nigh they moved their chairs nearer the "wireless" all claiming to be a little bit deaf in one ear or the other. In complete silence they listened to every word until the king came to that part of his speech when he said "I can no longer carry this great burden without the help and support of the woman I love."

"Heavenly God!" said Dundon. "One would think he owed money to the bank!"

"'Tis fine for him." said Big Mick. "What would he do if he had all his hay down in bad weather?"

"A foolish man." said Pad Jack. "Imagine giving up a good job for the sake of a woman."

They all lit their pipes to consider more fully the ups and downs of the abdication.

52

THE FINAL SKIRMISH

The "no free speech for traitors" campaign was the cause of many skirmishes in towns all over the country. There were occasions when the principal speakers failed to make their appearance, knowing that if they did their lives were in danger, especially where the Blueshirts were small in numbers.

This gave rise to the practice of lorry loads of Blueshirts travelling long distances to uphold the right of free speech and the defence of democracy. Needless to say, this was at their own expense, risk and peril.

On our way to some distant town we would be loudly cheered in some villages while in others we would be jeered at, while broken bottles and bricks rained down around us.

Whenever the IRA was successful in breaking up a public meeting the event was always celebrated by the writing of yet another pathetic patriotic verse such as the following:

"The King's assets –
Mulcahy's men
They marched it to
Kilmallock
But they didn't come again."

To tear the blue shirt off a lone man was considered a great day's work. The shirt would then be torn into shred and burned and the owner given a few good kicks for the road home. This was a time when it was foolish to be too audacious. To add to the political mix, something went wrong at GHQ and the organisation was split; one half supporting General O'Duffy and the other half supporting Commandant Cronin. This split caper is regarded as normal practice in every political organisation in Ireland. The rift between O'Duffy and Cronin made little difference to the average member. Some went one way, some the other way, but there were no hard feelings.

One Sunday morning the people in our area saw something very strange. They saw lorry loads of Blueshirts going towards Millstreet on their way to Macroom to commemorate someone or something. And they saw lorry loads of Blueshirts going in the opposite direction towards Mallow or further to commemorate something or somebody else. As the lorries passed each other there was great cheering and waving of Blueshirt flags. Whatever was wrong at HQ the men on the ground, sorry, the men on the lorries were far from being in any way downhearted.

A few of us rigged out in our blue shirts took up our position on the roadside ready to jump on the first lorry that came to a halt, be it going east or west. It made no difference to us. And it so happened we were taken on board a lorry going to Carrignavar via Mallow, to commemorate the shooting dead of Michael Patrick Lynch in a sales-yard in Cork exactly one year before at a sale of seized cattle.

We were packed tight and the only thing we could do was sing along with the others: "Pack up your troubles" followed by "We're here because we're here". And we had a new version composed by Con Fitzpatrick which surprised them all. Soon they all joined in singing with great gusto "*Chess pieces are, chess pieces are, chess pieces are, chess pieces are*".

In a short time we found ourselves going through Mallow and for some reason or another Mallow was regarded by many Blueshirts "as a right Bolshoi town full of IRA men".

We were in the last lorry and the lorries ahead of us were travelling at little more than walking pace watching out for an attack. Nothing happened until we were just clear of the town; five or six hags started yelling abuse and one of them turned her back to the lorries. Then bending down she lifted up her clothes exposing to everybody her bare backside. She began to beat her bottom with her free hand. I had never heard of anything like this but it must have been a terrible insult because three men leaped from the lorry ahead of us and while I never approved of violence towards women, I must say she got plenty of what she deserved. Hopefully she would keep her posterior under cover in future.

Now that we had disturbed the hornet's nest we would pay the price on our return journey. Friends of *Cuman na mBan* and the IRA would open a few Blueshirt heads, as a reprisal for our attempt at putting some manners and a little decorum on one of their supporters.

We reached our destination without any further trouble and in the graveyard at Dunbuileague we heard some lively speeches. We were told of the many graves up and down the country. Every graveyard had its quota of young men killed in the civil war for which de Valera was responsible. "But," said one speaker "search where you will, turn over every stone in every Irish graveyard, not once will you find the name de Valera". It soon became clear that this speaker had a very poor opinion of the leader of Fianna Fáil.

After the meeting we spent some time in a pub a few miles down the road. Obviously, it was a "Blueshirt pub" as our Blueshirt songs met with the approval of the landlord. Needless to say, he had no idea that a large quantity of his "empties" were being smuggled aboard the lorries so that we could retaliate if we were attacked in Mallow on our way home.

All good times come to an end and soon we were on the road again. After travelling a few miles the convoy came to a sudden stop just opposite a country forge. In a matter of minutes men were swarming all over the place looking for short iron bars and all sorts of things that could be used in self-defence.

An old Irish Guardsman, by the name of Jack Sheehan who had survived many battles, seemed very poorly protected. All he had was a neat walking cane. He seemed to enjoy the scramble for protective weapons.

"Is this all you have got?" I asked pointing to the walking-cane. He laughed and pointing towards some young men much better equipped, he retorted "If things go wrong this evening the air will be full of the grey hen's tail."

On the road once more all went well until we were within a couple of miles from Mallow and here a line of guards had the road blocked. Our leaders were called up and advised to go around by the beet factory and avoid trouble in the town. While our officers hesitated, shouts could be heard from down the line "No surrender to the bloody IRA", "We have a perfect right to go into town." And remarks were made about the "audacity" of the guards.

In the end a compromise was reached. The lorries would go via the beet factory and those who insisted on marching through the town were free to do so. It was arranged that the lorries would pick us up again at the railway arch at the western end of town after their detour.

Orders rang out "Get in line", "Form fours", "Left turn"; a new language to most of us. Instructors and trained soldiers seemed to be everywhere. They went up and down the line warning everybody "Don't break ranks", "Don't become isolated."

Satisfied at last that we were all properly briefed, the order rang out "By the right, quick march". This was it and we marched into town; eighty percent of us out of step without knowing it. We were insulted from the sidewalks and called – *traitors*, but our instructions were to keep in line and ignore the provocation. In good orderly ranks we were almost at the town hall before any missiles were thrown and these came mostly from upstairs windows. A man directly in front of me was hit by a heavy green bottle, a type of bottle seldom seen these days. The man stumbled, but before straightening himself he picked up the bottle, which was still intact, promising to give "some hure the contents of it". And still we went on and on. We were almost clear of the town proper before we had our first and only casualty. It happened like this. There was a house a few yards in off the road. Quietly a man carrying a pail of liquid, which definitely came from no tap or well, flung the contents of the pail over the Blueshirts nearest to him and then darted for the safety of the house. But there was already a man on his heels and the culprit was not able to fully close the door. However, help was at hand. The Blueshirt had his arm and baton trapped tightly and had there been no help available from outside he might well have had his arm made into strawberry jam by his own baton. It took half a dozen of us to force the door sufficiently to secure the release of the man's arm.

The lorries were waiting for us at the railway arch and we stood around for a while going over the day's events and getting rid of our extra "ammo" such as bottles and bars, by taking aim at a huge advertisement for some kind of sauce. The Chef with his white coat and tall white hat got a good dressing.

Then the lorries, which had gone in the opposite direction in the morning, arrived. They also had a badly wounded man, hit by a broken bottle as they drove out of Millstreet. Common sense prevailed. They decided to make the detour and avoid the town. They drove away shouting "Up Cronin" and we responded shouting "Up Duffy". What a day!

53

THE SPANISH CIVIL WAR

Before the outbreak of the Spanish Civil War one could be forgiven for thinking all the wars were over. The Irish had stopped fighting the ancient enemy and, for all practical purposes, amongst themselves; the few childish skirmishes now taking place were of little account and provoked no great excitement.

Life down on the farm became dull. The never-ending unsuitable weather, bad crops, poor prices and unemployment were for ever the topic of conversation. I found it difficult to work up an interest in these matters having long ago made up my mind, like the present-day holiday maker, to do anything to get away from it all. There was an unfair fight going on in Abyssinia between Mussolini and Haile Selassi. And I remember how one Italian bomber pilot described a bombing raid on some poor African village. "It opened up," said he "like a flowering rose." Little did I think then that one day I would meet the Emperor Haile Selassi. But that is another story.

The war in Spain was a different matter. Spain became the ideological battleground of Europe. Thousands of volunteers flocked to Spain from many different countries and for many different reasons. Large contingencies arrived from Russia to support the communists and this gave Hitler and Mussolini the excuse to send men and aircraft to General Franco; fascist confronting bolshoi, a very dangerous international situation. However, your average Irishman would consider a fall in the price of pigs as worse than the outcome of any war as far away as Europe.

The Roman Catholic clergy availed of every opportunity to support Franco on the grounds that there was no religious freedom in Russia and public opinion in the Irish Free State came down firmly on the side of General Franco and on the crest of this wave of support for Franco our own General O'Duffy announced that he was forming an Irish Brigade who would fight for freedom of worship, christianity and democracy in the battlefields of Spain. Thousands of young Blueshirts answered the call and within weeks a large contingent sailed out from Galway. Already quite a number of IRA men had sailed out to join the international brigade to fight for communism. Public opinion was very much opposed to this and their numbers were small in comparison. One of the nice things about this set-up was the prospect of meeting these IRA men face to face and fully armed across "no man's land". I could not afford to miss this opportunity of seeing what real war was like. It seemed to me, now was the time to separate the men from the boys. The fact that I might be killed or lose an arm or a leg never entered my head. Many young men feel like that and never count the cost. Admittedly there are others who do. These are far more cautious as we shall see.

There was this man in Dublin who was the principal organiser and anyone wishing to join O'Duffy's Brigade was advised to write to him submitting personal details such as age, previous army training etc. I sat down and wrote him a letter and it must have been a very impressive document because within a few days I received a letter containing instructions on how to form my own section. I should get as many as possible, but five would be an acceptable number. Pay would commence on the day of embarkation, and there was a hint it would be unwise to carry large sums of Irish money. To me this seemed straightforward enough and I set about getting my men together, keeping in mind the strict warning not to reveal the post of embarkation or the date of departure. This was easy because these matters were kept secret and I was informed I would receive ample notification of how, where and when. All I had to do was find five or six young men of military age with a love of adventure or a lust for foreign travel. I would point out to them the benefit of a free trip to Spain with the opportunity of participating in real war and helping to polish off the danger of communism once and for all. I let them know there would be no rushing home to Mom who would put them to bed and dry their clothes and promise not to wake them until the bacon and cabbage was on the table. I supplied no misinformation, letting them know from the start that the war in Spain would not be a matter of getting on your bike and cycling around from one safe house to another like Michael Collins. In real war you don't "go on the run," you stand your ground and if you are fatally wounded "you roll to your rifle and blow out your brains and go to your God like a soldier."

I had no difficulty finding five volunteers. They all seemed eager to be off. Every one of them warned me to let them know as soon as possible and "the sooner the better". I will not reveal the names of the men concerned. Four of them died from natural causes and the fifth would probably deny ever being such a fool.

Day after day we waited and then out of the blue arrived detailed instructions.

"All volunteers must be ready and waiting under cover at the Post Office at 8.00 pm on the evening of January 6, 1937.

Regarding transport, a car will stop at the Post Office. The driver will go through the motions of putting water in the engine. Leave cover immediately and get in the car. Ask no question."

At this time the sixth of January was a very important Church Holyday, almost as important as Christmas. It was fondly called the women's Christmas and every effort would be made to make it a happy occasion for mothers and maiden aunts. The usual big supper would be laid on, a sort of an endless affair with wine and sweet cake and novelties, making it more difficult for poor young Johnny to break away from the family circle and head off into the unknown. Generals and military men are heartless and no allowance is ever made for

Christmas parties or family celebrations. When you join the army you can forget Santa.

I set out to round up my volunteers. In other words, I would let them know the count down was ended. ***Zero hour 8.00 pm***.

I went to volunteer number one –

"Well feck him." said he. "My uncle is coming home from America next week and he wants to take me out to his ranch near Lakeview which is so big no one knows the boundary. There would be holy war if I was not here. Feck him anyway."

I went to volunteer number two –

"Talk about misfortune." said he. "I have a bloody carbuncle under my arm and another one coming and the doctor said to avoid sea water at all costs because one can get a carbuncle in the brain by coming in contact with sea water. Talk about bad luck."

I went to volunteer number three –

"Great God, wait till I tell you. I gave a hint to the oul lad about going to the war in Spain and Jaysus if he didn't give himself a stroke giving out about the Pope and Duffy and Franco. Feckers who would sweep away an only son. He is in the bed and can't move a hand or a leg. 'Tis fine for the rest of ye. I must wait for the funeral."

I went to volunteer number four –

"Do you mean to say you have not heard about my predicament? The wan is in the family way and the priest tells me I am the father. I told him there were more fathers than one and that I was not one of them and sez I she won't get the better of 'em, sez I. I can't feck off to Spain now. I must stay and stand my ground."

Morale was low as I made my way to the home of volunteer number five –

I consoled myself by thinking all available excuses were used up.

"Merciful God." said number five. "One trouble never comes alone. I am ate with an attack of bloody piles and bummed up the way I am I'd be of little help to Franco."

The complete failure of all my plans left me speechless. All I could say was one word, "unbelievable".

"If you don't believe me I will show you. Do you want to take a look."

I had never heard of piles and I had no idea of where I should look and to cover up my ignorance I said "I believe you."

He is the only one of the faithless volunteers still alive. Apparently, he could have had a worse complaint.

Now drawing very close to my four score years I have this to say. 'Never in a long life with its many ups and downs did I ever break a promise. Of course, I would be there at the appointed time and place – alone and pleased the cowards were remaining where they belonged close to Dad-da and Mom-ma.'

Knowing that the faithless five would remain silent for a long time was some consolation. Nevertheless having failed to find one single man ready to fight for Franco or follow Duffy to Spain was a "damn tough bullet to chew".

It was now 2.00 pm in the afternoon of D Day and who did I see cycling towards me but my old friend Janie Dunne. Why I overlooked him in the first place I will never know.

"Well, Janie." said I. "How are things?"

"Never worse. The moment I have a few quid collected I'm getting out of this cursed country."

"Janie." said I. "I can get you out of this country tonight, free of charge, provided you are willing to fight for General Franco in Spain for a week or two or until we turn the tide in his favour."

"Will we be paid and given pensions?"

"Automatically," said I. "Automatically."

"I always wanted to go to Australia," said Janie. "Is Australia far from Spain?"

"Just like Cork and Kerry. You can step across from one to the other." I remembered from our school days geography was not one of his favourite subjects.

"In that case," said he. "I'm your man."

I warned him to be at the Post Office at eight o'clock.

During the remainder of the evening at home I behaved as normal, doing little things like bringing in coal and firewood and watching for an opportunity to smuggle out a nice leather "grip" or "doctor's bag" which Aunt Kate brought from America. It was a gift from Howard Bush. However, the Bush family were not as famous then as they are now. But that is beside the point. I put some nice cake and some bread and some lemonade in the bag to take the empty look out of it. And when the time was right I stole away under cover of darkness. Even at this early stage of the adventure having a hold of this "doctor's bag" gave me some comfort. I suppose a sort of child's bottle syndrome. To make matters worse, physically, it was a typical January night, cold, stormy and wet. But from another point of view this bad weather served to keep most people indoors and we would not be under observation as we made our getaway.

I looked in the window of the Post Office. It was five minutes to eight by the big wall wagger. There was no trace of Janie.

Like it or not time will come and pass over the death of nations pitiless and unconcerned – in the same way, pitilessly it came to eight o'clock. I had taken shelter in the wood across the road from the Post Office; at the same time keeping everything under observation, hoping against hope that Janie would arrive. A minute later a car came to a halt and a man got out and opened the bonnet. From my position, in the shade, I saw him take a white jug from the car. There was no need for any further delay. This was it.

Picking up my "doctor's bag" I went towards him. "I am afraid," said I "I will be your only passenger."

"We allow for all that," said he. "We will have a full load before we reach our destination."

We were just about to drive away when I spotted a bicycle light coming around the Fairfield turn. "Wait a minute," said I. "This could be Janie." And it was Janie. I should have remembered that Janie was always late for everything.

He jumped off his bike in the middle of the road. "Don't leave it there." ordered the driver. Janie took hold of the bike and swinging it round and round like a hammer thrower he sent the bike crashing into the wood saying "there won't be much trace of that when we return."

'Nine hundred and ninety-nine can't bide
The shame, the mocking, and the laughter
But the thousandth man will stand by your side
To the gallows - foot - and after!'

To me just then Janie Dunne was the thousandth man, a man without piles, boils, or carbuncles, a man without excuses.

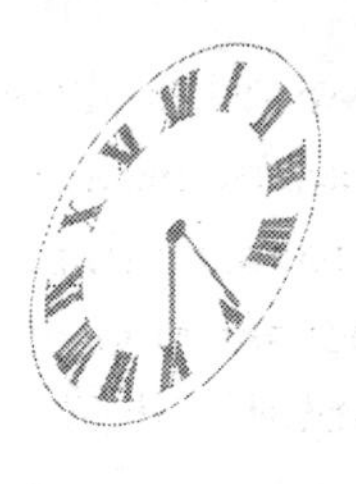

54

On Our Way

A few miles west of Mallow the car slowed down and we came to a halt in front of ornamental gates with a cut-stone lion rampant on each pier. A man came out of the shadows and joined us in the back. Not a word was spoken. A few minutes later we picked up another man near the entrance to Mallow Castle. At last the driver made up his mind to give us a little information.

"The port of embarkation is in Waterford. So we have quite a long run. The boat is not due in for several hours. We will be there in ample time, don't worry."

The man who joined us at Mallow Castle was, in our view, far too old for war. But looking at it another way he did not have much to lose. He would be dying shortly in any case from old age.

He was a hard man to describe. He carried a bag with a strap over his shoulder. He wore boots. He was well-dressed and spoke as only well-educated men can speak.

"We'd better get to know each other," said he. "My name is Fitzpatrick and my reason for being on this trip is simple. I had a shipload of fruit from south America torpedoed off the Azores. I will be demanding compensation from the new Spanish Government whenever things return to normal."

Then the other fellow spoke. "My name is O'Leary – O'Leary, the wild man, they call me. I am sick and tired of pulling beet, standing in cold water up to my knees because the floods came out and covered all the beet. And to make things worse, we had to load the cursed beet into small boats and float it down the river to a strand; after unloading it on the strand it had to be loaded again into carts and taken to the road and unloaded again and when we had sufficient beet out on the road we then had to fork it into lorries. O'Leary, the wild man, is finished with beet-forks and beet-knives. Give me a machine-gun and by God, Franco will win the war."

"How we will cope with war conditions is problematical." said Fitzpatrick.

Janie spoke next. "My name is Dunne from Dromskehey and people are always mixing me up with Janie Dundon from Dromina. I'm the only Dunne and there is a big difference between Dunne and Dundon."

"'Tis bad to be done once, but being done twice is terrible," said O'Leary. "But why are you coming to the war?"

"Because I have no intention of spending the rest of my life feeding pigs and being told what to do. I want a war pension."

"A truly philosophical view of war and the outcome of war," said Fitzpatrick.

I now felt duty bound to at least give my newly found friends my name and address.

"Are you in any way related to James Forrest of Lombardstown?" inquired Fitzpatrick.

"He is my uncle."

"My God," exclaimed Fitzpatrick. "What a coincidence. Did you ever hear the story of how your uncle James climbed the highest mountain in South America?"

"Yes. I heard the story many times from my uncle and he said the mountain was so high that the man who was with him claimed he could see the town of Kanturk from the top of it."

"I wouldn't doubt Jim to make a joke of it, but I will tell you something. This war will be a cake-walk compared to climbing that mountain. It has not been climbed since and that was over twenty years ago. How time flies."

Needless to say the man with the most experience took charge of the conversation and every subject he brought up was given full consideration.

"I don't fancy the damn Bay of Biscay this time of year," said Fitzpatrick. "And I doubt very much if the organisers of this expeditionary force will provide a proper troop ship. We will have poor facilities and a rough passage. Be prepared for the worst."

"Conditions will be rageous." said the beet-puller. "If they are anything like pulling beet in January for ten bob a week, O'Leary, the wild man, is ready to face anything, even the bay of the North Pole."

In a short while we found ourselves entering the town of Fermoy and *surprise, surprise* we were just in time to join a convoy of eight or ten vehicles all full of men travelling to the port of embarkation. Slowly we drove through the town and we were wondering what the hold-up was all about. Then we saw the car ahead of us stop and a priest wearing vestments and a stole over his shoulders blessing the men inside and sprinkling holy water on the car, which was a waste really because the rain washed it away immediately. We were next and now we could see things much better. There were three priests. One wearing a biretta, probably a Canon, and he held an ornate holy water pot while another made full use of the sprinkler. Another gave us his blessing. By keeping an eye on Fitzpatrick we learned how to behave during the ceremony. Fitzpatrick removed his hat and made the sign of the cross and the two boys followed suit by doing likewise. The moment the car moved the two "*government haybarn*" caps were put back in place. In another town in County Waterford we were blessed all over again and the overall effect of all these blessings nearly put the hearts crossways in us. One could see that the clergy took it for granted we were facing certain death.

Fitzpatrick remarked "We are being well looked after spiritually." And he hoped our bodily needs would be equally catered for. Alas! The organisers had other things to think about.

On our way to Lismore and Cappoquin we got to know each other better. Anyone could see that Fitzpatrick was a man that knew his way about and as we drove into Dungarvan he ventured to say. "Dungarvan. It is unlikely we sail from here?"

"No," said the driver. "Not from here. At a guess I'd say we are about half way to the boat."

Janie told us he had never heard of Dungarvan and O'Leary, the wild man, told him to "take a good look at the town because it is almost certain you will never see it again."

"Never say never." commented Fitzpatrick.

In this way we kept the conversation going as we passed Kilmeadon, Kilmacthomas and Waterford City and then on to a road which seemed to be leading to some place of little importance. Certainly not to any big city. The road was like a ten-mile glow worm. We could see little except the red tail lights of dozens and dozens of cars and buses wind their way to a place called Passage East. Passage East was a small seaside village in or near the Waterford harbour and as Janie put it, "We were there before we knew where we were." It was raining and a bitterly cold wind swept in from the sea. The only lights in the village were on the pier and already groups of men were congregated around their bits and pieces of baggage. Heavy showers of sleety rain would force them to retreat and seek shelter around corners and in doorways in the village. Lights began to appear in several houses as people got out of bed to investigate what was causing all the commotion, as almost a thousand men shouted and joked with each other around the streets. When the showers were over the vigil began again, from time to time a ship would be observed coming up the harbour towards us. Bags and suitcases would be realigned but hopes were dashed as ship after ship ignored our situation and went on their own legitimate business to Waterford. At this very time several countries had signed a "non-intervention" pact forbidding the transport of any more volunteers to Spain, lest what was in fact a civil war might develop into a war between nations. This was why our port of embarkation had to be top secret. Nevertheless a ship could slip into a small port and be on its way before the machinery of state could swing into action. The only policeman in Passage East was under arrest. Our key men took every precaution and things should run smoothly.

Janie and I decided to leave the pier and go on a walk-about. In the middle of the village we saw a large crowd. Obviously there was something going on and we pushed forward into the inner circle just in time to stand in front of the crowd and have our pictures taken by flash-light. This was something we had not seen before and little did we think the two of us would appear in a big picture in the Dublin papers next morning under the caption "*Some of the Volunteers who left for Spain.*" And of course, there would be the usual write-up. Now our former neighbours would know where to find us. It could be anywhere in the trenches around Madrid, Zaragossa, Seville or Sabinaninago.

We continued our tour of inspection and we found the local schoolhouse was full of volunteers. It proved to be our HQ for here were all the "top brass" sitting in comfort around a blazing fire. O'Leary, the wild man, was already proving his worth. He was standing on a desk ripping down long ceiling boards while others smashed them up and put them on the fire. This was not vandalism in the strict sense of the word. It was in fact very charitable work saving the lives of men who otherwise might have died of exposure. All night long Passage East resounded to the noise of young men passing jests and singing, always gazing seawards as if heaven instead of hell was out there. We noticed the head men never rushed to the pier. They gave us the impression they knew exactly when the boat would arrive. We took another walk-about and we climbed the high hill which overhangs the village. Getting to the top of the hill was no problem. We were young and active then. Today it would be utterly impossible. How the years take their toll.

All this time I held on firmly to my "doctor's bag" and on reaching the top it was my intention to share its contents with

Janie. We found another man sitting on some steps. To us he also seemed too old for war and Janie said to him. "Are you going to the war?"

"Yes. I am coming with you to the war and I hope I will not have to come back. Life for me is over, finished and done with."

"Why do you feel like this?" I asked as I opened the bag. And starting to divide the contents, sharing and sharing alike with the old man and Janie, I waited for an answer.

"Ah," said he. "You are young men without a care in the world. Little, indeed very little, do you know about life. And you know nothing whatever about life in other countries. I left Ireland many years ago, found work in Liverpool, married a fine girl. For twenty five years we were happy. Now it is all over." I asked him what happened. He continued gazing out to sea and then he answered. My daughter had a B.L.A.C.K. baby. He spelled it out. He could not say the word. After a suitable pause Janie said. "'Twas bad alright."

We left him there gazing seawards, seeking death.

We returned to the schoolhouse.

It looked as if zero hour was nigh. Farewell speeches were being made. Captain Lynch was standing on a desk. "Go in God's holy name," said he. "You brave sons of holy Ireland. Remember you are now part of the finest army in the world. Uphold the dignity of this noble army. Draw from sentiments of reverence and fervour for the Holy Roman Catholic Church which you hold with confidence and pride, animated and supported by our Holy Father the Pope. I know you will return glorious and victorious." He then called on everyone to join him in a verse of "Hail Glorious St. Patrick." Most of the men joined in the singing but many remained silent.

Straight away another speaker mounted the desk.

"Gentlemen. You have come in your thousands from every corner of this great country and Britain, to follow the footsteps of the great crusaders who left home for exactly the same reason. Our cause is the same. Every enemy of the cross is our enemy. Every enemy of the Church is our enemy. Every enemy of the Pope is our enemy. I call on you now to join me in "Faith of Our Fathers" before we board ship and lay down our lives."

Before the hymn got under way a man sitting with his back to the wall shouted. "Bullshit! When are we to eat. We want bread."

It was obvious he had the sympathy and support of many. The supply situation got immediate attention. We were all asked to contribute towards a van-load of bread and we were reminded that Irish money would be of no use to us on board ship. Most of us emptied our pockets. In all I'd say several hundred pounds were handed over to the owner of an old battered van, which he intended to abandon on the pier. Now he would give it one more run on an errand of mercy. He was to load the van to capacity with food enough to make everybody happy. He was warned not to delay or he might miss the boat.

"Jay-sus," said O'Leary, the wild man. "You will want help at that." And he jumped in beside the driver and that was the last we saw of them. They probably went into business together. Slowly the hours went by. There was rumour and counter rumour and lots of unverified information and four letter words.

In the late hours of the morning a telegram arrived from Dublin . . . our ship was under arrest somewhere off the south coast . . . we were told to return home . . . we were on our own.

What a confetic mess. There were in Passage East on the morning of January 7, 1937 nine hundred men stranded, hungry, cold, and mostly penniless after "the collection." All the cars and buses had left for home the previous night having dumped us at the port of embarkation. Between us, Janie and myself, had the grand total of one halfpenny and we had that by accident. Had I known it was in another pocket it would have been handed over with the rest of our money. Truly, *fools and their money soon part.*

"Janie." I said. "How long do you think it will take us to get home?"

"How far is it?"

"Almost 200 miles. One hundred and eighty to be exact."

Janie considered this information for some time before answering.

"About three weeks." was his well considered reply.

"Janie," said I. "You will be picking up your bike to night at 8.00 o'clock. And you can confirm this by looking in the Post Office window."

I knew it would take some doing but I was determined. Provided we were back inside twenty four hours, no one would believe we were in Passage East save those who read the Dublin papers. The *Cork Examiner* did not have our picture in the morning. However, the *Evening Echo* had us as large as life on the front page. Luckily the evening papers were not available in rural areas. We might and only might get away without being definitely identified.

55

The Retreat From Passage East

Generals and army Commanders as a rule find it much more difficult to retreat than advance and it is during a retreat that the quality of leadership is fully and properly tested. A badly conducted retreat can result in the destruction of a whole army.

I was always under the impression that, given the opportunity I could and would prove myself capable. Here was the challenge. I would bring my section, consisting of one man, safely home over an almost two hundred mile trek – in eight hours.

It was close to midday when we turned our backs to Passage East. We had no money; we had no food, no transport and no very clear recollection of the various towns and villages we should pass through on our return journey. My companion would do all in his power to prove his estimate of three weeks to be correct. He would dispute every turn and every crossroads, making no secret of his firm belief that trying to reach home in one day was nothing short of lunatic. Perhaps it was a forlorn hope. Only time could tell.

We were only a few hundred yards out from the village when a car pulled up and the lady driver offered us a lift into the city. She began by apologising for the lack of food and drink in the village. "Had we known about it," said she "things would have been very different." She stopped the car near a fine hotel and told us she would be honoured if we joined her for a good midday meal. We were more than glad to accept the offer. In a matter of minutes we were dining like high ranking officers. When the meal was over she opened her handbag and placed a ten shilling note between us on the table saying "You may find that useful before you reach home." I refused to take it. Remember a ten shilling note at that time would do more for you than a fifty pound note today. "I will not put it back in my bag," said she. "You may as well take it rather than leave it to the waitress." I knew she was in earnest. "We will take it and be very glad to have it." I told her. "On one condition – you give us your name and address." She wrote out:

Mrs Bridie Kavanagh
Passage East
Co Waterford

In due course I returned the ten shilling note. As a matter of fact I remained in constant communication with her for over thirty years, sending her letters and post cards from all over the world. Then one day a letter came edged in black telling me our friend had passed away. It was from her daughter, Mrs Nora Larkin (same address). Many of you might think the story of the good Samaritan is just another tall tale. You are wrong. There are wonderful people, marvellous people out there in the world and we are very seldom totally on our own.

Cars were scarce and hitch-hiking was not as highly developed as it is nowadays. Prodding the air with your thumb would get you nowhere. I found that by holding up my "doctor's bag" we could bring most cars to a halt and we lost no time in reaching Kilmacthomas. After that we had to do a little walking but we kept on the move. Once a young priest out for a walk tried to catch up with us but we increased the pace and he soon gave up. Again I held up my "doctor's bag" and again we were lucky. This driver took us right through to Cappoquin. Actually, it was nice to get out and walk for a little while before flagging down another obliging driver.

It so happened that we were again on foot with the village of Kilmeadon about a half a mile ahead and now we were slowly but surely being overtaken by a red-coated horseman. He drew level with us and it was obvious he was going to maintain his position. He had probably read the morning paper and knew all about the debacle of the previous night.

"Tell me," said he. "Would you people be Blueshirts by any chance?"

There was a lot riding on the answer to that question and I decided to plunge in at the deep end. We might as well be *"hung for a sheep as a lamb"*.

"We were side by side with Michael Patrick Lynch the day they shot him dead in Cork." completely untrue of course but it was an attempt to impress our horseman friend.

"And," said he "I heard all about Passage East on the radio. Would you by any chance be disappointed volunteers?"

"Heart-broken would be more like it. But there will be another day."

"Never mind," said he. "As far as I am concerned I think you have already proved yourselves valiant men. Men of incredible courage. Allow me to stand you a few drinks when we reach the village."

When we reached the village we walked right into a meeting of the Waterford Hounds. A large group of people and horses were standing around outside a very picturesque public house.

The noise and laughter coming from inside suggested to our ears that the place was full of men in good humour. Our friend handed over his horse to a caretaker who seemed to be there for the purpose and then he marched the two of us in and right up to the crowded bar. He ordered "three pints." Needless to say, we were not experienced "pint" drinkers but there is a widespread belief in this country that a good "pint" drinker is good enough company for any man. We bluffed our way and thanked him and then it happened.

Raising his voice above all the noise and clatter he began. "Gentleman let me introduce my two friends who are returning from Passage East after an abortive attempt to reach the Irish Brigade and General O'Duffy now fighting to take Madrid. They have requested me not to parade their courage on another occasion as Blueshirts."

Men jostled each other trying to have a word with us and all of them stood us pints. Soon the counter was black with pints awaiting attention.

Then a man, straight as a ram-rod, and with the finest waxed moustache I had ever seen came towards us. I knew instinctively he was an old soldier. "There must be something else we can do," said he by way of inquiry. Just then I had no ready answer but another huntsman took up the slack. "Well, Khyber," said the huntsman. "What do you think of these two fearless young soldiers? It seemed to me the man with the enormous moustache was known locally as Khyber and this in turn indicated he had seen service in India. In actual fact I had just finished reading "*Kim*" and I felt I knew a good deal about India. Trying to strike the right note I turned towards the man called Khyber.

"In our situation which only a man like yourself can understand we are more or less in the look out for a "*rupee*." The mention of the word "*rupee*" reminded him of better days. We shook hands vigorously and he started to quote:

"*Never was isle so little*

Never was sea so lone."

He waited for me to continue, not knowing that I liked reading Kipling.

"*But over the scud and the palm-trees*".

I waited but the man called Khyber was satisfied. I had established my credentials.

"Boys," said he "why don't we throw a few bob together and give these brave men their fare home".

"I will second that," said the horseman who first met us. Khyber took off his hat, pitched in a pocket full of silver and sent the hat on its way around the crowd. Unfortunately, the crowd had decreased a little as it was now almost moving-off time.

Nevertheless, there was quite a lot of half crowns and other miscellaneous coins in the hat when it arrived back and Khyber turned it upside down on the counter. No attempt was made to count it. He simply made two parts of the heap, pushing one part towards me and the other part towards Janie saying

"*Quo fas et gloria ducant*".

"What's that?" said Janie entering the conversation for the first time.

"That," said he. "is the motto of the Royal Artillery." And in a moment he was gone to join the hunt.

"A nice man," said Janie. "I think I will grow a moustache like that."

Janie, while not quite drunk, had certainly too much drink taken and I feared we would have trouble when he suggested we should follow the hunt for a few miles. There was a thirsty-looking fellow eyeing the dozen or more pints as yet untasted, which stood in front of us, and I said to him "Give us a hand here. We must be going."

"No problem," said he. "No problem. Leave the lot to me."

We were out just in time to see the hunt move off. Janie had no eye for the beauty of the scene; instead he wanted to go off with some idlers to some vantage point and wait for the kill. "Do you know I hate foxes and badgers?"

"Janie," said I. "We have other things to think about." And a car came along travelling westwards. Once again my "doctor's bag" was effective. "Where to?" asked the driver.

"Cork," said I meaning the county rather than the city.

After travelling five or six miles the driver said "OK. This is as far as I go. Keep on this road. It's the road to Fermoy." Fermoy was music to my ears. I knew if I reached Fermoy we could afford to take the train to Banteer, which was the nearest station to home. On shank's mare once more we took the opportunity of counting our money. We had over six pounds each and we had the ten shilling note and the original halfpenny and as usual when people are too well off, people start trouble. Janie sat down and looking straight at me:

"Can I ask you a fair question?" said he.

"Certainly."

"Where are we now?"

"We are on the road to Fermoy. I don't exactly know where we are."

"I knew it. I knew it all the time. I knew we would end up nowhere. We'd better go back."

From here on I got little or no co-operation from Janie. He believed we were on the wrong road and that further effort was useless. "What you are trying to do is impossible. I know we are lost."

I tried to instil some hope in him by repeating a verse we had both learned in school.

"*Remember Janie,*

The passing stranger scaled the wall.

Where weary men might turn."

"Where did you hear that foolishness?" said Janie and just then there came a bus and we got on. We sat apart and after a while the conductor came round making a leisurely call on everyone with his "fares please," and a few words about the weather. When he came to Janie things took a turn for the worse.

"Where are you taking us?"

"Fermoy, in ten minutes."

"We thought you were taking us to Cork. We won't pay you for taking us to the wrong place."

Before things got out of hand I felt I had to butt in. "Look," said I. "We have a bit of a problem as you can see."

"And so have I," said the conductor. "What happens if an inspector finds you travelling without tickets and refusing to pay."

"We want no trouble. We will hop off at the next stop. He was a reasonable man. Ready to do anything for a quiet life.

At the verge of town the bus halted and a few people got off. We joined them. All that remained now was a short walk to the railway station and our troubles were over.

I thought it would please Janie if I allowed him to get the tickets and thus let him share some responsibility for our great achievement in coming so far without any great difficulty.

I said to him. "Go to the booking office and get two single tickets to Banteer and ask when is the next train."

I remained where I was, expecting no trouble. Unfortunately, Janie had no idea of the inner workings of the Great Southern and Western Railway. As a rule the booking office is closed and is opened always five minutes before the arrival of a train. This gives plenty of time to the few people travelling to obtain tickets.

Finding the office closed Janie set out to locate the Station Master.

Being on legitimate business he saw no harm in walking into the Station Master's private house and finding no one in the first compartment continued his search. Upstairs he came face to face with the Station Master.

"Who the hell are you and what are you doing here?"

"My name is Janie Dunne and I want two tickets to Banteer."

"I don't give a damn who you are, get outside my door."

"I have a great mind to give you a good belt in the gob," said Janie. "And you can stuff your tickets."

That is the story as he told it to me, but knowing Janie I am afraid there was much more to it than that. No way would Janie agree to travel on the train from Fermoy after the acceleration. "I won't give him the satisfaction," said Janie and now I had to try and find a car on the road to Mallow. It was now quite dark and I had no idea what kind of vehicle I was flagging down with my "doctor's bag." It turned out to be an ESB van and the driver told us we were in luck. He was going direct to Mallow.

There was only room for two in front and we fixed Janie up nicely on top of tools and overalls. He seemed to be happy enough. Then the back doors were closed and locked; this left Janie sitting in the blind dark with no view of anything inside or outside.

We were about half way to Mallow when Janie began to belt the sides of the van with a hammer shouting "*Let me out. Let me out.* This is worse than the time of the bloody Black and Tans. *Let me out.*" We came to a sudden stop and we rushed to the rear doors and opened them as quickly as possible while Janie continued to shout and hammer.

He leaped out saying, "We are on the wrong road. Too many turns. He was totally disorientated and to make matters worse there was heavy rain.

"I will hold on to the roof-rack," said Janie.

"You bloody well will not," said the driver. "Do you think I will drive through the town with you doing the ape, swinging from the roof-rack. Get back in there or you may bloody-well walk it."

The rain may well have been the deciding factor. Reluctantly, he resumed his seat. Again the doors were closed and locked. The driver and myself resumed normal conversation. "I don't care what you say, anyone volunteering to go to the Spanish Civil War must be mad and that guy in the back is a pure nut-case." At last I had to admit to myself, that Janie was a headstrong fellow and that was the reason he was not one of the five original volunteers. Yet with all his faults he was an upright, downright honest man and people put up with him for the sake of peace.

Finally, we entered the town and having had a good long talk with the driver about national and international affairs, he said he would take us to the station. Forgetting about Janie he took the right-hand turn for the station far too sharply and Janie again, taken by surprise, lost his balance – creating bedlam as we drove into the station yard. "Fek-eee my bloody head is broke. 'Tis worse than the war." We released him as quickly as possible. Nevertheless quite a few spectators had gathered round. This could develop into an embarrassing situation. Everything depended on how Janie would react and his reactions were always unpredictable and difficult to anticipate.

He leaped out, looked towards the bright lights. "Jay-sus. Good God – Mallow," and turning to the driver he continued "You are one sound man. Better'n that hure Franco any day."

The driver extricated himself from Janie's embrace and sitting in he drove away.

He had a queer story for the lads at Tarrant's Bar later in the evening.

People were beginning to line up outside the office but we had one more call to make before joining the queue.

They were all strangers to us except one man and we thought if we kept quiet we would remain unnoticed . . .

The man we were afraid might recognize us was Big Con. He was a Fianna Fáil County Councillor at this time and every man, woman and child in North Cork had great respect for him. And apart altogether from party politics his good nature and jovial outlook endeared him to friend and opponent alike.

Just as he was about to buy his ticket he gave a side glance at those of us in line and for a brief moment we thought, "he didn't see us." And then we heard him say to the ticket seller, "A single and two halves to Banteer. I see a couple of neighbours childer heading my way. He handed each of us a hal-price ticket saying. "There will be a car to meet me at Banteer and we can drop you off anywhere around the Post Office."

"The Post Office will be grand," said Janie. "My bike is there." Ah! How the mighty had fallen. All last night and for most of the day we were gallant soldiers and heroes. Now we were home and neighbour's children once again. The railway company had no objection to us travelling as children, a truly humiliating experience for both of us.

However, we showed no resentment or indignation towards Big Con. He would save us a four mile walk from the station to the Post Office. He asked us no embarrassing questions. Instead he spent his time asking about the fathers and the mothers, Mrs Cronin's bad pains, the new priest and the old doctor and the football team. He was truly a man of the people who kept himself in touch.

We were hopeful very few people would become aware of our escapade. We feared becoming the butt of many jokes, most of them in bad taste. The so-called volunteers, who had boils and piles and strokes and carbuncles and rich uncles would no doubt be surprised to see me back from Spain so soon and I in turn would be equally surprised at their return to full health. In less than a week everything should be back to normal.

For me, the old excuse would work again. As for Janie, he was not even on speaking terms with his father so he required no excuse. He came and went wherever and whenever he liked. His mother believed he was a good boy and prayed he would not fall into bad company.

56

Joking Set Aside

The first thing we did on reaching the Post Office was peep in the window and have one last look at the old familiar eight-day clock. It was exactly 8.00 pm.

A lot had happened during the past twenty-four hours. I had done what I set out to do earlier that day namely, to get back from Passage East in less than eight hours in mid-winter.

I was so happy about this I felt like asking Janie to join me in a trip around the world to find out if we could reduce the present record of eighty days to half that number, but somehow I got the feeling that he was in bad humour. He was in fact in very bad humour.

Our failure to reach the war zone had a profound effect upon him.

Standing beside his retrieved bicycle, hand on saddle, *government haybarn* cap pulled well down over one ear, he began cursing Franco, the Pope, Duffy, de Valera, the British Government and the Russians; as if they all had conspired to prevent him drawing a war pension for the rest of his life.

"Let me tell you this," said he. "I will never again join any army or organisation, or any club or company or religion. Enough is enough. By the Lord God I won't even join my hands."

He jumped on his bike and without another word he rode away into the darkness.

The nag-nag of wanderlust returned with even greater force. I answered the call and when I returned after years in scorching deserts in yet another war and sampling life in various other lands the Irish Free State had passed into history.

Que sera, sera. Like the bubble on the fountain, thou art gone!

And for ever.